ORDER OF
CHRISTIAN FUNERALS

Study Edition

THE ROMAN RITUAL

REVISED BY DECREE OF THE
SECOND VATICAN ECUMENICAL
COUNCIL AND PUBLISHED BY
AUTHORITY OF POPE PAUL VI

GEOFFREY CHAPMAN
LONDON

ORDER OF CHRISTIAN FUNERALS

**APPROVED FOR USE IN THE DIOCESES OF ENGLAND
AND WALES, AND SCOTLAND**

Study Edition

Prepared by
Liturgy Office of the Bishops' Conference of England and Wales
and
International Commission on English in the Liturgy
A Joint Commission of Catholic Bishops' Conferences

GEOFFREY CHAPMAN
an imprint of Cassell Publishers Limited
Villiers House, 41/47 Strand, London WC2N 5JE, England

ISBN 0 225 66649 9

First published 1991

Concordat cum originali: Jennifer Demolder, Peter Gallacher, 1 June 1990
Nihil obstat: Anton Cowan
Imprimatur: ✠ John Crowley, V.G., Bishop in Central London, Westminster, 29 June 1990

The *Nihil obstat* and *Imprimatur* are a declaration that a book or pamphlet is considered
to be free from doctrinal or moral error. It is not implied that those who have granted
the *Nihil obstat* and *Imprimatur* agree with the contents, opinions, or statements expressed.

ACKNOWLEDGEMENTS

The English translation, original texts, general introduction, pastoral notes, arrangement,
and design of *Order of Christian Funerals* © 1989, 1985, International Committee on English
in the Liturgy, Inc. (ICEL); excerpts from the English translation of *The Roman Missal*
© 1973, ICEL; excerpts from the English translation of *Holy Communion and Worship of
the Eucharist outside Mass* © 1974, ICEL; excerpts from *Pastoral Care of the Sick: Rites of Anointing
and Viaticum* © 1982, ICEL. All rights reserved.

Pastoral notes and arrangement of Part III, various pastoral notes related specifically to
the celebration of funerals in England and Wales, and Scotland, and editorial arrangement of related rites and various rites of committal (rite numbers 3, 8 through 12, and
18 through 21) © 1990, Liturgy Office of the Bishops' Conference of England and Wales.

The introductory verse, hymns, antiphons, responsories, and intercessions of the office
for the dead from *The Divine Office*, © 1974, the hierarchies of Australia, England and
Wales, and Ireland.

The Scripture readings used in this volume are taken from *The Jerusalem Bible*. Excerpts
from *The Jerusalem Bible*, copyright © 1966 by Darton, Longman & Todd, Ltd. Used by
permission of the publisher.

Psalm texts from *The Psalms: A New Translation* © The Grail (England) 1963. The complete psalms first published in 1963 by and available through Wm. Collins, Sons & Company, Ltd. The texts for the Canticle of Zechariah and the Canticle of Mary © The Grail
(England). Used by permission.

Texts of Isaiah 38:10-14, 17-20 and Philippians 2:6-11 are reproduced with permission from
the *Revised Standard Version, Common Bible*, copyright © 1973 by the Division of Christian
Education, National Council of the Churches of Christ in the U.S.A.

Text of 'Remember Those, O Lord', © 1969, James Quinn, S.J. By permission of Geoffrey
Chapman, an imprint of Cassell Publishers Ltd.

Prayer texts of committal, 'In sure and certain hope . . .' and 'Into your hands, O merciful Saviour, . . .', used by permission, from the *Book of Common Prayer*, 1979, published
by The Church Pension Fund.

Paragraph number 229 based on note contained in the *Book of Alternative Services of the
Anglican Church of Canada* © 1985 by the General Synod of the Anglican Church of Canada.

Printed and bound in Great Britain by
Biddles Ltd, Guildford and King's Lynn

EPISCOPAL CONFERENCE OF ENGLAND AND WALES

AND

EPISCOPAL CONFERENCE OF SCOTLAND

DECREE

The *Order of Christian Funerals* as the revised English version of the *Ordo Exsequiarum* was approved by the Bishops' Conference of England and Wales on 10 April 1986 and confirmed by the Congregation for Divine Worship (Prot. n. 516/86) on 26 June 1987, and by the Bishops' Conference of Scotland on 7 April 1987, and confirmed by the Congregation for Divine Worship (Prot. n. 265/88) on 18 December 1988.

On All Souls Day, 2 November 1990, this edition may be published and from that day on be used for the celebration of funerals in England and Wales, and Scotland. From Easter Sunday 1991 the use of this edition is mandatory and no previous version may be used.

✠ George Basil Hume
President
Bishops' Conference of England and Wales

✠ Thomas Joseph Winning
President
Bishops' Conference of Scotland

CONTENTS

EDITORIAL NOTE

Beginning with the General Introduction, the numbering system in this book diverges from the Latin edition of *Ordo Exsequiarum*. The new numbering system appears at the left-hand side of the page. The corresponding number from the Latin edition appears in the right-hand margin. A text having a number on the left but no reference number in the right-hand margin is either newly composed or is a text from *The Roman Missal, Holy Communion and Worship of the Eucharist outside Mass, The Divine Office,* or *Pastoral Care of the Sick: Rites of Anointing and Viaticum*.

'Funeral rites' is a general designation used of all the liturgical celebrations in this book. 'Funeral liturgy' is a more particular designation applied to the two forms of liturgical celebration presented under the headings 'Funeral Mass' and 'Funeral Liturgy outside Mass'.

For ease of celebration each rite is set out in full with alternatives incorporated in sequence. Further alternative texts for particular circumstances are contained in Part V.

CONGREGATION FOR DIVINE WORSHIP

Prot. no. 720/69

DECREE

By means of the funeral rites it has been the practice of the Church, as a tender mother, not simply to commend the dead to God but also to raise high the hope of its children and to give witness to its own faith in the future resurrection of the baptized with Christ.

Vatican Council II accordingly directed in the Constitution on the Liturgy that the funeral rites be revised in such a way that they would more clearly express the paschal character of the Christian's death and also that the rites for the burial of children would have a proper Mass (art. 81-82).

The Consilium prepared the desired rites and put them into trial use in different parts of the world. Now Pope Paul VI by his apostolic authority has approved and ordered the publication of these rites as henceforth obligatory for all those using the Roman Ritual.

Also by order of Pope Paul this Congregation for Divine Worship promulgates the *Order of Funerals*, stipulating that its effective date is 1 June 1970.

The Congregation further establishes that until 1 June 1970, when Latin is used in celebrating funerals there is an option to use either the present rite or the rite now in the Roman Ritual; after 1 June 1970 only this new *Order of Funerals* is to be used.

Once the individual conferences of bishops have prepared a vernacular version of the rite and received its confirmation from this Congregation, they have authorization to fix any other, feasible effective date prior to 1 June 1970 for use of the *Order of Funerals*.

All things to the contrary notwithstanding.

Congregation for Divine Worship, 15 August 1969, the solemnity of the Assumption.

Benno Cardinal Gut
Prefect

A. Bugnini
Secretary

ORDER OF
CHRISTIAN FUNERALS

Why do you search for the Living One among the dead?

ORDER OF
CHRISTIAN FUNERALS

GENERAL INTRODUCTION

1   In the face of death, the Church confidently proclaims that God has created each person for eternal life and that Jesus, the Son of God, by his death and resurrection, has broken the chains of sin and death that bound humanity. Christ 'achieved his task of redeeming humanity and giving perfect glory to God, principally by the paschal mystery of his blessed passion, resurrection from the dead, and glorious ascension.'[1]

2   The proclamation of Jesus Christ 'who was put to death for our sins and raised to life to justify us' (Romans 4:25) is at the centre of the Church's life. The mystery of the Lord's death and resurrection gives power to all of the Church's activity. 'For it was from the side of Christ as he slept the sleep of death upon the cross that there came forth the sublime sacrament of the whole Church.'[2] The Church's liturgical and sacramental life and proclamation of the Gospel make this mystery present in the life of the faithful. Through the sacraments of baptism, confirmation, and eucharist, men and women are initiated into this mystery. 'You have been taught that when we were baptized in Christ Jesus we were baptized into his death; in other words when we were baptized we went into the tomb with him and joined him in death, so that as Christ was raised from the dead by the Father's glory, we too might live a new life. If in union with Christ we have imitated his death, we shall also imitate him in his resurrection' (Romans 6:3-5).

3   In the eucharistic sacrifice, the Church's celebration of Christ's Passover from death to life, the faith of the baptized in the paschal mystery is renewed and nourished. Their union with Christ and with each other is strengthened: 'Because there is one bread, we who are many, are one body, for we all partake of the one bread' (1 Corinthians 10:17).

4   At the death of a Christian, whose life of faith was begun in the waters of baptism and strengthened at the eucharistic table, the Church intercedes on behalf of the deceased because of its confident belief that death is not the end nor does it break the bonds forged in life. The Church also ministers to the sorrowing and consoles them in the funeral rites with the comforting word of God and the sacrament of the eucharist.

---

[1] Vatican Council II, Constitution on the Liturgy *Sacrosanctum Concilium*, art. 5.
[2] Ibid.

5   Christians celebrate the funeral rites to offer worship, praise, and thanksgiving to God for the gift of a life which has now been returned to God, the author of life and the hope of the just. The Mass, the memorial of Christ's death and resurrection, is the principal celebration of the Christian funeral.

6   The Church through its funeral rites commends the dead to God's merciful love and pleads for the forgiveness of their sins. At the funeral rites, especially at the celebration of the eucharistic sacrifice, the Christian community affirms and expresses the union of the Church on earth with the Church in heaven in the one great communion of saints. Though separated from the living, the dead are still at one with the community of believers on earth and benefit from their prayers and intercession. At the rite of final commendation and farewell, the community acknowledges the reality of separation and commends the deceased to God. In this way it recognises the spiritual bond that still exists between the living and the dead and proclaims its belief that all the faithful will be raised up and reunited in the new heavens and a new earth, where death will be no more.

7   The celebration of the Christian funeral brings hope and consolation to the living. While proclaiming the Gospel of Jesus Christ and witnessing to Christian hope in the resurrection, the funeral rites also recall to all who take part in them God's mercy and judgment and meet the human need to turn always to God in times of crisis.

MINISTRY AND PARTICIPATION

8   'If one member suffers in the body of Christ which is the Church, all the members suffer with that member' (1 Corinthians 12:26). For this reason, those who are baptized into Christ and nourished at the same table of the Lord are responsible for one another. When Christians are sick, their brothers and sisters share a ministry of mutual charity and 'do all that they can to help the sick return to health, by showing love for the sick, and by celebrating the sacraments with them'.[3] So too when a member of Christ's Body dies, the faithful are called to a ministry of consolation to those who have suffered the loss of one whom they love. Christian consolation is rooted in that hope that comes from faith in the saving death and resurrection of the Lord Jesus Christ. Christian hope faces the reality of death and the anguish of grief but trusts confidently that the power of sin and death has been vanquished by the risen Lord. The Church calls each member of Christ's Body — priest, deacon, layperson — to participate in the ministry

---

[3] See Roman Ritual, *Pastoral Care of the Sick: Rites of Anointing and Viaticum*, General Introduction, no. 33.

of consolation: to care for the dying, to pray for the dead, to comfort those who mourn.

COMMUNITY

9   The responsibility for the ministry of consolation rests with the believing community, which heeds the words and example of the Lord Jesus: 'Blessed are they who mourn; they shall be consoled' (Matthew 5:3). Each Christian shares in this ministry according to the various gifts and offices in the Church. As part of the pastoral ministry, priests and other ministers should instruct the parish community on the Christian meaning of death and on the purpose and significance of the Church's liturgical rites for the dead. Information on how the parish community assists families in preparing for funerals should also be provided.

By giving instruction, priests should lead the community to a deeper appreciation of its role in the ministry of consolation and to a fuller understanding of the significance of the death of a fellow Christian. Often the community must respond to the anguish voiced by Martha, the sister of Lazarus: 'Lord, if you had been here, my brother would never have died' (John 11:21) and must console those who mourn, as Jesus himself consoled Martha: 'Your brother will rise again. . . . I am the resurrection and the life: those who believe in me, though they should die, will come to life; and those who are alive and believe in me will never die' (John 11:25-26). The faith of the Christian community in the resurrection of the dead brings support and strength to those who suffer the loss of those whom they love.

10   Members of the community should console the mourners with words of faith and support and with acts of kindness, for example, assisting them with some of the routine tasks of daily living. Such assistance may allow members of the family to devote time to planning the funeral rites with the priest and other ministers and may also give the family time for prayer and mutual comfort.

11   The community's principal involvement in the ministry of consolation is expressed in its active participation in the celebration of the funeral rites, particularly the vigil for the deceased, the funeral liturgy, and the rite of committal. For this reason these rites should be scheduled at times that permit as many of the community as possible to be present. The assembly's participation can be assisted by the preparation of booklets that contain an outline of the rite, the texts and songs belonging to the people, and directions for posture, gesture, and movement.

12   At the vigil for the deceased or on another occasion before the eucharistic celebration, the presiding minister should invite all to be present at the funeral liturgy and to take an active part in it. The minister may also describe the funeral liturgy and explain why the community gathers to

hear the word of God proclaimed and to celebrate the eucharist when one of the faithful dies.

The priest and other ministers should also be mindful of those persons who are not members of the Catholic Church, or Catholics who are not involved in the life of the Church.

13 As a minister of reconciliation, the priest should be especially sensitive to the possible needs for reconciliation felt by the family and others. Funerals can begin the process of reconciling differences and supporting those ties that can help the bereaved adjust to the loss brought about by death. With attentiveness to each situation, the priest can help to begin the process of reconciliation when needed. In some cases this process may find expression in the celebration of the sacrament of penance, either before the funeral liturgy or at a later time.

LITURGICAL MINISTERS

Presiding Minister

14 Priests, as teachers of faith and ministers of comfort, preside at the funeral rites, especially the Mass; the celebration of the funeral liturgy is especially entrusted to priests. When no priest is available, deacons, as ministers of the word, of the altar, and of charity, preside at funeral rites. When no priest or deacon is available for the vigil and related rites or the rite of committal, a layperson presides.

Other Liturgical Ministers

15 In the celebration of the funeral rites laymen and laywomen may serve as readers, musicians, ushers, pall-bearers, and, according to existing norms, as special ministers of the eucharist. Priests should instil in these ministers an appreciation of how much the reverent exercise of their ministries contributes to the celebration of the funeral rites. Family members should be encouraged to take an active part in these ministries, but they should not be asked to assume any role that their grief or sense of loss may make too burdensome.

MINISTRY FOR THE MOURNERS AND THE DECEASED

FAMILY AND FRIENDS

16 In planning and carrying out the funeral rites the priest and all other ministers should keep in mind the life of the deceased and the circumstances of death. They should also take into consideration the spiritual and psychological needs of the family and friends of the deceased to express grief and their sense of loss, to accept the reality of death, and to comfort one another.

17 Whenever possible, ministers should involve the family in planning the funeral rites: in the choice of texts and rites provided in the ritual, in the selection of music for the rites, and in the designation of liturgical ministers.

Planning of the funeral rites may take place during the visit of the priest or other minister at some appropriate time after the death and before the vigil service. Ministers should explain to the family the meaning and significance of each of the funeral rites, especially the vigil, the funeral liturgy, and the rite of committal.

If pastoral and personal considerations allow, the period before death may be an appropriate time to plan the funeral rites with the family and even with the family member who is dying. Although planning the funeral before death should be approached with sensitivity and care, it can have the effect of helping the one who is dying and the family face the reality of death with Christian hope. It can also help relieve the family of numerous details after the death and may allow them to benefit more fully from the celebration of the funeral rites.

Deceased

18 Through the celebration of the funeral rites, the Church manifests its care for the dead, both baptized members and catechumens. In keeping with the provisions of *Codex Iuris Canonici*, can. 1183, the Church's funeral rites may be celebrated for a child who died before baptism and whose parents intended to have the child baptized. The Church's funeral rites may also be celebrated for a person baptized into another Church or ecclesial community but who was seeking to be received into full communion with the Catholic Church.

At the discretion of the local Ordinary, the Church's funeral rites may be celebrated for a baptized member of another Church or ecclesial community provided this would not be contrary to the wishes of the deceased person and provided the minister of the Church or ecclesial community in which the deceased person was a regular member or communicant is unavailable.

19 Since in baptism the body was marked with the seal of the Trinity and became the temple of the Holy Spirit, Christians respect and honour the bodies of the dead and the places where they rest. Any customs associated with the preparation of the body of the deceased should always be marked with dignity and reverence and never with the despair of those who have no hope. Preparation of the body should include prayer, especially at those intimate moments reserved for family members. For the final disposition of the body, it is the ancient Christian custom to bury or entomb the bodies of the dead; cremation is permitted, unless it is evident that cremation was chosen for anti-Christian motives. In the case of a body

donated to science, the funeral rites may be celebrated in the absence of the body, while the rite of committal is held over until such time as final interment or cremation takes place.

20   In countries or regions where an undertaker, and not the family or community, carries out the preparation and transfer of the body, the priest and other ministers are to ensure that the undertakers appreciate the values and beliefs of the Christian community.

The family and friends of the deceased should not be excluded from taking part in the services sometimes provided by undertakers, for example, the preparation and laying out of the body.

LITURGICAL ELEMENTS

21   Since liturgical celebration involves the whole person, it requires attentiveness to all that affects the senses. The readings and prayers, psalms and songs should be proclaimed or sung with understanding, conviction, and reverence. Music for the assembly should be truly expressive of the texts and at the same time simple and easily sung. The ritual gestures, processions, and postures should express and foster an attitude of reverence and reflectiveness in those taking part in the funeral rites. The funeral rites should be celebrated in an atmosphere of simple beauty, in a setting that encourages participation. Liturgical signs and symbols affirming Christian belief and hope in the paschal mystery are abundant in the celebration of the funeral rites, but their undue multiplication or repetition should be avoided. Care must be taken that the choice and use of signs and symbols are in accord with the culture of the people.

THE WORD OF GOD

Readings

22   In every celebration for the dead, the Church attaches great importance to the reading of the word of God. The readings proclaim to the assembly the paschal mystery, teach remembrance of the dead, convey the hope of being gathered together again in God's kingdom, and encourage the witness of Christian life. Above all, the readings tell of God's designs for a world in which suffering and death will relinquish their hold on all whom God has called his own. A careful selection and use of readings from Scripture for the funeral rites will provide the family and the community with an opportunity to hear God speak to them in their needs, sorrows, fears, and hopes.

23   In the celebration of the liturgy of the word at the funeral liturgy, the biblical readings may not be replaced by non-biblical readings. But dur-

ing prayer services with the family non-biblical readings may be used in addition to readings from Scripture.

24 Liturgical tradition assigns the proclamation of the readings in the celebration of the liturgy of the word to readers and the deacon. The presiding minister proclaims the readings only when there are no assisting ministers present. Those designated to proclaim the word of God should prepare themselves to exercise this ministry.[4]

Psalmody

25 The psalms are rich in imagery, feeling, and symbolism. They powerfully express the suffering and pain, the hope and trust of people of every age and culture. Above all the psalms sing of faith in God, of revelation and redemption. They enable the assembly to pray in the words that Jesus himself used during his life on earth. Jesus, who knew anguish and the fear of death, 'offered up prayer and entreaty, aloud and in silent tears, to the one who had the power to save him out of death. . . . Although he was Son, he learned to obey through suffering; but having been made perfect, he became for all who obey him the source of eternal salvation . . .' (Hebrews 5:7-9). In the psalms the members of the assembly pray in the voice of Christ, who intercedes on their behalf before the Father.[5] The Church, like Christ, turns again and again to the psalms as a genuine expression of grief and of praise and as a sure source of trust and hope in times of trial. Priests and other ministers are, therefore, to make an earnest effort through an effective catechesis to lead their communities to a clearer and deeper grasp of at least some of the psalms provided for the funeral rites.

26 The psalms are designated for use in many places in the funeral rites (for example, as responses to the readings, for the processions, for use at the vigil for the deceased). Since the psalms are songs, whenever possible, they should be sung.

Homily

27 A brief homily based on the readings is always given after the gospel reading at the funeral liturgy and may also be given after the readings at the vigil service; but there is never to be a eulogy. Attentive to the grief of those present, the homilist should dwell on God's compassionate love and on the paschal mystery of the Lord, as proclaimed in the Scripture readings. The homilist should also help the members of the assembly to understand that the mystery of God's love and the mystery of Jesus' victorious death and resurrection were present in the life and death of the

---

[4] See Lectionary for Mass (2nd *editio typica*, 1981), General Introduction, nos. 49, 52, and 55.

[5] See General Instruction of the Liturgy of the Hours, no. 109.

deceased and that these mysteries are active in their own lives as well. Through the homily members of the family and community should receive consolation and strength to face the death of one of their members with a hope nourished by the saving word of God. Laypersons who preside at the funeral rites give an instruction on the readings.

PRAYERS AND INTERCESSIONS

28   In the presidential prayers of the funeral rites the presiding minister addresses God on behalf of the deceased and the mourners in the name of the entire Church. From the variety of prayers provided the minister in consultation with the family should carefully select texts that truly capture the unspoken prayers and hopes of the assembly and also respond to the needs of the mourners.

29   Having heard the word of God proclaimed and preached, the assembly responds at the vigil and at the funeral liturgy with prayers of intercession for the deceased and all the dead, for the family and all who mourn, and for all in the assembly. The holy people of God, confident in their belief in the communion of saints, exercise their royal priesthood by joining together in this prayer for all those who have died.[6]

Several models of intercessions are provided within the rites for adaptation to the circumstances.

MUSIC

30   Music is integral to the funeral rites. It allows the community to express convictions and feelings that words alone may fail to convey. It has the power to console and uplift the mourners and to strengthen the unity of the assembly in faith and love. The texts of the songs chosen for a particular celebration should express the paschal mystery of the Lord's suffering, death, and triumph over death and should be related to the readings from Scripture.

31   Since music can evoke strong feelings, the music for the celebration of the funeral rites should be chosen with great care. The music at funerals should support, console, and uplift the participants and should help to create in them a spirit of hope in Christ's victory over death and in the Christian's share in that victory.

32   Music should be provided for the vigil and funeral liturgy and, whenever possible, for the funeral processions and the rite of committal. The specific notes that precede each of these rites suggest places in the rites where music is appropriate. Many musical settings used by the parish community

---

[6] See *De Oratione communi seu fidelium* (2nd ed., Vatican Polyglot Press, 1966), chapter 1, no. 3, p. 7: tr., *Documents on the Liturgy* (The Liturgical Press, 1982), no. 1893.

during the liturgical year may be suitable for use at funerals. Efforts should be made to develop and expand the parish's repertoire for use at funerals.

33   An organist or other instrumentalist, a cantor, and, whenever possible, even a choir should assist the assembly's full participation in singing the songs, responses, and acclamations of these rites.

SILENCE

34   Prayerful silence is an element important to the celebration of the funeral rites. Intervals of silence should be observed, for example, after each reading and during the final commendation and farewell, to permit the assembly to reflect upon the word of God and the meaning of the celebration.

SYMBOLS

Easter Candle and Other Candles

35   The Easter candle reminds the faithful of Christ's undying presence among them, of his victory over sin and death, and of their share in that victory by virtue of their initiation. It recalls the Easter Vigil, the night when the Church awaits the Lord's resurrection and when new light for the living and the dead is kindled. During the funeral liturgy and also during the vigil service, when celebrated in the church, the Easter candle may be placed beforehand near the position the coffin will occupy at the conclusion of the procession.

According to local custom, other candles may also be placed near the coffin during the funeral liturgy as a sign of reverence and solemnity.

Holy Water

36   Blessed or holy water reminds the assembly of the saving waters of baptism. In the rite of reception of the body at the church, its use calls to mind the deceased's baptism and initiation into the community of faith. In the rite of final commendation the gesture of sprinkling may also signify farewell.

Incense

37   Incense is used during the funeral rites as a sign of honour to the body of the deceased, which through baptism became the temple of the Holy Spirit. Incense is also used as a sign of the community's prayers for the deceased rising to the throne of God and as a sign of farewell.

Other Symbols

38   If it is the custom in the local community, a pall may be placed over the coffin when it is received at the church. A reminder of the baptismal

garment of the deceased, the pall is a sign of the Christian dignity of the person. The use of the pall also signifies that all are equal in the eyes of God (see James 2:1-9).

A Book of the Gospels or a Bible may be placed on the coffin as a sign that Christians live by the word of God and that fidelity to that word leads to eternal life.

A cross may be placed on the coffin as a reminder that the Christian is marked by the cross in baptism and through Jesus' suffering on the cross is brought to the victory of his resurrection.

Fresh flowers, used in moderation, can enhance the setting of the funeral rites.

Only Christian symbols may rest on or be placed near the coffin during the funeral liturgy. Any other symbols, for example, national flags, or flags or insignia of associations, have no place in the funeral liturgy.

Liturgical Colour

39   The liturgical colour chosen for funerals should express Christian hope in the light of the paschal mystery, but without being offensive to human grief.

White expresses the hope of Easter, the fulfilment of baptism, and the wedding garment necessary for the kingdom. Violet recalls the eschatological expectation of Advent and the Lenten preparation for the paschal mystery. Black is used as a token of mourning, but, in our society, increasingly without the associations of Christian hope.

The choice should be made in the light of local custom and perceptions, and in consultation with the family and community.

RITUAL GESTURES AND MOVEMENT

40   The presiding minister or an assisting minister may quietly direct the assembly in the movements, gestures, and posture appropriate to the particular ritual moment or action.

41   Processions, especially when accompanied with music and singing, can strengthen the bond of communion in the assembly. For processions, ministers of music should give preference to settings of psalms and songs that are responsorial or litanic in style and that allow the people to respond to the verses with an invariable refrain. During the various processions, it is preferable that the pallbearers carry the coffin as a sign of reverence and respect for the deceased. Family members or friends will be especially appropriate for this task. The mourners who follow the coffin may carry lighted candles which can be set down around the catafalque or the grave.

42   Processions continue to have special significance in funeral celebrations, as in Christian Rome where funeral rites consisted of three 'stages'

or 'stations' joined by two processions. Christians accompanied the body on its last journey. From the home of the deceased the Christian community proceeded to the church singing psalms. When the service in the church concluded, the body was carried in solemn procession to the grave or tomb. During the final procession the congregation sang psalms praising the God of mercy and redemption and antiphons entrusting the deceased to the care of the angels and saints. The funeral liturgy mirrored the journey of human life, the Christian pilgrimage to the heavenly Jerusalem.

In many places and situations a solemn procession on foot to the church or to the place of committal may not be possible. Nevertheless at the conclusion of the funeral liturgy an antiphon or versicle and response may be sung as the body is taken to the entrance of the church. Psalms, hymns, or liturgical songs may also be sung when the participants gather at the place of committal.

SELECTION OF RITES FROM THE ORDER OF CHRISTIAN FUNERALS

43　The *Order of Christian Funerals* makes provision for the minister, in consultation with the family, to choose those rites and texts that are most suitable to the situation: those that most closely apply to the needs of the mourners, the circumstances of the death, and the customs of the local Christian community. The minister and family may be assisted in the choice of a rite or rites by the reflections preceding each rite or group of rites.

44　Part I, 'Funeral Rites', of the *Order of Christian Funerals* provides those rites that may be used in the funerals of Christians and is divided into three groups of rites that correspond in general to the three principal ritual moments in Christian funerals: 'Vigil and Related Rites and Prayers', 'Funeral Liturgy', and 'Rite of Committal'.

45　The section entitled 'Vigil and Related Rites and Prayers' includes rites that may be celebrated between the time of death and the funeral liturgy or, should there be no funeral liturgy, before the rite of committal. The vigil is the principal celebration of the Christian community during the time before the funeral liturgy. It may take the form of a liturgy of the word or of some part of the office for the dead. Two vigil services are provided: 'Vigil for the Deceased' and 'Vigil for the Deceased with Reception at the Church'. The second service is used when the vigil is celebrated in the church and the body is to be received at this time.

This section also includes 'Prayers' and 'Related Rites' which provide four brief rites that may be used on other occasions: 'Prayers after Death', 'Gathering in the Presence of the Body', 'Simple Form of the Reception of the Body', and 'Gathering of the Family and Transfer of the Body'. These rites are examples or models of what can be done and should be adapted to the circumstances.

46 The section entitled 'Funeral Liturgy' provides two forms of the funeral liturgy, the central celebration of the Christian community for the deceased: 'Funeral Mass' and 'Funeral Liturgy outside Mass'. When one of its members dies, the Church especially encourages the celebration of the Mass. When Mass cannot be celebrated (see no. 189), the second form of the funeral liturgy may be used and a Mass for the deceased should be celebrated, if possible, at a later time.

47 The section entitled 'Rite of Committal' includes seven forms in all: The 'Rite of Committal at a Cemetery' and 'Rite of Committal at a Crematorium' are used when the final commendation is celebrated as part of the conclusion of the funeral liturgy. The 'Rite of Committal at a Cemetery with Final Commendation' and 'Rite of Committal at a Crematorium with Final Commendation' are used when the final commendation does not take place during the funeral liturgy, or when the funeral liturgy does not immediately precede the committal.

The 'Rite of Committal for Burial' and 'Rite of Committal for Cremation' are intended for use at a cemetery or crematorium chapel when no other liturgical celebration at all has taken place, and they incorporate elements of the funeral liturgy itself.

A seventh form is provided for the burial of ashes.

48 Part II, 'Funeral Rites for Children', provides an adaptation of the principal rites in Part I: 'Vigil for a Deceased Child', 'Funeral Liturgy', and 'Rite of Committal'. These rites may be used in the funerals of infants and young children, including those of early school age. The rites in Part II include texts for use in the case of a baptized child and in the case of a child who died before baptism.

In some instances, for example, the death of an infant, the vigil and funeral liturgy may not be appropriate. Only the rite of committal and perhaps one of the forms of prayer with the family as provided in 'Related Rites and Prayers' may be desirable. Part II does not contain 'Related Rites and Prayers', but the rites from Part I may be adapted.

49 Part III, 'Funerals for Catechumens: Guidelines and Texts', includes guidelines and texts for such celebrations.

Part IV, 'Office for the Dead', includes 'Morning Prayer' and 'Evening Prayer'.

Part V, 'Additional Texts', contains: a collection of prayers for particular categories of persons, for example, priests, married couples, young people; and specific circumstances, for example, suicide, violent death, long illness; a variety of prayers for mourners; and processional psalms.

PART I
FUNERAL RITES

God is not the God of the dead but of the living;
for in him all are alive

PART I
FUNERAL RITES

50   Part I of the *Order of Christian Funerals* is divided into three groups of rites that correspond in general to the three principal ritual moments in the funerals of Christians: 'Vigil and Related Rites and Prayers', 'Funeral Liturgy', and 'Rite of Committal'. The minister, in consultation with those concerned, chooses from within these three groups of rites those that best correspond to the particular needs and customs of the mourners. This choice may be assisted by the reflections given in the General Introduction and in the introduction to each rite or group of rites.

VIGIL
AND RELATED RITES
AND PRAYERS

Do not let your hearts be troubled; trust in God still

VIGIL
AND RELATED RITES
AND PRAYERS

51 The rites provided here may be celebrated between the time of death and the funeral liturgy or, should there be no funeral liturgy, before the rite of committal.

The principal rite for this time is the vigil, of which two forms are presented here: 'Vigil for the Deceased', and 'Vigil for the Deceased with Reception at the Church', for convenient use in accord with the circumstances.

Four other rites are provided. Two rites are given in the section entitled 'Prayers': 'Prayers after Death' may be used when the minister first meets with the family; and 'Gathering in the Presence of the Body' could be used when the family first gathers around the body of the deceased. It is suggested that these might be led by a family member or a parishioner who exercises a pastoral ministry to the bereaved. Two rites are given in the section entitled 'Related Rites': 'Simple Form of the Reception of the Body' is for use when the body is to be received at the church but the vigil or funeral liturgy is not held at once; and 'Gathering of the Family and Transfer of the Body' could be used on the day of the funeral, in the home or funeral home, immediately before the body is taken to the church or place of committal.

Any of these rites may be led either by a priest, a deacon, or a lay person. They are examples or models of what can be done and should be adapted to the circumstances.

52 The time immediately following death is often one of bewilderment and may involve shock or heart-rending grief for the family and close friends. The ministry of the Church at this time is one of gently accompanying the mourners in their initial adjustment to the fact of death and to the sorrow this entails. Through a careful use of the rites contained in this section, the minister helps the mourners to express their sorrow and to find strength and consolation through faith in Christ and his resurrection to eternal life. The members of the Christian community offer support to the mourners, especially by praying that the one they have lost may have eternal life.

53 Ministers should be aware that the experience of death can bring about in the mourners possible needs for reconciliation. With attentiveness to each situation, the minister can help to begin the process of reconciliation. In some cases this process may find expression in the celebration of the sacrament of penance, either before the funeral liturgy or at a later time.

1 PRAYERS

PRAYERS AFTER DEATH

Blessed are the sorrowing; they shall be consoled

54   This rite provides a model of prayer that may be used when the minister first meets with the family following death. The rite follows a common pattern of reading, response, prayer, and blessing and may be adapted according to the circumstances.

55   The presence of the minister and the calming effect of familiar prayers can comfort the mourners as they begin to face their loss. When the minister is present with the family at the time death occurs, this rite can be used as a quiet and prayerful response to the death. In other circumstances, for example, in the case of sudden or unexpected death, this form of prayer can be the principal part of the first pastoral visit of the minister.

56   The initial pastoral visit can be important as the first tangible expression of the community's support for the mourners. A minister unfamiliar with the family or the deceased person can learn a great deal on this occasion about the needs of the family and about the life of the deceased. The minister may also be able to form some preliminary judgments to help the family in planning the funeral rites. If circumstances allow, some first steps in the planning may take place at this time.

OUTLINE OF THE RITE

Invitation to Prayer
Reading
The Lord's Prayer
Concluding Prayers
Blessing

PRAYERS AFTER DEATH

INVITATION TO PRAYER

57 Using one of the following greetings, or in similar words, the minister greets those present.

A In this moment of sorrow
the Lord is in our midst
and consoles us with his word:
Blessed are the sorrowful; they shall be comforted.

B Praised be God, the Father of our Lord Jesus Christ,
the Father of mercies,
and the God of all consolation!
He comforts us in all our afflictions
and thus enables us to comfort those who grieve
with the same consolation
we have received from him.

The minister then invites those present to pray in silence.

READING

58 The minister or one of those present proclaims the reading. One of the following or another Scripture reading is read.

A Matthew 18:19-20

Jesus said: 'If two of you on earth agree to ask anything at all, it will be granted to you by my Father in heaven. For where two or three meet in my name, I shall be there with them.'

B John 11:21-24

Martha said to Jesus, 'If you had been here, my brother would not have died, but I know that, even now, whatever you ask of God, he will grant you.' 'Your brother,' said Jesus to her, 'will rise again.' Martha said, 'I know he will rise again at the resurrection on the last day.' Jesus said:

'I am the resurrection and the life.
If anyone believes in me, even though he dies he will live,
and whoever lives and believes in me
will never die.
Do you believe this?'
'Yes, Lord,' she said, 'I believe that you are the Christ, the Son
of God, the one who was to come into this world.'

C   Luke 20:35-38

Jesus said: 'Those who are judged worthy of a place in the other
world and in the resurrection from the dead do not marry because they can no longer die, for they are the same as the angels,
and being children of the resurrection they are sons of God. And
Moses himself implies that the dead rise again, in the passage
about the bush where he calls the Lord the God of Abraham,
the God of Isaac and the God of Jacob. Now he is God, not of
the dead, but of the living; for to him all men are in fact alive.'

THE LORD'S PRAYER

59   Using one of the following invitations, or in similar words,
the minister invites those present to pray the Lord's Prayer.

A   With God there is mercy and fullness of redemption; let us pray
as Jesus taught us:

B   Let us pray for the coming of the kingdom as Jesus taught us:

C   In love, God calls us his children, for that indeed is what we
are. We ask for the strength we need by praying in the words
Jesus gave us:

All:
Our Father . . .

CONCLUDING PRAYERS

60   A prayer for the deceased person is then said. This prayer
may be followed by a prayer for the mourners. When the deceased is a child prayers should be taken from no. 580, 25-26
and no. 581, 8-15 (see p. 407).

For the deceased person

The minister says the following prayer or one of those provided in no. 580, p. 407.

Holy Lord, almighty and eternal God,   167
hear our prayers for your servant N.,
whom you have summoned out of this world.
Forgive his/her sins and failings
and grant him/her a place of refreshment, light, and peace.
Let him/her pass unharmed through the gates of death
to dwell with the blessed in light,
as you promised to Abraham and his children for ever.
Accept N. into your safe-keeping
and on the great day of judgment
raise him/her up with all the saints
to inherit your eternal kingdom.

We ask this through Christ our Lord.

R. Amen.

For the mourners

The minister may then say the following prayer or one of those provided in no. 581, p. 407.

Father of mercies and God of all consolation,   34
you pursue us with untiring love
and dispel the shadow of death
with the bright dawn of life.

[Comfort your family in their loss and sorrow.
Be our refuge and our strength, O Lord,
and lift us from the depths of grief
into the peace and light of your presence.]

Your Son, our Lord Jesus Christ,
by dying has destroyed our death,
and by rising, restored our life.
Enable us therefore to press on toward him,
so that, after our earthly course is run,
he may reunite us with those we love,
when every tear will be wiped away.

We ask this through Christ our Lord.

R. Amen.

BLESSING

The minister says:

Blessed are those who have died in the Lord;
let them rest from their labours for their good deeds
   go with them.

For children

Jesus said: 'Let the childen come to me. Do not keep them from
me. The kingdom of God belongs to such as these.'

A gesture, for example, signing the forehead of the deceased with
the sign of the cross, may accompany the following words.

Eternal rest grant unto him/her, O Lord.

R. And let perpetual light shine upon him/her.

May he/she rest in peace.

R. Amen.

May his/her soul and the souls of all the faithful departed,
through the mercy of God, rest in peace.

R. Amen.

A   A minister who is a priest or deacon says:

May the peace of God,
which is beyond all understanding,
keep your hearts and minds
in the knowledge and love of God
and of his Son, our Lord Jesus Christ.

R. Amen.

May almighty God bless you,
the Father, and the Son, ✠ and the Holy Spirit.

R. Amen.

B

May the love of God and the peace of the Lord Jesus Christ
console you
and gently wipe every tear from your eyes.

R. Amen.

May almighty God bless you,
the Father, and the Son, ✠ and the Holy Spirit.

R. Amen.

C

May the love of God and the peace of the Lord Jesus Christ
bless and console us
and gently wipe every tear from our eyes:
in the name of the Father,
and of the Son, and of the Holy Spirit.

R. Amen.

GATHERING IN THE PRESENCE OF THE BODY

If we have died with Christ, we believe we shall also live with him

62   This rite provides a model of prayer that may be used when the family first gathers in the presence of the body, when the body is to be prepared for burial, or after it has been prepared. The family members, in assembling in the presence of the body, confront in the most immediate way the fact of their loss and the mystery of death. Because cultural attitudes and practices on such occasions may vary, the minister should adapt the rite.

If the family does not gather until the day of the funeral, the rite, 'Gathering of the Family and Transfer of the Body', p. 71, may be more appropriate.

63   Through the presence of the minister and others and through the celebration of this brief rite, the community seeks to be with the mourners in their need and to provide an atmosphere of sensitive concern and confident faith. In prayer and gesture those present show reverence for the body of the deceased as a temple of the life-giving Spirit and ask, in that same Spirit, for the eternal life promised to the faithful.

64   The minister should try to be as attentive as possible to the particular needs of the mourners. The minister begins the rite at an opportune moment and, as much as possible, in an atmosphere of calm and recollection. The pause for silent prayer after the Scripture verse can be especially helpful in this regard.

OUTLINE OF THE RITE

Sign of the Cross
Scripture Verse
Sprinkling with Holy Water
Psalm
The Lord's Prayer
Concluding Prayer
Blessing

GATHERING IN THE PRESENCE OF THE BODY

SIGN OF THE CROSS

> 65   The minister and those present sign themselves with the sign
> of the cross as the minister says:

In the name of the Father, and of the Son, and of the Holy Spirit.

R. Amen.

SCRIPTURE VERSE

> 66   One of the following or another brief Scripture verse is read.

A   Matthew 11:28-30

My brothers and sisters, Jesus says: 'Come to me, all you who
labour and are overburdened, and I will give you rest. Shoulder my yoke and learn from me, for I am gentle and humble
in heart, and you will find rest for your souls. Yes, my yoke is
easy and my burden light.'

B   John 14:1-3

My brothers and sisters, Jesus says:
   'Do not let your hearts be troubled.
   Trust in God still and trust in me.
   There are many rooms in my Father's house;
   if there were not, I should have told you.
   I am going now to prepare a place for you,
   and after I have gone and prepared you a place,
   I shall return to take you with me,
   so that where I am
   you may be too.'

> Pause for silent prayer.

Sprinkling with Holy Water

> 67 Using one of the following texts, the minister may sprinkle the body with holy water.

A   The Lord is our shepherd
and leads us to streams of living water.

B   Let this water call to mind our baptism into Christ,
who by his death and resurrection has redeemed us.

C   The Lord God lives in his holy temple yet abides in our midst.
Since in baptism N. became God's temple
and the Spirit of God lived in him/her,
with reverence we bless his/her mortal body.

Psalm

> 68 One of the following or another suitable psalm is sung or said.

A   R. I hope in the Lord, I trust in his word.

Psalm 129 (130)

Out of the depths I cry to you, O Lord,
Lord, hear my voice!
O let your ears be attentive
to the voice of my pleading. R.

If you, O Lord, should mark our guilt,
Lord, who would survive?
But with you is found forgiveness:
for this we revere you. R.

My soul is waiting for the Lord,
I count on his word.
My soul is longing for the Lord
more than watchman for daybreak. R.

Because with the Lord there is mercy
and fullness of redemption,
Israel indeed he will redeem
from all its iniquity. R.

B   R. I will walk in the presence of the Lord, in the land of the living.

> Psalm 114 and 115 (115 and 116)

How gracious is the Lord, and just;
our God has compassion.
The Lord protects the simple hearts;
I was helpless so he saved me. R.

I trusted, even when I said:
'I am sorely afflicted,'
and when I said in my alarm:
'No man can be trusted.' R.

O precious in the eyes of the Lord
is the death of his faithful.
Your servant, Lord, your servant am I;
you have loosened my bonds. R.

The Lord's Prayer

69   Using one of the following invitations, or in similar words,
the minister invites those present to pray the Lord's Prayer.

A   With God there is mercy and fullness of redemption; let us pray as Jesus taught us:

B   Let us pray for the coming of the kingdom as Jesus taught us:

C   In love, God calls us his children, for that indeed is what we are. We ask for the strength we need by praying in the words Jesus gave us:

All:
Our Father . . .

Concluding Prayer

70   The minister says one of the following prayers or one of those
provided in nos. 580-581, p. 407. When the deceased is a child
prayers should be taken from no. 580, 25-26 and no. 581, 8-15
(see p. 407).

A   God of faithfulness,   30
in your wisdom you have called your servant N.
  out of this world;
release him/her from the bonds of sin,
and welcome him/her into your presence,
so that he/she may enjoy eternal light and peace
and be raised up in glory with all your saints.

We ask this through Christ our Lord.

R. Amen.

B   Into your hands, O Lord,   168
we humbly entrust our brother/sister N.
In this life you embraced him/her with your tender love;
deliver him/her now from every evil
and bid him/her enter eternal rest.

The old order has passed away:
welcome him/her then into paradise,
where there will be no sorrow, no weeping nor pain,
but the fullness of peace and joy
with your Son and the Holy Spirit
for ever and ever.

R. Amen.

BLESSING

The minister says:

Blessed are those who have died in the Lord;
let them rest from their labours for their good deeds
  go with them.

For children

Jesus said: 'Let the childen come to me. Do not keep them from
me. The kingdom of God belongs to such as these.'

A gesture, for example, signing the forehead of the deceased with
the sign of the cross, may accompany the following words.

Eternal rest grant unto him/her, O Lord.

R. And let perpetual light shine upon him/her.

May he/she rest in peace.

R. Amen.

May his/her soul and the souls of all the faithful departed,
through the mercy of God, rest in peace.

R. Amen.

A   A minister who is a priest or deacon says:

May the peace of God,
which is beyond all understanding,
keep your hearts and minds
in the knowledge and love of God
and of his Son, our Lord Jesus Christ.

R. Amen.

May almighty God bless you,
the Father, and the Son, ✠ and the Holy Spirit.

R. Amen.

B   A minister who is a priest or deacon says:

May the love of God and the peace of the Lord Jesus Christ
console you
and gently wipe every tear from your eyes.

R. Amen.

May almighty God bless you,
the Father, and the Son, ✠ and the Holy Spirit.

R. Amen.

C   A lay minister invokes God's blessing and signs himself or herself with the sign of the cross, saying:

May the love of God and the peace of the Lord Jesus Christ
bless and console us
and gently wipe every tear from our eyes:
in the name of the Father,
and of the Son, and of the Holy Spirit.

R. Amen.

2 VIGIL FOR THE DECEASED

Happy now are the dead who die in the Lord;
they shall find rest from their labours

72   The vigil for the deceased is the principal rite celebrated by the Christian community in the time following death and before the funeral liturgy, or if there is no funeral liturgy, before the rite of committal. It may take the form either of a liturgy of the word (nos. 87-99, 100-125) or of some part of the office for the dead (see Part IV, p. 378). Two vigil services are provided: 'Vigil for the Deceased' and 'Vigil for the Deceased with Reception at the Church.' The second service is used when the vigil is celebrated in the church and begins with the reception of the body.

73   The vigil may be celebrated in the home of the deceased, in the funeral home, parlour or chapel of rest, or in some other suitable place. It may also be celebrated in the church, but at a time well before the funeral liturgy, so that the funeral liturgy will not be lengthy and the liturgy of the word repetitious. Adaptations of the vigil will often be suggested by the place in which the celebration occurs. A celebration in the home of the deceased, for example, may be simplified and shortened.

   If the reception of the body at church is celebrated apart from the vigil or the funeral liturgy, the 'Simple Form of Reception at the Church', p. 63, may be used.

74   At the vigil the Christian community keeps watch with the family in prayer to the God of mercy and finds strength in Christ's presence. It is the first occasion among the funeral rites for the solemn reading of the word of God. In this time of loss the family and community turn to God's word as the source of faith and hope, as light and life in the face of darkness and death. Consoled by the redeeming word of God and by the abiding presence of Christ and his Spirit, the assembly at the vigil calls upon the Father of mercy to receive the deceased into the kingdom of light and peace.

STRUCTURE AND CONTENT OF THE VIGIL

75   The vigil in the form of the liturgy of the word consists of the introductory rites, the liturgy of the word, the prayer of intercession, and a concluding rite.

INTRODUCTORY RITES

76   The introductory rites gather the faithful together to form a community and to prepare all to listen to God's word. The introductory rites of

the vigil for the deceased include the greeting, an opening song, an invitation to prayer, a pause for silent prayer, and an opening prayer.

In the vigil for the deceased with reception at the church, the rite of reception forms the introductory rites (nos. 100-104). In this case the family and others who have accompanied the body are greeted at the entrance of the church. The body is then sprinkled with holy water and, if it is the custom, the pall is placed on the coffin by family members, friends, or the minister. The entrance procession follows, during which a hymn or psalm is sung. At the conclusion of the procession a symbol of the Christian life may be placed on the coffin. Then the invitation to prayer, a pause for silent prayer, and an opening prayer conclude the introductory rites.

The opening song or entrance song should be a profound expression of belief in eternal life and the resurrection of the dead, as well as a prayer of intercession for the dead.

Liturgy of the Word

77   The proclamation of the word of God is the high point and central focus of the vigil. The liturgy of the word usually includes a first reading, responsorial psalm, gospel reading, and homily. A reader proclaims the first reading. The responsorial psalm should be sung, whenever possible. If an assisting deacon is present, he proclaims the gospel reading. Otherwise the presiding minister proclaims the gospel reading.

78   The purpose of the readings at the vigil is to proclaim the paschal mystery, teach remembrance of the dead, convey the hope of being gathered together in God's kingdom, and encourage the witness of Christian life. Above all, the readings tell of God's designs for a world in which suffering and death will relinquish their hold on all whom God has called his own. The responsorial psalm enables the community to respond in faith to the reading and to express its grief and its praise of God. In the selection of readings the needs of the mourners and the circumstances of the death should be kept in mind.

79   A homily based on the readings is given at the vigil to help those present find strength and hope in God's saving word.

Prayer of Intercession

80   In the prayer of intercession the community calls upon God to comfort the mourners and to show mercy to the deceased. The prayer of intercession takes the form of a litany, the Lord's Prayer, and a concluding prayer.

After this prayer and before the blessing or at some other suitable time during the vigil, a member of the family or a friend of the deceased may speak in remembrance of the deceased.

CONCLUDING RITE

81   The vigil concludes with a blessing, which may be followed by a liturgical song or a few moments of silent prayer or both.

MINISTRY AND PARTICIPATION

82   Members of the local parish community should be encouraged to participate in the vigil as a sign of concern and support for the mourners. In many circumstances the vigil will be the first opportunity for friends, neighbours, and members of the local parish community to show their concern for the family of the deceased by gathering for prayer. The vigil may also serve as an opportunity for participation in the funeral by those who, because of work or other reasons, cannot be present for the funeral liturgy or the rite of committal.

83   The full participation by all present is to be encouraged. This is best achieved through careful planning of the celebration. Whenever possible, the family of the deceased should take part in the selection of texts and music and in the designation of liturgical ministers.

84   Besides the presiding minister, other available ministers (a reader, a cantor, an acolyte) should exercise their ministries. Family members may assume some of these liturgical roles, unless their grief prevents them from doing so.

The presiding minister and assisting ministers should vest for the vigil according to local custom. If the vigil is celebrated in the church, a priest or deacon who presides wears an alb or surplice with stole.

85   As needs require, and especially if the funeral liturgy or rite of committal is not to take place for a few days, the vigil may be celebrated more than once and should be adapted to each occasion.

86   Music is integral to any vigil, especially the vigil for the deceased. In the difficult circumstances following death, well-chosen music can touch the mourners and others present at levels of human need that words alone often fail to reach. Such music can enliven the faith of the community gathered to support the family and to affirm hope in the resurrection.

Whenever possible, an instrumentalist and a cantor or leader of song should assist the assembly's full participation in the singing.

In the choice of music for the vigil, preference should be given to the singing of the opening song and the responsorial psalm. The litany, the Lord's Prayer, and a closing song may also be sung.

OUTLINE OF THE RITE

INTRODUCTORY RITES

Greeting
Opening Song
Invitation to Prayer
Opening Prayer

LITURGY OF THE WORD

First Reading
Responsorial Psalm
Gospel
Homily

PRAYER OF INTERCESSION

Litany
The Lord's Prayer
Concluding Prayer

CONCLUDING RITE

Blessing

VIGIL FOR THE DECEASED

INTRODUCTORY RITES

GREETING

> 87 Using one of the following greetings, or in similar words, the minister greets those present.

A   May the God of hope give you the fullness of peace, and may the Lord of life be always with you.

R. And also with you.

B   The grace and peace of God our Father and the Lord Jesus Christ be with you.

R. And also with you.

C   The grace and peace of God our Father, who raised Jesus from the dead, be always with you.

R. And also with you.

D   May the Father of mercies, the God of all consolation, be with you.

R. And also with you.

OPENING SONG

> 88 The celebration continues with a song.

Invitation to Prayer

89 In the following or similar words, the minister invites those present to pray.

My brothers and sisters, we believe that all the ties of friendship and affection which knit us as one throughout our lives do not unravel with death.

Confident that God always remembers the good we have done and forgives our sins, let us pray, asking God to gather N. to himself.

Pause for silent prayer.

Opening Prayer

90 The minister says one of the following prayers or one of those provided in nos. 580-581, p. 407.

A   Lord our God,
the death of our brother/sister N.
recalls our human condition
and the brevity of our lives on earth.
But for those who believe in your love
death is not the end,
nor does it destroy the bonds
that you forge in our lives.
We share the faith of your Son's disciples
and the hope of the children of God.
Bring the light of Christ's resurrection
to this time of testing and pain
as we pray for N. and for those who love him/her,
through Christ our Lord.

R. Amen.

O God,   171
   glory of believers and life of the just,
   by the death and resurrection of your Son, we are redeemed:
   have mercy on your servant N.,
   and make him/her worthy to share the joys of paradise,
   for he/she believed in the resurrection of the dead.

   We ask this through Christ our Lord.

   R. Amen.

LITURGY OF THE WORD

91 The celebration continues with the liturgy of the word. Other readings, psalms, and gospel readings are found in the Lectionary, Volume III.

First Reading

92 A reader proclaims the first reading.

A reading from the second letter of Saint Paul
to the Corinthians   5:1, 6-10

We have an everlasting home in heaven.

We know that when the tent that we live in on earth is folded up, there is a house built by God for us, an everlasting home not made by human hands, in the heavens.

We are always full of confidence, then, when we remember that to live in the body means to be exiled from the Lord, going as we do by faith and not by sight—we are full of confidence, I say, and actually want to be exiled from the body and make our home with the Lord.

Whether we are living in the body or exiled from it, we are intent on pleasing him. For all the truth about us will be brought out in the law court of Christ, and each of us will get what he deserves for the things he did in the body, good or bad.

This is the Word of the Lord.

93   The following or another suitable psalm is sung or said.

R. The Lord is my light and my help.

   Or:

R. I am sure I shall see the Lord's goodness in the land of the
living.

Psalm 26 (27)   110

The Lord is my light and my help;
whom shall I fear?
The Lord is the stronghold of my life;
before whom shall I shrink? R.

There is one thing I ask of the Lord,
for this I long,
to live in the house of the Lord,
all the days of my life,
to savour the sweetness of the Lord,
to behold his temple. R.

O Lord, hear my voice when I call;
have mercy and answer.
It is your face, O Lord, that I seek;
hide not your face. R.

I am sure I shall see the Lord's goodness
in the land of the living.
Hope in him, hold firm and take heart.
Hope in the Lord! R.

GOSPEL

94 The gospel reading is then proclaimed.

A reading from the holy gospel according to Luke   12:35-40   134

Be prepared.

Jesus said to his disciples:

'See that you are dressed for action and have your lamps lit. Be like men waiting for their master to return from the wedding feast, ready to open the door as soon as he comes and knocks.

'Happy those servants whom the master finds awake when he comes. I tell you solemnly, he will put on an apron, sit them down at table and wait on them. It may be in the second watch he comes, or in the third, but happy those servants if he finds them ready.

'You may be quite sure of this, that if the householder had known at what hour the burglar would come, he would not have let anyone break through the wall of his house.

'You too must stand ready, because the Son of Man is coming at an hour you do not expect.'

This is the Gospel of the Lord.

HOMILY

95 A brief homily on the readings is then given.

PRAYER OF INTERCESSION

LITANY

96   The minister leads those present in the following litany.

Let us turn to Christ Jesus with confidence and faith in the power of his cross and resurrection:

A reader or the minister then continues:
Risen Lord, pattern of our life for ever:
Lord, have mercy.

R.   Lord, have mercy.

Promise and image of what we shall be:
Lord, have mercy.

R.   Lord, have mercy.

Son of God who came to destroy sin and death:
Lord, have mercy.

R.   Lord, have mercy.

Word of God who delivered us from the fear of death:
Lord, have mercy.

R.   Lord, have mercy.

Crucified Lord, forsaken in death, raised in glory:
Lord, have mercy.

R.   Lord, have mercy.

Lord Jesus, gentle Shepherd who bring rest to our souls, give peace to N. for ever:
Lord, have mercy.

R.   Lord, have mercy.

Lord Jesus, you bless those who mourn and are in pain. Bless N.'s family and friends who gather around him/her today:
Lord, have mercy.

R.   Lord, have mercy.

The Lord's Prayer

97 Using one of the following invitations, or in similar words, the minister invites those present to pray the Lord's Prayer.

A   [Friends/Brothers and sisters], our true home is heaven. Therefore let us pray to our heavenly Father as Jesus taught us:

B   With God there is mercy and fullness of redemption; let us pray as Jesus taught us:

C   Let us pray for the coming of the kingdom as Jesus taught us:

All:
Our Father . . .

Concluding Prayer

98 The minister says one of the following prayers or one of those provided in nos. 580-581, p. 407.

A   Lord Jesus, our Redeemer,   169
you willingly gave yourself up to death,
so that all might be saved and pass from death to life.
We humbly ask you to comfort your servants in their grief
and to receive N. into the arms of your mercy.
You alone are the Holy One,
you are mercy itself;
by dying you unlocked the gates of life
    for those who believe in you.
Forgive N. his/her sins,
and grant him/her a place of happiness, light, and peace
in the kingdom of your glory for ever.
R. Amen.

B   Lord God,
you are attentive to the voice of our pleading.
Let us find in your Son
comfort in our sadness,
certainty in our doubt,
and courage to live through this hour.
Make our faith strong
through Christ our Lord.

R. Amen.

> A member or a friend of the family may speak in remembrance
> of the deceased.

CONCLUDING RITE

BLESSING

> 99   The minister says:

Blessed are those who have died in the Lord;
let them rest from their labours for their good deeds
    go with them.

> A gesture, for example, signing the forehead of the deceased with
> the sign of the cross, may accompany the following words.

Eternal rest grant unto him/her, O Lord.

R. And let perpetual light shine upon him/her.

May he/she rest in peace.

R. Amen.

May his/her soul and the souls of all the faithful departed,
through the mercy of God, rest in peace.

R. Amen.

A   A minister who is a priest or deacon says:

May the peace of God,
which is beyond all understanding,
keep your hearts and minds
in the knowledge and love of God
and of his Son, our Lord Jesus Christ.

R. Amen.

May almighty God bless you,
the Father, and the Son, ✠ and the Holy Spirit.

R. Amen.

B   A minister who is a priest or deacon says:

May the love of God and the peace of the Lord Jesus Christ
console you
and gently wipe every tear from your eyes.

R. Amen.

May almighty God bless you,
the Father, and the Son, ✠ and the Holy Spirit.

R. Amen.

C   A lay minister invokes God's blessing and signs himself or herself with the sign of the cross, saying:

May the love of God and the peace of the Lord Jesus Christ
bless and console us
and gently wipe every tear from our eyes:
in the name of the Father,
and of the Son, and of the Holy Spirit.

R. Amen.

The vigil may conclude with a song or a few moments of silent prayer or both.

OUTLINE OF THE RITE

INTRODUCTORY RITES

Greeting
Sprinkling with Holy Water
Entrance Procession
[Placing of the Pall]
[Placing of Christian Symbols]
Invitation to Prayer
Opening Prayer

LITURGY OF THE WORD

First Reading
Responsorial Psalm
Gospel
Homily

PRAYER OF INTERCESSION

Litany
The Lord's Prayer
Concluding Prayer

CONCLUDING RITE

Blessing

VIGIL FOR THE DECEASED
WITH RECEPTION AT THE CHURCH

INTRODUCTORY RITES

GREETING

100 The minister, with assisting ministers, goes to the door of the church and, using one of the following greetings, or in similar words, greets those present.

A May the God of hope give you the fullness of peace, and may the Lord of life be always with you.

R. And also with you.

B The grace and peace of God our Father and the Lord Jesus Christ be with you.

R. And also with you.

C The grace and peace of God our Father, who raised Jesus from the dead, be always with you.

R. And also with you.

D May the Father of mercies, the God of all consolation, be with you.

R. And also with you.

SPRINKLING WITH HOLY WATER

101 The minister then sprinkles the coffin with holy water, saying:

In the waters of baptism
N. died with Christ and rose with him to new life.
May he/she now share with him eternal glory.

Entrance Procession

102 The Easter candle may be placed beforehand near the position the coffin will occupy at the conclusion of the procession. The minister and assisting ministers precede the coffin and the mourners into the church. During the procession a psalm, song, or responsory is sung.

Placing of the Pall

103 If it is the custom in the local community, the pall is then placed on the coffin by family members, friends, or the minister.

Placing of Christian Symbols

104 A symbol of the Christian life, such as a Book of the Gospels, a Bible, or a cross, may be carried in procession, then placed on the coffin, either in silence or as one of the following texts is said.

A   Book of the Gospels or Bible

In life N. cherished the Gospel of Christ.
May Christ now greet him/her with these words of eternal life:
Come, blessed of my Father!

B   Cross

In baptism N. received the sign of the cross.
May he/she now share
in Christ's victory over sin and death.

Invitation to Prayer

105 In the following or similar words, the minister invites those present to pray.

My brothers and sisters, we believe that all the ties of friendship and affection which knit us as one throughout our lives do not unravel with death.

Confident that God always remembers the good we have done and forgives our sins, let us pray, asking God to gather N. to himself.

Pause for silent prayer.

Opening Prayer

106 The minister says one of the following prayers or one of those provided in nos. 580-581, p. 407.

A   Lord, in our grief we turn to you.   33
    Are you not the God of love
    always ready to hear our cries?

   Listen to our prayers for your servant N.,
   whom you have called out of this world:
   lead him/her to your kingdom of light and peace
   and count him/her among the saints in glory.

   We ask this through Christ our Lord.

   R. Amen.

B   Lord Jesus, our Redeemer,   169
    you willingly gave yourself up to death,
    so that all might be saved and pass from death to life.
    We humbly ask you to comfort your servants in their grief
    and to receive N. into the arms of your mercy.
    You alone are the Holy One,
    you are mercy itself;
    by dying you unlocked the gates of life
       for those who believe in you.
    Forgive N. his/her sins,
    and grant him/her a place of happiness, light, and peace
    in the kingdom of your glory for ever.

   R. Amen.

LITURGY OF THE WORD

107 The celebration continues with the liturgy of the word. Other readings, psalms, and gospel readings are found in the Lectionary, Volume III.

FIRST READING

108 A reader proclaims the first reading.

A reading from the first letter of Saint John   3:1-2   103

We shall see God as he really is.

Think of the love that the Father has lavished on us,
by letting us be called God's children;
and that is what we are.
Because the world refused to acknowledge him,
therefore it does not acknowledge us.

My dear people, we are already the children of God
but what we are to be in the future
has not yet been revealed;
all we know is, that when it is revealed
we shall be like him
because we shall see him as he really is.

This is the Word of the Lord.

RESPONSORIAL PSALM

109 The following or another suitable psalm is sung or said.

R. The Lord is compassion and love.   113
     Or:

R. The salvation of the just comes from the Lord.

Psalm 102 (103)

The Lord is compassion and love,
slow to anger and rich in mercy.
He does not treat us according to our sins
nor repay us according to our faults. R.

As a father has compassion on his sons,
the Lord has pity on those who fear him;
for he knows of what we are made,
he remembers that we are dust. R.

As for man, his days are like grass;
he flowers like the flower of the field;
the wind blows and he is gone
and his place never sees him again. R.

But the love of the Lord is everlasting
upon those who hold him in fear;
his justice reaches out to children's children
when they keep his covenant in truth. R.

GOSPEL

110 The gospel reading is then proclaimed.

A reading from the holy gospel according to John   14:1-6   143

There are many rooms in my Father's house.

Jesus said to his disciples:

'Do not let your hearts be troubled.
Trust in God still, and trust in me.
There are many rooms in my Father's house;
if there were not, I should have told you.
I am going now to prepare a place for you,
and after I have gone and prepared you a place,
I shall return to take you with me;
so that where I am
you may be too.
You know the way to the place where I am going.'

Thomas said, 'Lord, we do not know where you are going, so how can we know the way?' Jesus said:

'I am the Way, the Truth and the Life.
No one can come to the Father except through me.'

This is the Gospel of the Lord.

HOMILY

111 A brief homily on the readings is then given.

PRAYER OF INTERCESSION

LITANY

112 The minister leads those present in the following litany.

Let us turn to Christ Jesus with confidence and faith in the power of his cross and resurrection:

A reader or the minister then continues:
Risen Lord, pattern of our life for ever:
Lord, have mercy.

R. Lord, have mercy.

Promise and image of what we shall be:
Lord, have mercy.

R. Lord, have mercy.

Son of God who came to destroy sin and death:
Lord, have mercy.

R. Lord, have mercy.

Word of God who delivered us from the fear of death:
Lord, have mercy.

R. Lord, have mercy.

Crucified Lord, forsaken in death, raised in glory:
Lord, have mercy.

R. Lord, have mercy.

Lord Jesus, gentle Shepherd who bring rest to our souls, give peace to N. for ever:
Lord, have mercy.

R. Lord, have mercy.

Lord Jesus, you bless those who mourn and are in pain. Bless N.'s family and friends who gather around him/her today:
Lord, have mercy.

R. Lord, have mercy.

THE LORD'S PRAYER

113 Using one of the following invitations, or in similar words, the minister invites those present to pray the Lord's Prayer.

A [Friends/Brothers and sisters], our true home is heaven. Therefore let us pray to our heavenly Father as Jesus taught us:

B With God there is mercy and fullness of redemption; let us pray as Jesus taught us:

C Let us pray for the coming of the kingdom as Jesus taught us:

All:
Our Father . . .

CONCLUDING PRAYER

114 The minister says one of the following prayers or one of those provided in nos. 580-581, p. 407.

A Lord God, in whom all find refuge,
we appeal to your boundless mercy:
grant to the soul of your servant N.
a kindly welcome,
cleansing of sin,
release from the chains of death,
and entry into everlasting life.
We ask this through Christ our Lord.
R. Amen.

B Lord God,
you are attentive to the voice of our pleading.
Let us find in your Son
comfort in our sadness,
certainty in our doubt,
and courage to live through this hour.
Make our faith strong
through Christ our Lord.
R. Amen.

A member or a friend of the family may speak in remembrance of the deceased.

CONCLUDING RITE

BLESSING

115 The minister says:

Blessed are those who have died in the Lord;
let them rest from their labours for their good deeds
    go with them.

A gesture, for example, signing the forehead of the deceased with
the sign of the cross, may accompany the following words.

Eternal rest grant unto him/her, O Lord.

R. And let perpetual light shine upon him/her.

May he/she rest in peace.

R. Amen.

May his/her soul and the souls of all the faithful departed,
through the mercy of God, rest in peace.

R. Amen.

A   A minister who is a priest or deacon says:

May the peace of God,
which is beyond all understanding,
keep your hearts and minds
in the knowledge and love of God
and of his Son, our Lord Jesus Christ.

R. Amen.

May almighty God bless you,
the Father, and the Son, ✠ and the Holy Spirit.

R. Amen.

B   A minister who is a priest or deacon says:

May the love of God and the peace of the Lord Jesus Christ
console you
and gently wipe every tear from your eyes.

R. Amen.

May almighty God bless you,
the Father, and the Son, ✠ and the Holy Spirit.

R. Amen.

C   A lay minister invokes God's blessing and signs himself or herself with the sign of the cross, saying:

May the love of God and the peace of the Lord Jesus Christ
bless and console us
and gently wipe every tear from our eyes:
in the name of the Father,
and of the Son, and of the Holy Spirit.

R. Amen.

The vigil may conclude with a song or a few moments of silent
prayer or both.

3 RELATED RITES

SIMPLE FORM OF RECEPTION
AT THE CHURCH

If we have died with Christ, we believe we shall also live with him.

116 If the body is to be received in church but the vigil and remaining stages of the funeral liturgy do not take place at once, this simple rite of reception at the church may be used.

OUTLINE OF THE RITE

Greeting
Sprinkling with Holy Water
Entrance Procession
[Placing of the Pall]
Opening Prayer
Scripture Verse
[Intercessions]
The Lord's Prayer
Blessing

SIMPLE FORM OF RECEPTION
AT THE CHURCH

GREETING

> 117 The minister goes to the door of the church and, using one of the following greetings, or in similar words, greets those present.

A   May the God of hope give you the fullness of peace, and may the Lord of life be always with you.

    R. And also with you.

B   The grace and peace of God our Father and the Lord Jesus Christ be with you.

    R. And also with you.

C   The grace and peace of God our Father, who raised Jesus from the dead, be always with you.

    R. And also with you.

D   May the Father of mercies, the God of all consolation, be with you.

    R. And also with you.

SPRINKLING WITH HOLY WATER

> 118 The minister then sprinkles the coffin with holy water, saying:

In the waters of baptism
N. died with Christ and rose with him to new life.
May he/she now share with him eternal glory.

119 The Easter candle may be placed beforehand near the position the coffin will occupy at the conclusion of the procession. The minister precedes the coffin and the mourners into the church. During the procession the following psalm or another suitable psalm, song, or responsory is sung.

R. Let us go to God's house, rejoicing.

Or:

R. I rejoiced when I heard them say: 'Let us go to God's house.'

Psalm 121 (122)   115

I rejoiced when I heard them say:
'Let us go to God's house.'
And now our feet are standing
within your gates, O Jerusalem. R.

Jerusalem is built as a city
strongly compact.
It is there that the tribes go up,
the tribes of the Lord. R.

For Israel's law it is,
there to praise the Lord's name.
There were set the thrones of judgment
of the house of David. R.

For the peace of Jerusalem pray:
'Peace be to your homes!
May peace reign in your walls,
in your palaces, peace!' R.

For love of my brethren and friends
I say: 'Peace upon you!'
For love of the house of the Lord
I will ask for your good. R.

PLACING OF THE PALL

120 If it is the custom in the local community, the pall is then placed on the coffin by family members, friends, or the minister.

Opening Prayer

121 The minister says the following prayer or one of those provided in nos. 580-581, p. 407.

Lord God,
you are attentive to the voice of our pleading.
Let us find in your Son
comfort in our sadness,
certainty in our doubt,
and courage to live through this hour.
Make our faith strong
through Christ our Lord.

R. Amen.

Scripture Verse

122 One of the following or another brief Scripture verse is read.

A   Matthew 11:28-30

My brothers and sisters, Jesus says: 'Come to me, all you who labour and are overburdened, and I will give you rest. Shoulder my yoke and learn from me, for I am gentle and humble in heart, and you will find rest for your souls. Yes, my yoke is easy and my burden light.'

B   John 14:1-3

My brothers and sisters, Jesus says:
'Do not let your hearts be troubled.
Trust in God still and trust in me.
There are many rooms in my Father's house;
if there were not, I should have told you.
I am going now to prepare a place for you,
and after I have gone and prepared you a place,
I shall return to take you with me,
so that where I am
you may be too.'

Intercessions

123 After the Scripture verse a period of silent prayer or intercessions may follow.

The Lord's Prayer

124 Using one of the following invitations, or in similar words,
the minister invites those present to pray the Lord's Prayer.

A With God there is mercy and fullness of redemption; let us pray
as Jesus taught us:

B Let us pray for the coming of the kingdom as Jesus taught us:

All:
Our Father . . .

Blessing

125 The minister says:

Blessed are those who have died in the Lord;
let them rest from their labours for their good deeds
go with them.

For children

Jesus said: 'Let the childen come to me. Do not keep them from
me. The kingdom of God belongs to such as these.'

A gesture, for example, signing the forehead of the deceased with
the sign of the cross, may accompany the following words.

Eternal rest grant unto him/her, O Lord.

R. And let perpetual light shine upon him/her.

May he/she rest in peace.

R. Amen.

May his/her soul and the souls of all the faithful departed,
through the mercy of God, rest in peace.

R. Amen.

A   A minister who is a priest or deacon says:

May the peace of God,
which is beyond all understanding,
keep your hearts and minds
in the knowledge and love of God
and of his Son, our Lord Jesus Christ.

R. Amen.

May almighty God bless you,
the Father, and the Son, ✠ and the Holy Spirit.

R. Amen.

B   A minister who is a priest or deacon says:

May the love of God and the peace of the Lord Jesus Christ
console you
and gently wipe every tear from your eyes.

R. Amen.

May almighty God bless you,
the Father, and the Son, ✠ and the Holy Spirit.

R. Amen.

C   A lay minister invokes God's blessing and signs himself or herself with the sign of the cross, saying:

May the love of God and the peace of the Lord Jesus Christ
bless and console us
and gently wipe every tear from our eyes:
in the name of the Father,
and of the Son, and of the Holy Spirit.

R. Amen.

The rite may conclude with a song.

GATHERING OF THE FAMILY
AND TRANSFER OF THE BODY
TO THE CHURCH
OR TO THE PLACE OF COMMITTAL

Your life is hidden now with Christ in God

126 This rite may be used for prayer with the family and close friends on the day of the funeral, as they gather, perhaps for the first time since the death, at home or at the funeral home, and prepare to accompany the body of the deceased in the procession to the church or to the place of committal. It is a model, for adaptation by the minister according to the circumstances.

127 The procession to the church is a rite of initial separation of the mourners from the deceased; the procession to the place of committal is the journey to the place of final separation of the mourners from the deceased. Because the transfer of the body may be an occasion of great emotion for the mourners, the minister and other members of the community should make every effort to be present to support them. Reverent celebration of the rite can help reassure the mourners and create an atmosphere of calm preparation before the procession.

OUTLINE OF THE RITE

Sign of the Cross

Invitation

Scripture Verse

Psalm

Litany

The Lord's Prayer

Concluding Prayer

Invitation to the Procession

Procession to the Church
or to the Place of Committal

GATHERING OF THE FAMILY AND TRANSFER OF THE BODY TO THE CHURCH OR TO THE PLACE OF COMMITTAL

SIGN OF THE CROSS

128 The minister and those present sign themselves with the sign of the cross as the minister says:

In the name of the Father, and of the Son, and of the Holy Spirit.

R. Amen.

INVITATION

129 In the following or similar words, the minister addresses those present.

Dear friends in Christ, in the name of Jesus and of his Church, we gather to pray for N., that God may bring him/her to everlasting peace and rest.

We share the pain of loss, but the promise of eternal life gives us hope. Let us comfort one another with these words:

SCRIPTURE VERSE

130 One of the following or another brief Scripture verse is read.

A   Matthew 11:28-30

My brothers and sisters, Jesus says: 'Come to me, all you who labour and are overburdened, and I will give you rest. Shoulder my yoke and learn from me, for I am gentle and humble in heart, and you will find rest for your souls. Yes, my yoke is easy and my burden light.'

B   Colossians 3:3-4

My brothers and sisters, we read in sacred Scripture:

You have died, and now the life you have is hidden with Christ
in God. But when Christ is revealed — and he is your life — you
too will be revealed in all your glory with him.

C   Romans 6:8-9

My brothers and sisters, we read in sacred Scripture:

We believe that having died with Christ we shall return to life
with him: Christ, as we know, having been raised from the dead
will never die again. Death has no power over him any more.

          Pause for silent prayer.

Psalm

          131 One of the following or another suitable psalm is sung or
          said.

A   R. I hope in the Lord, I trust in his word.

          Psalm 129 (130)

Out of the depths I cry to you, O Lord,
Lord, hear my voice!
O let your ears be attentive
to the voice of my pleading. R.

If you, O Lord, should mark our guilt,
Lord, who would survive?
But with you is found forgiveness:
for this we revere you. R.

My soul is waiting for the Lord,
I count on his word.
My soul is longing for the Lord
more than watchman for daybreak. R.

Because with the Lord there is mercy
and fullness of redemption,
Israel indeed he will redeem
from all its iniquity. R.

B   R. I will walk in the presence of the Lord in the land of the
living.

Psalm 114 and 115 (115 and 116)

How gracious is the Lord, and just;
our God has compassion.
The Lord protects the simple hearts;
I was helpless so he saved me. R.

I trusted, even when I said:
'I am sorely afflicted,'
and when I said in my alarm:
'No man can be trusted.' R.

O precious in the eyes of the Lord
is the death of his faithful.
Your servant, Lord, your servant am I;
you have loosened my bonds. R.

LITANY

132 The minister leads those present in the following litany.

Dear friends, our Lord comes to raise the dead and comforts
us with the solace of his love. Let us praise the Lord Jesus Christ.

A reader or the minister then continues:

Word of God, Creator of the earth to which N. now returns:
in baptism you called him/her to eternal life to praise your
Father for ever:
Lord, have mercy.

R. Lord, have mercy.

Son of God, you raise up the just and clothe them with the glory
of your kingdom:
Lord, have mercy.

R. Lord, have mercy.

Crucified Lord, you protect the soul of N. by the power of your
cross, and on the day of your coming you will show mercy to
all the faithful departed:
Lord, have mercy.

R. Lord, have mercy.

Judge of the living and the dead, at your voice the tombs will open and all the just who sleep in your peace will rise and sing the glory of God:
Lord, have mercy.

R. Lord, have mercy.

All praise to you, Jesus our Saviour, death is in your hands and all the living depend on you alone:
Lord, have mercy.

R. Lord, have mercy.

THE LORD'S PRAYER

133 In the following or similar words, the minister invites those present to pray the Lord's Prayer.

With faith and hope we pray to the Father in the words Jesus taught his disciples:

All:

Our Father . . .

CONCLUDING PRAYER

134 The minister says one of the following prayers or one of those provided in nos. 580-581, p. 407.

A Lord,
N. is gone now from this earthly dwelling
and has left behind those who mourn his/her absence.
Grant that as we grieve for our brother/sister
we may hold his/her memory dear
and live in hope of the eternal kingdom
where you will bring us together again.

We ask this through Christ our Lord.

R. Amen.

B   Lord, in our grief we turn to you.   33
      Are you not the God of love
      always ready to hear our cries?

      Listen to our prayers for your servant N.,
      whom you have called out of this world:
      lead him/her to your kingdom of light and peace
      and count him/her among the saints in glory.

      We ask this through Christ our Lord.

      R. Amen.

C   God of all consolation,   176
      open our hearts to your word,
      so that, listening to it, we may comfort one another,
      finding light in time of darkness
      and faith in time of doubt.

      We ask this through Christ our Lord.

      R. Amen.

          The minister invites those present to pray in silence while all
          is made ready for the procession to the church or place of com-
          mittal.

INVITATION TO THE PROCESSION

          135 In the following or similar words, the minister invites those
          present to join in the procession.

      The Lord guards our coming in and our going out.
      May God be with us today
      as we make this last journey with our brother/sister.

Procession to the Church or to the Place of Committal

136 During the procession, psalms and other suitable songs may be sung. If this is not possible, a psalm is sung or recited either before or after the procession. The following psalm and others provided in no. 582, p. 407, may be used.

R. I rejoiced when I heard them say: 'Let us go to God's house.'

Or:

R. Let us go to God's house, rejoicing.

Psalm 121 (122)

I rejoiced when I heard them say:
'Let us go to God's house.'
And now our feet are standing
within your gates, O Jerusalem. R.

Jerusalem is built as a city
strongly compact.
It is there that the tribes go up,
the tribes of the Lord. R.

For Israel's law it is,
there to praise the Lord's name.
There were set the thrones of judgment
of the house of David. R.

For the peace of Jerusalem pray:
'Peace be to your homes!
May peace reign in your walls,
in your palaces, peace!' R.

For love of my brethren and friends
I say: 'Peace upon you!'
For love of the house of the Lord
I will ask for your good. R.

FUNERAL LITURGY

All will be brought to life in Christ

FUNERAL LITURGY

137 The funeral liturgy is the central liturgical celebration of the Christian community for the deceased. Two forms of the funeral liturgy are presented here: 'Funeral Mass' and 'Funeral Liturgy outside Mass.'

When one of its members dies, the Church encourages the celebration of the Mass. But when Mass cannot be celebrated (see no. 189), the second form of the funeral liturgy is used. When the funeral liturgy is celebrated outside Mass before the committal, a Mass for the deceased should be scheduled, if possible, for the family and friends at a convenient time after the funeral.

138 At the funeral liturgy the community gathers with the family and friends of the deceased to give praise and thanks to God for Christ's victory over sin and death, to commend the deceased to God's tender mercy and compassion, and to seek strength in the proclamation of the paschal mystery. Through the Holy Spirit the community is joined together in faith as one Body in Christ to reaffirm in sign and symbol, word and gesture that each believer through baptism shares in Christ's death and resurrection and can look to the day when all the elect will be raised up and united in the kingdom of light and peace.

STRUCTURE AND CONTENT OF THE FUNERAL LITURGY

139 The funeral Mass includes the reception of the body, if this has not already occurred, the celebration of the liturgy of the word, the liturgy of the eucharist, and the final commendation and farewell. The funeral liturgy outside Mass includes all these elements except the liturgy of the eucharist. Both the funeral Mass and the funeral liturgy outside Mass may be followed by the procession to the place of committal.

RECEPTION AT THE CHURCH

140 Since the church is the place where the community of faith assembles for worship, the rite of reception of the body at the church has great significance. The church is the place where the Christian life is begotten in baptism, nourished in the eucharist, and where the community gathers to commend one of its deceased members to the Father. The church is at once a symbol of the community and of the heavenly liturgy that the celebration of the liturgy anticipates. In the act of receiving the body, the members of the community acknowledge the deceased as one of their own, as one who was welcomed in baptism and who held a place in the assembly. Through the use of various baptismal symbols the community shows the reverence due to the body, the temple of the Spirit, and in this way pre-

pares for the funeral liturgy in which it asks for a share in the heavenly banquet promised to the deceased and to all who have been washed in the waters of rebirth and marked with the sign of faith.

141 Any national flags or the flags or insignia of associations to which the deceased belonged are to be removed from the coffin at the entrance of the church. They may be replaced after the coffin has been taken from the church.

142 The rite of reception takes place at the beginning of the funeral liturgy, usually at the entrance of the church. It begins with a greeting of the family and others who have accompanied the coffin to the door of the church. The minister sprinkles the coffin with holy water in remembrance of the deceased person's initiation and first acceptance into the community of faith. The entrance procession follows. The minister precedes the coffin and the mourners into the church. If the Easter candle is used on this occasion, it may be placed beforehand near the position the coffin will occupy at the conclusion of the procession. A funeral pall, a reminder of the garment given at baptism, and therefore signifying life in Christ, may then be placed on the coffin by family members, friends, or the minister.

    The coffin should be placed before the altar, or in some other suitable place in view of the congregation and in proximity to the altar. If a catafalque is used, it should be of worthy design and harmonize with the sanctuary furnishings. Care should be taken that the placing of the catafalque and coffin does not impede either the view of the congregation or the movement of ministers and people.

143 If in this rite a symbol of the Christian life is to be placed on the coffin, it is carried in the procession and is placed on the coffin by a family member, friend, or the minister at the conclusion of the procession.

144 To draw the community together in prayer at the beginning of the funeral liturgy, the procession should be accompanied, whenever possible, by the singing of the entrance song. This song ought to be a profound expression of belief in eternal life and the resurrection of the dead as well as a prayer of intercession for the deceased.

145 If the rite of reception has already taken place, the funeral Mass begins in the usual way and the funeral liturgy outside Mass begins with the entrance song, followed by the greeting and an invitation to prayer.

LITURGY OF THE WORD

146 The reading of the word of God is an essential element of the celebration of the funeral liturgy. The readings proclaim the paschal mystery, teach remembrance of the dead, convey the hope of being gathered together again in God's kingdom, and encourage the witness of Christian life. Above all,

the readings tell of God's design for a world in which suffering and death will relinquish their hold on all whom God has called his own.

147 Depending on pastoral circumstances, there may be either one or two readings before the gospel. When there is a first and second reading before the gospel reading, it is preferable to have a different reader for each.

148 The responsorial psalm enables the community to respond in faith to the first reading. Through the psalms the community expresses its grief and praise, and acknowledges its Creator and Redeemer as the sure source of trust and hope in times of trial. Since the responsorial psalm is a song, whenever possible, it should be sung. Psalms may be sung responsorially, with the response sung by the assembly and all the verses by the cantor or choir, or directly, with no response and all the verses sung by all or by the cantor or choir. When not sung, the responsorial psalm after the reading should be recited in a manner conducive to meditation on the word of God.[1]

149 In the *alleluia*, or the gospel acclamation, the community welcomes the Lord who is about to speak to it. If the *alleluia* is not sung, it is omitted. The cantor or choir sings the *alleluia* or Lenten acclamation first and the people repeat it. The verse is then sung by the cantor or choir and the *alleluia* or Lenten acclamation is then sung once more by all.

150 A brief homily based on the readings should always be given at the funeral liturgy, but never any kind of eulogy. The homilist should dwell on God's compassionate love and on the paschal mystery of the Lord as proclaimed in the Scripture readings. Through the homily, the community should receive the consolation and strength to face the death of one of its members with a hope that has been nourished by the proclamation of the saving word of God.

151 In the intercessions the community responds to the proclamation of the word of God by prayer for the deceased and all the dead, for the bereaved and all who mourn, and for all in the assembly. The intercessions provided may be used or adapted to the circumstances, or new intercessions may be composed.

LITURGY OF THE EUCHARIST

152 At the funeral Mass, the community, having been spiritually renewed at the table of God's word, turns for spiritual nourishment to the table of the eucharist. The community with the priest offers to the Father the sacrifice of the New Covenant and shares in the one bread and the one cup. In partaking of the body of Christ, all are given a foretaste of eternal life

---

[1] See *Lectionary for Mass* (2nd *editio typica*, 1981), General Introduction, no. 22.

in Christ and are united with Christ, with each other, and with all the faithful, living and dead: 'Because there is one bread, we who are many are one body, for we all partake of the one bread' (1 Corinthians 10:17).

153 The liturgy of the eucharist takes place in the usual manner at the funeral Mass. Members of the family or friends of the deceased should bring the gifts to the altar. Instrumental music or a song (for example, Psalm 17[18]:1-6, Psalm 62[63], Psalm 65[66]:13-20, or Psalm 137[138]) may accompany the procession with the gifts. Before the priest washes his hands, he may incense the gifts and the altar. Afterward the deacon or other minister may incense the priest and the congregation.

Those eucharistic prayers which contain special texts of intercession for the dead are especially appropriate for use at the funeral Mass. Since music gives greater solemnity to a ritual action, the singing of the people's parts of the eucharistic prayer should be encouraged, that is, the responses of the preface dialogue, the Sanctus, the memorial acclamation, and the Great Amen.

To reinforce and to express more fully the unity of the congregation during the communion rite, the people may sing the Lord's Prayer, the doxology, the Lamb of God, and a song for the communion procession (for example, Psalm 22[23], Psalm 26[27], Psalm 33[34], Psalm 62[63], or Psalm 120[121]).

FINAL COMMENDATION AND FAREWELL

154 At the conclusion of the funeral liturgy, the rite of final commendation and farewell is celebrated, unless it is to be celebrated later at the place of committal.

155 The final commendation is a final farewell by the members of the community, an act of respect for one of their members, whom they entrust to the tender and merciful embrace of God. This act of last farewell also acknowledges the reality of separation and affirms that the community and the deceased, baptized into the one Body, share the same destiny, resurrection on the last day. On that day the one Shepherd will call each by name and gather the faithful together in the new and eternal Jerusalem.

156 The rite begins with the minister's opening words and a few moments of silent prayer. The opening words serve as a brief explanation of the rite and as an invitation to pray in silence for the deceased. The pause for silence allows the bereaved and all present to relate their own feelings of loss and grief to the mystery of Christian hope in God's abundant mercy and his promise of eternal life.

Where this is customary, the body may then be sprinkled with holy water and incensed, or this may be done during or after the song of farewell. The sprinkling is a reminder that through baptism the person was marked for eternal life and the incensation signifies respect for the body as the temple of the Holy Spirit.

The song of farewell, which should affirm hope and trust in the paschal mystery, is the climax of the rite of final commendation. It should be sung to a melody simple enough for all to sing. It may take the form of a responsory or even a hymn. When singing is not possible, invocations may be recited by the assembly.

A prayer of commendation concludes the rite. In this prayer the community calls upon God's mercy, commends the deceased into God's hands, and affirms its belief that those who have died in Christ will share in Christ's victory over death.

PROCESSION TO THE PLACE OF COMMITTAL

157 At the conclusion of the funeral liturgy, the procession is formed and the body is accompanied to the place of committal. This final procession of the funeral rite mirrors the journey of human life as a pilgrimage to God's kingdom of peace and light, the new and eternal Jerusalem.

158 Especially when accompanied with music and singing, the procession can help to reinforce the bond of communion between the participants. Whenever possible, psalms or songs may accompany the entire procession from the church to the place of committal. In situations where a solemn procession on foot from the church to the place of committal is not possible, an antiphon or song may be sung as the body is being taken to the entrance of the church. Psalms, hymns, or liturgical songs may also be sung by the participants as they gather at the place of committal.

MINISTRY AND PARTICIPATION

159 Because the funeral liturgy is the central celebration for the deceased, it should be scheduled for a time that permits as many of the Christian community as possible to be present. The full and active participation of the assembly affirms the value of praying for the dead, gives strength and support to the bereaved, and is a sure sign of faith and hope in the paschal mystery. Every effort, therefore, should be made by the various liturgical ministers to encourage the active participation of the family and of the entire assembly.

160 The priest is the ordinary presiding minister of the funeral liturgy. Except for Mass, a deacon may conduct the funeral liturgy. If pastoral need requires, the conference of bishops, with the permission of the Apostolic See, may decide that laypersons also preside at the funeral liturgy outside Mass.

161 Whenever possible, ministers should involve the family in the planning of the funeral liturgy: in the choice of readings, prayers, and music for the liturgy and in the designation of ushers, pallbearers, readers, acolytes, special ministers of the eucharist, when needed, and musicians. The family should also be given the opportunity to designate persons who will place the pall or other Christian symbols on the coffin during the rite of reception of the body at the church, who will carry the coffin, and who will bring the gifts to the altar at Mass.

162 An organist or other instrumentalist, a cantor, and, whenever possible, a choir should be present to assist the congregation in singing the songs, responses, and acclamations of the funeral liturgy. Those who are regular participants at weekday Mass should be encouraged to become familiar with a repertoire of appropriate chants, so that they can sustain and lead the assembly's singing.

4 FUNERAL MASS

Until the Lord comes, you are proclaiming his death

163 When one of its members dies, the Church encourages the celebration of the Mass. In the proclamation of the Scriptures, the saving word of God through the power of the Spirit becomes living and active in the minds and hearts of the community. Having been strengthened at the table of God's word, the community calls to mind God's saving deeds and offers the Father in the Spirit the eucharistic sacrifice of Christ's Passover from death to life, a living sacrifice of praise and thanksgiving, of reconciliation and atonement. Communion nourishes the community and expresses its unity. In communion, the participants have a foretaste of the heavenly banquet that awaits them and are reminded of Christ's own words: 'Whoever eats my flesh and drinks my blood shall live for ever' (John 6:55). Confident in Jesus' presence among them in the living word, the living sacrifice, the living meal, those present in union with the whole Church offer prayers and petitions for the deceased, whom they entrust to God's merciful love.

164 The funeral Mass is ordinarily celebrated in the parish church, but, at the discretion of the local Ordinary, it may be celebrated in the home of the deceased or some other place.

165 The Mass texts are those of the Roman Missal and the Lectionary for Mass, 'Masses for the Dead.' The intercessions should be adapted to the circumstances. Models are given in place.

166 In the choice of music for the funeral Mass, preference should be given to the singing of the acclamations, the responsorial psalm, the entrance and communion songs, and especially the song of farewell at the final commendation.

OUTLINE OF THE RITE

INTRODUCTORY RITES

Greeting
Sprinkling with Holy Water
Entrance Procession
[Placing of the Pall]
[Placing of Christian Symbols]
Opening Prayer

LITURGY OF THE WORD

Readings
Homily
General Intercessions
   Intercessions
   Concluding Prayer

LITURGY OF THE EUCHARIST

FINAL COMMENDATION

Invitation to Prayer
Silence
Signs of Farewell
Song of Farewell
Prayer of Commendation

PROCESSION TO
THE PLACE OF COMMITTAL

FUNERAL MASS

167 If the rite of reception of the body takes place at the beginning of the funeral Mass, the introductory rites are those given here and the usual introductory rites for Mass, including the penitential rite, are omitted.

If the rite of reception of the body has already taken place, the Mass begins in the usual way, with the entrance procession, the greeting, and the penitential rite.

INTRODUCTORY RITES

GREETING

168 The priest, with assisting ministers, goes to the door of the church and, using one of the following greetings, or in similar words, greets those present.

A   The grace of our Lord Jesus Christ and the love of God and the fellowship of the Holy Spirit be with you all.

   R. And also with you.

B   The grace and peace of God our Father and the Lord Jesus Christ be with you.

   R. And also with you.

C   The grace and peace of God our Father, who raised Jesus from the dead, be always with you.

   R. And also with you.

D   May the Father of mercies, the God of all consolation, be with you.

   R. And also with you.

Sprinkling with Holy Water

169 Using one of the following texts, the priest then sprinkles
the coffin with holy water.

A   In the waters of baptism
N. died with Christ and rose with him to new life.
May he/she now share with him eternal glory.

B   The Lord is our shepherd
and leads us to streams of living water.

C   Let this water call to mind our baptism into Christ,
who by his death and resurrection has redeemed us.

D   The Lord God lives in his holy temple yet abides in our midst.
Since in baptism N. became God's temple
and the Spirit of God lived in him/her,
with reverence we bless his/her mortal body.

Entrance Procession

170 The Easter candle may be placed beforehand near the position the coffin will occupy at the conclusion of the procession.
The priest and assisting ministers precede the coffin and the
mourners into the church. During the procession a hymn or song
may be sung.

Placing of the Pall

171 If it is the custom in the local community, the pall is then
placed on the coffin by family members, friends, or the priest.

Placing of Christian Symbols

172 A symbol of the Christian life, such as a Book of the Gospels,
a Bible, or a cross, may be carried in procession, then placed
on the coffin, either in silence or as one of the following texts
is said.

A   Book of the Gospels or Bible

In life N. cherished the Gospel of Christ.
May Christ now greet him/her with these words of eternal life:
Come, blessed of my Father!

B   Cross

In baptism N. received the sign of the cross.
May he/she now share
in Christ's victory over sin and death.

On reaching the altar, the priest, with the assisting ministers,
makes the customary reverence, kisses the altar, and (if incense
is used) incenses it. Then he goes to the chair.

OPENING PRAYER

173 When all have reached their places, the priest invites the
assembly to pray.

Let us pray.

After a brief period of silent prayer, the priest sings or says one
of the following prayers or one of those provided in no. 580-581,
p. 407, or one from the Roman Missal.

A   Almighty God and Father,   170
it is our certain faith
that your Son, who died on the cross, was raised from the dead,
the firstfruits of all who have fallen asleep.
Grant that through this mystery
your servant N., who has gone to his/her rest in Christ,
may share in the joy of his resurrection.

We ask this through our Lord Jesus Christ, your Son,
who lives and reigns with you and the Holy Spirit,
one God, for ever and ever.

R. Amen.

B   O God,
to whom mercy and forgiveness belong,
hear our prayers on behalf of your servant N.,
whom you have called out of this world;
and because he/she put his/her hope and trust in you,
command that he/she be carried safely home to heaven
and come to enjoy your eternal reward.

We ask this through our Lord Jesus Christ, your Son,
who lives and reigns with you and the Holy Spirit,
one God, for ever and ever.

R. Amen.

C   O God,
in whom sinners find mercy and the saints find joy,
we pray to you for our brother/sister N.,
whose body we honour with Christian burial,
that he/she may be delivered from the bonds of death.
Admit him/her to the joyful company of your saints
and raise him/her on the last day
to rejoice in your presence for ever.

We ask this through our Lord Jesus Christ, your Son,
who lives and reigns with you and the Holy Spirit,
one God, for ever and ever.

R. Amen.

D   During the Easter season   173

God of loving kindness,
listen favourably to our prayers:
strengthen our belief that your Son has risen from the dead
and our hope that your servant N. will also rise again.

We ask this through our Lord Jesus Christ, your Son,
who lives and reigns with you and the Holy Spirit,
one God, for ever and ever.

R. Amen.

LITURGY OF THE WORD

READINGS

174 After the introductory rites, the liturgy of the word is celebrated. Depending upon pastoral circumstances, either one or two readings may be read before the gospel.

HOMILY

175 A brief homily is given after the gospel reading.

GENERAL INTERCESSIONS

176 The general intercessions then take place.

INTERCESSIONS

177 One of the following sets of intercessions may be used or adapted to the circumstances, or new intercessions may be composed.

A   The priest begins:

God, the almighty Father, raised Christ his Son from the dead; 200
with confidence we ask him to save all his people, living and dead:

A deacon or reader then continues:

For N. who in baptism was given the pledge of eternal life, that
he/she may now be admitted to the company of the saints.
Lord, in your mercy:

R. Hear our prayer.

For our brother/sister who ate the body of Christ, the bread
of life, that he/she may be raised up on the last day.
Lord, in your mercy:

R. Hear our prayer.

[For a deacon: For our brother N., who proclaimed the Good
News of Jesus Christ and served the needs of the poor, that he
may be welcomed into the sanctuary of heaven.
Lord, in your mercy:

R. Hear our prayer.]

[For a bishop or priest: For our brother N., who served the Church as a priest, that he may be given a place in the liturgy of heaven. Lord, in your mercy:

R. Hear our prayer.]

For our deceased relatives and friends and for all who have helped us, that they may have the reward of their goodness. Lord, in your mercy:

R. Hear our prayer.

For those who have fallen asleep in the hope of rising again, that they may see God face to face. Lord, in your mercy:

R. Hear our prayer.

For the family and friends of our brother/sister N., that they may be consoled in their grief by the Lord, who wept at the death of his friend Lazarus. Lord, in your mercy:

R. Hear our prayer.

For all of us assembled here to worship in faith, that we may be gathered together again in God's kingdom. Lord, in your mercy:

R. Hear our prayer.

B   The priest begins:

My dear friends, let us join with one another in praying to God, 201 not only for our departed brother/sister, but also for the Church, for peace in the world, and for ourselves.

      A deacon or reader then continues:

That the bishops and priests of the Church, and all who preach the Gospel, may be given the strength to express in action the word they proclaim. We pray to the Lord:

R. Lord, hear our prayer.

That those in public office may promote justice and peace. We pray to the Lord:

R. Lord, hear our prayer.

That those who bear the cross of pain in mind or body may never feel forsaken by God.
We pray to the Lord:

R. Lord, hear our prayer.

That God may deliver the soul of his servant N. from punishment and from the powers of darkness.
We pray to the Lord:

R. Lord, hear our prayer.

That God in his mercy may blot out all his/her offences.
We pray to the Lord:

R. Lord, hear our prayer.

That God may establish him/her in light and peace.
We pray to the Lord:

R. Lord, hear our prayer.

That God may call him/her to happiness in the company of all the saints. We pray to the Lord:

R. Lord, hear our prayer.

That God may welcome into his glory those of our family and friends who have departed this life.
We pray to the Lord:

R. Lord, hear our prayer.

That God may give a place in the kingdom of heaven to all the faithful departed.
We pray to the Lord:

R. Lord, hear our prayer.

CONCLUDING PRAYER

178 The priest says one of the following prayers or one of those provided in no. 580, p. 407.

A   God, our shelter and our strength,
you listen in love to the cry of your people:
hear the prayers we offer for our departed brother/sister N.
Cleanse him/her and all the faithful departed of their sins
and grant them the fullness of redemption.

We ask this through Christ our Lord.

R. Amen.

B   O God,
Creator and Redeemer of all the faithful,
grant to the souls of your departed servants
release from all their sins.
Hear our prayers for those we love
and give them the pardon they have always desired.

We ask this through Christ our Lord.

R. Amen.

LITURGY OF THE EUCHARIST

179 The liturgy of the eucharist is celebrated in the usual manner, as found in the Roman Missal.

180 If the final commendation is to be celebrated at the place of committal, the procession to the place of committal (no. 187) begins following the prayer after communion.

FINAL COMMENDATION

181 Following the prayer after communion, the priest goes to a place near the coffin. If incense and holy water are to be used, they are carried by the assisting ministers.

A member or a friend of the family may speak in remembrance of the deceased before the final commendation begins.

INVITATION TO PRAYER

182 Using one of the following invitations, or in similar words, the priest begins the final commendation.

A   Before we go our separate ways, let us take leave of our brother/   185
sister. May our farewell express our affection for him/her; may
it ease our sadness and strengthen our hope. One day we shall
joyfully greet him/her again when the love of Christ, which conquers all things, destroys even death itself.

B   Trusting in God, we have prayed together for N. and now we   186
come to the last farewell. There is sadness in parting, but we
take comfort in the hope that one day we shall see N. again
and enjoy his/her friendship. Although this congregation will
disperse in sorrow, the mercy of God will gather us together
again in the joy of his kingdom. Therefore let us console one
another in the faith of Jesus Christ.

C   Our brother/sister N. has fallen asleep in Christ. Confident in   183
our hope of eternal life, let us commend him/her to the loving
mercy of our Father and let our prayers go with him/her. He/she
was adopted as God's son/daughter in baptism and was nourished at the table of the Lord; may he/she now inherit the promise of eternal life and take his/her place at the table of God's
children in heaven.

Let us pray also on our own behalf, that we who now mourn
and are saddened may one day go forth with our brother/sister
to meet the Lord of life when he appears in glory.

D   The following text should not be used if cremation is to follow.   46
65

With faith in Jesus Christ, we must reverently bury the body
of our brother/sister.

Let us pray with confidence to God, in whose sight all creation
lives, that he will raise up in holiness and power the mortal
body of our brother/sister and command his/her soul to be numbered among the blessed.

May God grant him/her a merciful judgment, deliverance from
death, and pardon of sin. May Christ the Good Shepherd carry
him/her home to be at peace with the Father. May he/she rejoice for ever in the presence of the eternal King and in the
company of all the saints.

E   The following text should not be used if cremation is to follow.

Because God has chosen to call our brother/sister N. from this life to himself, we commit his/her body to the earth, for we are dust and unto dust we shall return.

But the Lord Jesus Christ will change our mortal bodies to be like his in glory, for he is risen, the first-born from the dead.

So let us commend our brother/sister to the Lord, that the Lord may embrace him/her in peace and raise up his/her body on the last day.

Silence

183   All pray in silence.

Signs of Farewell

184   The coffin may now be sprinkled with holy water and incensed, or this may take place during or after the song of farewell.

Song of Farewell

185   The song of farewell is then sung. One of the following texts or another suitable hymn or song may be sung.

A   I know that my Redeemer lives,   189
And on that final day of days,
His voice shall bid me rise again:
Unending joy, unceasing praise!

This hope I cherish in my heart:
To stand on earth, my flesh restored,
And, not a stranger but a friend,
Behold my Saviour and my Lord.

Tune: LM, for example, Duke Street

B   Saints of God, come to his/her aid! 47
66
Hasten to meet him/her, angels of the Lord!
R. Receive his/her soul and present him/her
to God the Most High.

May Christ, who called you, take you to himself;
may angels lead you to the bosom of Abraham.
R. Receive his/her soul and present him/her
to God the Most High.

Eternal rest grant unto him/her, O Lord,
and let perpetual light shine upon him/her.
R. Receive his/her soul and present him/her
to God the Most High.

Prayer of Commendation

186 The priest then says one of the following prayers.

A   Into your hands, Father of mercies, 48
we commend our brother/sister N.
in the sure and certain hope
that, together with all who have died in Christ,
he/she will rise with him on the last day.

[We give you thanks for the blessings
which you bestowed upon N. in this life:
they are signs to us of your goodness
and of our fellowship with the saints in Christ.]

Merciful Lord,
turn toward us and listen to our prayers:
open the gates of paradise to your servant
and help us who remain
to comfort one another with assurances of faith,
until we all meet in Christ
and are with you and with our brother/sister for ever.

We ask this through Christ our Lord.

R. Amen.

B   To you, O Lord, we commend the soul of N., your servant;   192
    in the sight of this world he/she is now dead;
    in your sight may he/she live for ever.
    Forgive whatever sins he/she committed through human
        weakness
    and in your goodness grant him/her everlasting peace.

    We ask this through Christ our Lord.

    R. Amen.

PROCESSION TO THE
PLACE OF COMMITTAL

187 The deacon or, in the absence of a deacon, the priest says:

In peace let us take N. to his/her place of rest.

If a symbol of the Christian life has been placed on the coffin,
it should be removed at this time.

The procession then begins: the priest and assisting ministers
precede the coffin; the family and mourners follow.

One or more of the following texts or other suitable songs may
be sung during the procession to the entrance of the church. The
singing may continue during the journey to the place of committal.

A   The following antiphon may be sung with verses from Psalm
        24 (25), p. 429.

May the angels lead you into paradise;   50
may the martyrs come to welcome you
and take you to the holy city,
the new and eternal Jerusalem.

B   The following antiphon may be sung with verses from Psalm
        114 (116), p. 430, or separately.

May choirs of angels welcome you   50
and lead you to the bosom of Abraham;
and where Lazarus is poor no longer
may you find eternal rest.

C   May saints and angels lead you on,
Escorting you where Christ has gone.
Now he has called you, come to him
Who sits above the seraphim.

Come to the peace of Abraham
And to the supper of the Lamb:
Come to the glory of the blessed,
And to perpetual light and rest.

D   Another suitable psalm may also be used.

5 FUNERAL LITURGY OUTSIDE MASS

I am the resurrection and the life; whoever believes in me shall never die

188 In the funeral liturgy outside Mass the community gathers to hear the message of Easter hope proclaimed in the liturgy of the word and to commend the deceased to God.

189 This rite may be used for various reasons:

1. when the funeral Mass is not permitted, namely, on solemnities of obligation, on Holy Thursday and the Easter Triduum, and on the Sundays of Advent, Lent, and the Easter Season;[1]

2. when in some places or circumstances it is not possible to celebrate the funeral Mass before the committal, for example, if a priest is not available;

3. when for pastoral reasons the priest and the family judge that the funeral liturgy outside Mass is a more suitable form of celebration.

190 The funeral liturgy outside Mass is ordinarily celebrated in the parish church, but may also be celebrated in the home of the deceased, a funeral home, parlour, chapel of rest, or cemetery chapel.

191 The readings are those of the Lectionary for Mass, 'Masses for the Dead.' The intercessions should be adapted to the circumstances; models are given in place. The celebration may also include holy communion.

192 In the choice of music for the funeral liturgy, preference should be given to the singing of the entrance song, the responsorial psalm, the gospel acclamation, and especially the song of farewell at the final commendation.

193 The minister who is a priest or deacon wears an alb with stole (a cope may be used, if desired); a layperson who presides wears the liturgical vestments approved for the region.

---

[1] See General Instruction of the Roman Missal, no. 336.

OUTLINE OF THE RITE

INTRODUCTORY RITES

Greeting
Sprinkling with Holy Water
Entrance Procession
[Placing of the Pall]
[Placing of Christian Symbols]
Invitation to Prayer
Opening Prayer

LITURGY OF THE WORD

Readings
Homily
General Intercessions
   Intercessions
   The Lord's Prayer
   [Concluding Prayer]

[LITURGY OF HOLY COMMUNION]

Communion
Silent Prayer
Prayer after Communion

FINAL COMMENDATION

Invitation to Prayer
Silence
Signs of Farewell
Song of Farewell
Prayer of Commendation

PROCESSION TO THE PLACE OF COMMITTAL

FUNERAL LITURGY OUTSIDE MASS

194 If the rite of reception of the body takes place at the beginning of the funeral liturgy, the introductory rites are those given here.

If the rite of reception of the body has already taken place, the liturgy begins with an entrance song and the greeting (no. 195), followed by the invitation to prayer (no. 200).

INTRODUCTORY RITES

GREETING

195 The presiding minister, with assisting ministers, goes to the door of the church and, using one of the following greetings, or in similar words, greets those present.

A   The grace of our Lord Jesus Christ and the love of God and the fellowship of the Holy Spirit be with you all.

    R. And also with you.

B   The grace and peace of God our Father and the Lord Jesus Christ be with you.

    R. And also with you.

C   The grace and peace of God our Father, who raised Jesus from the dead, be always with you.

    R. And also with you.

D   May the Father of mercies, the God of all consolation, be with you.

    R. And also with you.

Sprinkling with Holy Water

> 196 Using one of the following texts, the presiding minister then sprinkles the coffin with holy water.

A   In the waters of baptism
N. died with Christ and rose with him to new life.
May he/she now share with him eternal glory.

B   The Lord is our shepherd
and leads us to streams of living water.

C   Let this water call to mind our baptism into Christ,
who by his death and resurrection has redeemed us.

D   The Lord God lives in his holy temple yet abides in our midst.
Since in baptism N. became God's temple
and the Spirit of God lived in him/her,
with reverence we bless his/her mortal body.

Entrance Procession

> 197 The Easter candle may be placed beforehand near the position the coffin will occupy at the conclusion of the procession. The presiding minister and assisting ministers precede the coffin and the mourners into the church. During the procession a hymn or song may be sung.

Placing of the Pall

> 198 If it is the custom in the local community, the pall is then placed on the coffin by family members, friends, or the presiding minister.

Placing of Christian Symbols

> 199 A symbol of the Christian life, such as a Book of the Gospels, a Bible, or a cross, may be carried in procession, then placed on the coffin, either in silence or as one of the following texts is said.

A   Book of the Gospels or Bible

In life N. cherished the Gospel of Christ.
May Christ now greet him/her with these words of eternal life:
Come, blessed of my Father!

B   Cross

In baptism N. received the sign of the cross.
May he/she now share
in Christ's victory over sin and death.

On reaching the altar, the presiding minister, with the assisting
ministers, makes the customary reverence and goes to the chair.

Invitation to Prayer

200 When all have reached their places, the presiding minister,
using one of the following texts, or in similar words, invites the
assembly to pray.

A   My brothers and sisters, we believe that all the ties of friendship and affection which knit us as one throughout our lives
do not unravel with death.

Confident that God always remembers the good we have done
and forgives our sins, let us pray, asking God to gather N. to
himself.

B   Dear friends in Christ, in the name of Jesus and of his Church,
we gather to pray for N. that God may bring him/her to everlasting peace and rest.

We share the pain of loss, but the promise of eternal life gives
us hope. Let us comfort one another as we turn to God in prayer.

C   My brothers and sisters, we have come together to renew our
trust in Christ who, by dying on the cross, has freed us from
eternal death and, by rising, has opened for us the gates of heaven.

Let us pray for our brother/sister, that he/she may share in
Christ's victory, and let us pray for ourselves, that the Lord may
grant us the gift of his loving consolation.

Opening Prayer

201 After a brief period of silent prayer, the presiding minister says one of the following prayers or one of those provided in no. 580, p. 407.

A   Almighty God and Father,   170
     it is our certain faith
     that your Son, who died on the cross, was raised from the dead,
     the firstfruits of all who have fallen asleep.
     Grant that through this mystery
     your servant N., who has gone to his/her rest in Christ,
     may share in the joy of his resurrection.

     We ask this through our Lord Jesus Christ, your Son,
     who lives and reigns with you and the Holy Spirit,
     one God, for ever and ever.

     R. Amen.

B   O God,
     to whom mercy and forgiveness belong,
     hear our prayers on behalf of your servant N.,
     whom you have called out of this world;
     and because he/she put his/her hope and trust in you,
     command that he/she be carried safely home to heaven
     and come to enjoy your eternal reward.

     We ask this through our Lord Jesus Christ, your Son,
     who lives and reigns with you and the Holy Spirit,
     one God, for ever and ever.

     R. Amen.

C   O God,
     in whom sinners find mercy and the saints find joy,
     we pray to you for our brother/sister N.,
     [whose body we honour with Christian burial,]
     that he/she may be delivered from the bonds of death.
     Admit him/her to the joyful company of your saints
     and raise him/her on the last day
     to rejoice in your presence for ever.

We ask this through our Lord Jesus Christ, your Son,
who lives and reigns with you and the Holy Spirit,
one God, for ever and ever.

R. Amen.

D   During the Easter season

God of loving kindness,
listen favourably to our prayers:
strengthen our belief that your Son has risen from the dead
and our hope that your servant N. will also rise again.

We ask this through our Lord Jesus Christ, your Son,
who lives and reigns with you and the Holy Spirit,
one God, for ever and ever.

R. Amen.

LITURGY OF THE WORD

READINGS

202 After the introductory rites, the liturgy of the word is celebrated. Depending upon pastoral circumstances, either one or
two readings may be read before the gospel.

HOMILY

203 A brief homily is given after the gospel reading.

GENERAL INTERCESSIONS

204 The general intercessions then take place.

INTERCESSIONS

205 One of the following sets of intercessions may be used or adapted to the circumstances, or new intercessions may be composed.

A   The presiding minister begins:

God, the almighty Father, raised Christ his Son from the dead;   200
with confidence we ask him to save all his people, living and dead:

An assisting minister or reader then continues:

For N. who in baptism was given the pledge of eternal life, that he/she may now be admitted to the company of the saints.
Lord, in your mercy:

R. Hear our prayer.

For our brother/sister who ate the body of Christ, the bread of life, that he/she may be raised up on the last day.
Lord, in your mercy:

R. Hear our prayer.

For our deceased relatives and friends and for all who have helped us, that they may have the reward of their goodness.
Lord, in your mercy:

R. Hear our prayer.

For those who have fallen asleep in the hope of rising again, that they may see God face to face.
Lord, in your mercy:

R. Hear our prayer.

For the family and friends of our brother/sister N. that they may be consoled in their grief by the Lord, who wept at the death of his friend Lazarus.
Lord, in your mercy:

R. Hear our prayer.

For all of us assembled here to worship in faith, that we may be gathered together again in God's kingdom.
Lord, in your mercy:

R. Hear our prayer.

B   The presiding minister begins:

Brothers and sisters, Jesus Christ is risen from the dead and sits at the right hand of the Father, where he intercedes for his Church. Confident that God hears the voices of those who trust in the Lord Jesus, we join our prayers to his:

An assisting minister or reader then continues:

In baptism N. received the light of Christ. Scatter the darkness now and lead him/her over the waters of death.
Lord, in your mercy:

R. Hear our prayer.

Our brother/sister N. was nourished at the table of the Saviour. Welcome him/her into the halls of the heavenly banquet.
Lord, in your mercy:

R. Hear our prayer.

Many friends and members of our families have gone before us and await the kingdom. Grant them an everlasting home with your Son.
Lord, in your mercy:

R. Hear our prayer.

Many people die by violence, war, and famine each day. Show your mercy to those who suffer so unjustly these sins against your love, and gather them to the eternal kingdom of peace.
Lord, in your mercy:

R. Hear our prayer.

Those who trusted in the Lord now sleep in the Lord. Give refreshment, rest, and peace to all whose faith is known to you alone.
Lord, in your mercy:

R. Hear our prayer.

The family and friends of N. seek comfort and consolation. Heal their pain and dispel the darkness and doubt that come from grief.
Lord, in your mercy:

R. Hear our prayer.

We are assembled here in faith and confidence to pray for our brother/sister   Strengthen our hope so that we may live in the expectation of your Son's coming.
Lord, in your mercy:

R. Hear our prayer.

THE LORD'S PRAYER

> 206 Using one of the following invitations, or in similar words, the minister invites those present to pray the Lord's Prayer.

A   Now let us pray as Christ the Lord has taught us:

B   With longing for the coming of God's kingdom, let us offer our prayer to the Father:

> All say:

Our Father . . .

CONCLUDING PRAYER

> 207 If there is no communion, the presiding minister then says one of the following prayers.

A   God, our shelter and our strength,
you listen in love to the cry of your people:
hear the prayers we offer for our departed brother/sister N.
Cleanse him/her and all the faithful departed of their sins
and grant them the fullness of redemption.

We ask this through Christ our Lord.

R. Amen.

B   Lord God,
      giver of peace and healer of souls,
      hear the prayers of the Redeemer, Jesus Christ,
      and the voices of your people,
      whose lives were purchased by the blood of the Lamb.
      Forgive the sins of all who sleep in Christ
      and grant them a place in the kingdom.

      We ask this through Christ our Lord.

      R. Amen.

LITURGY OF HOLY COMMUNION

Communion

208 If there is to be communion, the presiding minister shows the eucharistic bread to those present, saying:

This is the Lamb of God
who takes away the sins of the world.
Happy are those who are called to his supper.

All then respond:

Lord, I am not worthy to receive you,
but only say the word and I shall be healed.

Those present then receive communion in the usual way.

Silent Prayer

209 A period of silence may be observed.

Prayer after Communion

210 When all have received communion, the presiding minister then says one of the following prayers.

Let us pray.

All pray in silence for a brief period, if this has not preceded.

A   Lord God,
     your Son Jesus Christ gave us
     the sacrament of his body and blood
     to guide us on our pilgrim way to your kingdom.
     May our brother/sister N., who shared in the eucharist,
     come to the banquet of life Christ has prepared for us.

     We ask this through Christ our Lord.

     R. Amen.

B   Father, all-powerful God,
     we pray for our brother/sister N.
     whom you have called from this world.
     May this eucharist cleanse him/her,
     forgive his/her sins,
     and raise him/her up to eternal joy in your presence.

     We ask this through Christ our Lord.

     R. Amen.

C   During the Easter season
     Lord God,
     may the death and resurrection of Christ
     which we celebrate in this eucharist
     bring our brother/sister N. the peace of your eternal home.

     We ask this in the name of Jesus the Lord.

     R. Amen.

D   For a catechumen
     Lord,
     hear the prayers of those who share in the body and blood
        of your Son.
     By these sacred mysteries
     you have filled them with hope of eternal life.
     May they be comforted in the sorrows of this present life.

     We ask this in the name of Jesus the Lord.

     R. Amen.

211 If the final commendation is to be celebrated at the place
of committal, the procession to the place of committal (no. 218)
now begins.

FINAL COMMENDATION

212 The presiding minister goes to a place near the coffin. If
incense and holy water are to be used, they are carried by the
assisting ministers.

A member or a friend of the family may speak in remembrance
of the deceased before the final commendation begins.

INVITATION TO PRAYER

213 Using one of the following invitations, or in similar words,
the presiding minister begins the final commendation.

A   Before we go our separate ways, let us take leave of our brother/   185
sister. May our farewell express our affection for him/her; may
it ease our sadness and strengthen our hope. One day we shall
joyfully greet him/her again when the love of Christ, which conquers all things, destroys even death itself.

B   Trusting in God, we have prayed together for N. and now we   186
come to the last farewell. There is sadness in parting, but we
take comfort in the hope that one day we shall see N. again
and enjoy his/her friendship. Although this congregation will
disperse in sorrow, the mercy of God will gather us together
again in the joy of his kingdom. Therefore let us console one
another in the faith of Jesus Christ.

C   Our brother/sister N. has fallen asleep in Christ. Confident in   183
    our hope of eternal life, let us commend him/her to the loving
    mercy of our Father and let our prayers go with him/her. He/she
    was adopted as God's son/daughter in baptism and was nour-
    ished at the table of the Lord; may he/she now inherit the prom-
    ise of eternal life and take his/her place at the table of God's
    children in heaven.

    Let us pray also on our own behalf, that we who now mourn
    and are saddened may one day go forth with our brother/sister
    to meet the Lord of life when he appears in glory.

D   The following text should not be used if cremation is to follow.   46
65

    With faith in Jesus Christ, we must reverently bury the body
    of our brother/sister.

    Let us pray with confidence to God, in whose sight all creation
    lives, that he will raise up in holiness and power the mortal
    body of our brother/sister and command his/her soul to be num-
    bered among the blessed.

    May God grant him/her a merciful judgment, deliverance from
    death, and pardon of sin. May Christ the Good Shepherd carry
    him/her home to be at peace with the Father. May he/she re-
    joice for ever in the presence of the eternal King and in the
    company of all the saints.

E   The following text should not be used if cremation is to follow.   184

    Because God has chosen to call our brother/sister N. from this
    life to himself, we commit his/her body to the earth, for we are
    dust and unto dust we shall return.

    But the Lord Jesus Christ will change our mortal bodies to be
    like his in glory, for he is risen, the first-born from the dead.

    So let us commend our brother/sister to the Lord, that the Lord
    may embrace him/her in peace and raise up his/her body on
    the last day.

SILENCE

214 All pray in silence.

SIGNS OF FAREWELL

215 The coffin may now be sprinkled with holy water and incensed, or this may take place during or after the song of farewell.

SONG OF FAREWELL

216 The song of farewell is then sung. One of the following texts or another suitable hymn or song may be sung.

A   I know that my Redeemer lives,   189
And on that final day of days,
His voice shall bid me rise again:
Unending joy, unceasing praise!

This hope I cherish in my heart:
To stand on earth, my flesh restored,
And, not a stranger but a friend,
Behold my Saviour and my Lord.

Tune: LM, for example, Duke Street

B   Saints of God, come to his/her aid!   47
Hasten to meet him/her, angels of the Lord!   66
R. Receive his/her soul and present him/her
to God the Most High.

May Christ, who called you, take you to himself;
may angels lead you to the bosom of Abraham.
R. Receive his/her soul and present him/her
to God the Most High.

Eternal rest grant unto him/her, O Lord,
and let perpetual light shine upon him/her.
R. Receive his/her soul and present him/her
to God the Most High.

Prayer of Commendation

217 The presiding minister then says one of the following prayers.

A   Into your hands, Father of mercies,   48
we commend our brother/sister N.
in the sure and certain hope
that, together with all who have died in Christ,
he/she will rise with him on the last day.

[We give you thanks for the blessings
which you bestowed upon N. in this life:
they are signs to us of your goodness
and of our fellowship with the saints in Christ.]

Merciful Lord,
turn toward us and listen to our prayers:
open the gates of paradise to your servant
and help us who remain
to comfort one another with assurances of faith,
until we all meet in Christ
and are with you and with our brother/sister for ever.

We ask this through Christ our Lord.

R. Amen.

B   To you, O Lord, we commend the soul of N. your servant;   192
in the sight of this world he/she is now dead;
in your sight may he/she live for ever.
Forgive whatever sins he/she committed through human
     weakness
and in your goodness grant him/her everlasting peace.

We ask this through Christ our Lord.

R. Amen.

PROCESSION TO THE PLACE OF COMMITTAL

218 The deacon or, in the absence of a deacon, the presiding minister says:

In peace let us take N. to his/her place of rest.

If a symbol of the Christian life has been placed on the coffin, it should be removed at this time.

The procession then begins: the presiding minister and assisting ministers precede the coffin; the family and mourners follow.

One or more of the following texts or other suitable songs may be sung during the procession to the entrance of the church. The singing may continue during the journey to the place of committal.

A   The following antiphon may be sung with verses from Psalm 24 (25), p. 429.

May the angels lead you into paradise;   50
may the martyrs come to welcome you
and take you to the holy city,
the new and eternal Jerusalem.

B   The following antiphon may be sung with verses from Psalm 114 (116), p. 430, or separately.

May choirs of angels welcome you   50
and lead you to the bosom of Abraham;
and where Lazarus is poor no longer
may you find eternal rest.

C   May saints and angels lead you on,
Escorting you where Christ has gone.
Now he has called you, come to him
Who sits above the seraphim.

Come to the peace of Abraham
And to the supper of the Lamb:
Come to the glory of the blessed,
And to perpetual light and rest.

D   Another suitable psalm may also be used.

RITE OF COMMITTAL

Joseph took Jesus down from the cross,
wrapped him in a shroud,
and laid him in a tomb

RITE OF COMMITTAL

219 The rite of committal, the conclusion of the funeral rites, is the final act of the community of faith in caring for the body of its deceased member. It may be celebrated at the grave, tomb, or crematorium and may be used for burial at sea. Whenever possible, the rite of committal is to be celebrated at the site of committal, that is, beside the open grave or place of interment, rather than at a cemetery chapel.

220 Seven forms of the rite of committal are provided here: The 'Rite of Committal at a Cemetery' and 'Rite of Committal at a Crematorium' are used when the final commendation is celebrated as part of the conclusion of the funeral liturgy. The 'Rite of Committal at a Cemetery with Final Commendation' and 'Rite of Committal at a Crematorium with Final Commendation' are used when the final commendation does not take place during the funeral liturgy, or when the funeral liturgy does not immediately precede the committal. The 'Rite of Committal for Burial' and 'Rite of Committal for Cremation' are intended for use at a cemetery or crematorium chapel when no other liturgical celebration at all has taken place, and they incorporate elements of the funeral liturgy itself. A seventh form is provided for the burial of ashes.

221 In committing the body to its resting place, the community expresses the hope that, with all those who have gone before marked with the sign of faith, the deceased awaits the glory of the resurrection. The rite of committal is an expression of the communion that exists between the Church on earth and the Church in heaven: the deceased passes with the farewell prayers of the community of believers into the welcoming company of those who need faith no longer but see God face to face.

STRUCTURE AND CONTENT OF THE RITE OF COMMITTAL

Committal at a Cemetery

222 Both the rite of committal and the rite of committal with final commendation begin with an invitation, Scripture verse, and a prayer over the place of committal. The several alternatives for the prayer over the place of committal take into account whether the grave, tomb, or resting place has already been blessed, and situations in which the final disposition of the body will actually take place at a later time.

223 The rite of committal continues with the words of committal, the intercessions, and the Lord's Prayer.

The rite of committal with final commendation continues with an invitation to prayer, a pause for silent prayer, the sprinkling and incensing of the body, where this is customary, the song of farewell, and the prayer of commendation.

224 The act of committal takes place after the words of committal (in the rite of committal with final commendation, after the prayer of commendation) or at the conclusion of the rite. The act of committal expresses the full significance of this rite. Through this act the community of faith proclaims that the grave or place of interment, once a sign of futility and despair, has been transformed by means of Christ's own death and resurrection into a sign of hope and promise.

225 Both forms of the rite conclude with a prayer over the people, which includes the verse *Eternal rest*, and a blessing. Depending on local custom, a song may then be sung and a gesture of final leave-taking may be made, for example, placing flowers or soil on the coffin.

COMMITTAL AT A CREMATORIUM

226 In the rite of committal at a crematorium, there is no prayer over the place of committal, but a brief prayer of commendation. This is normally followed by the signs of farewell: the coffin may be sprinkled with holy water and incensed, and the family and mourners may also sprinkle the coffin or make some other gesture of leavetaking. During the words of committal which follow, the coffin may be removed from view, if this is the custom. The rite concludes with the intercessions, the Lord's Prayer, and the prayer over the people. When the coffin is left in view throughout, the gesture of leavetaking may be performed at the end of the rite.

227 In the rite of committal with final commendation at a crematorium, the invitation and the Scripture verse are followed by an invitation to silent prayer and the signs of farewell. A song of farewell may be sung, after which a prayer of commendation and committal is said, during which the coffin may be removed from view. The rite concludes with the prayer over the people and a final song. When the coffin remains in view, however, the gesture of leavetaking may be performed at the end of the rite.

COMMITTAL WHEN NO OTHER LITURGY HAS TAKEN PLACE

228 It sometimes happens that the family of the deceased chooses to have only one funeral service, at the time of the committal itself. This will normally take place at the chapel in the cemetery or crematorium. Special orders of service are provided here which expand the rite of committal with elements from the other rites which have been foregone, for instance the reception of the body at the church and the liturgy of the word.

229 Many mourners who are not members of the Church, and who may not regard themselves as religious, are often among the most assiduous in attending funerals. While it may not have been the wish, either of the deceased or of the community, that the funeral should be celebrated in this way, arrangements are often made with the funeral director before contact has been made with the Church. It is important that the priest or minister bring out the particular insights and interpretations which Christian faith brings to bear on the reality of death and the experience of bereavement.

230 The 'Rite of Committal for Burial' and 'Rite of Committal for Cremation' follow an identical order until the end of the intercessions. When committal is by burial, there follows the procession to the grave where the rite of committal takes place. After an invitation and Scripture verse, a prayer over the grave is said, followed by the act of committal and the prayer over the people. When committal is by cremation, a prayer of commendation and committal follows, during which the coffin may be removed from view. The rite concludes with the prayer over the people.

MINISTRY AND PARTICIPATION

231 The community continues to show its concern for the mourners by participating in the rite of committal. The rite marks the separation in this life of the mourners from the deceased, and through it the community assists them as they complete their care for the deceased and lay the body to rest. The act of committal is a stark and powerful expression of this separation. When carried out in the midst of the community of faith, the committal can help the mourners to face the end of one relationship with the deceased and to begin a new one based on prayerful remembrance, gratitude, and the hope of resurrection and reunion. Members of the family and friends may assist in lowering the coffin into the grave.

By their presence and prayer members of the community signify their intention to continue to support the mourners in the time following the funeral.

232 The singing of well-chosen music at the rite of committal can help the mourners as they face the reality of the separation. At the rite of committal with final commendation and in the rites of committal for burial or cremation when no liturgy has preceded, whenever possible, the song of farewell should be sung. In all forms of the committal rite, a hymn or liturgical song that affirms hope in God's mercy and in the resurrection of the dead is desirable at the conclusion of the rite.

233 In the absence of a parish minister, a friend or member of the family should lead those present in the rite of committal.

The minister should vest according to local custom.

Committal at a Crematorium

234 Since the crematorium chapel will frequently be an interdenominational or even a neutral building, particular care should be taken to create as much of a Christian atmosphere and environment as possible.

If no Christian symbols are in evidence, pastors should see that at least a worthy copy of the Scriptures, a movable cross or crucifix, and authentic lighted candles are available for the duration of the service. If at all possible, servers should be on hand to carry a processional cross and candles.

Arrangements should be made for a worthy holy water vessel and a suitable incense burner to be kept at the chapel for use at committals.

235 Live music will almost always be preferable to recorded music. Pastors may have to arrange for copies of appropriate music to be kept at the chapel for the use of congregations. Where recorded music is habitually used, pastors should ensure that the crematorium authorities are supplied with recordings of good quality liturgical music.

236 When only a strictly limited time is allocated for a crematorium service, great care should be taken by the minister not to appear hurried. It may be preferable to omit some options altogether, so that the remaining items can be used with dignity, reverence, and sensitivity to the occasion.

237 Family and mourners, already distressed, may feel threatened or apprehensive in the unfamiliar environment of a crematorium. It may be helpful for individuals or a group from the parish community to accompany the mourners, to guide them to their places, help them with the books, and support them in prayer and singing.

Such a person or group could be a valuable link with the priest and the funeral director on occasions when the deceased and family are not known to either (as, for instance, when a duty priest is officiating at a city crematorium).

238 Usually funeral directors are responsible for carrying out the mourners' wishes with regard to the disposal of the ashes. If the family so wish, arrangements can be made for a priest or minister to say prayers at the interment of the ashes.

239 Cremated remains should not normally be scattered above ground, but reverently returned to the earth.

If this is done within a short time of cremation, it will not be necessary to repeat the entire rite of committal. A short rite for the burial of ashes is provided at p. 215.

240 If the interment of ashes takes place some considerable time after the cremation, or in a different place with a different gathering of people, then the 'Rite of Committal at a Cemetery with Final Commendation' should be celebrated.

241 In cases where the body of the deceased has not been recovered, after some tragedy or for other reasons, suitable adapted vigil rites can still be most helpful to the family and mourners, and the funeral liturgy can be held in the absence of the body.

The Easter candle may stand in place of the catafalque, and may be sprinkled and incensed at those points in the rite when the coffin would have been so reverenced.

The funeral liturgy should conclude with the final commendation and prayer over the people.

242 In the case of a body donated to science, the funeral rites may be celebrated in the absence of the body in the manner described above, while the rite of committal is held over until such time as final interment or cremation takes place.

OUTLINE OF THE·RITE

Invitation
Scripture Verse
Prayer over the Place of Committal

Committal
Intercessions
The Lord's Prayer
Concluding Prayer

Prayer over the People

6 RITE OF COMMITTAL AT A CEMETERY

[INCLUDING BURIAL AT SEA]

WHEN A FUNERAL LITURGY HAS IMMEDIATELY PRECEDED

INVITATION

243 When the funeral procession arrives at the place of committal, the minister says the following or a similar invitation.

Our brother/sister N. has gone to his/her rest in the peace of Christ. May the Lord now welcome him/her to the table of God's children in heaven. With faith and hope in eternal life, let us assist him/her with our prayers.

Let us pray to the Lord also for ourselves. May we who mourn be reunited one day with N.; together may we meet Christ Jesus when he who is our life appears in glory.

SCRIPTURE VERSE

244 One of the following or another brief Scripture verse is read. The minister first says:

We read in sacred Scripture:

A   Matthew 25:34   119

Come, you whom my Father has blessed, says the Lord;
  inherit the kingdom prepared for you since the foundation
    of the world.

B   John 6:39   121

This is the will of my Father, says the Lord,
  that I should lose nothing of all that he has given to me,
  and that I should raise it up on the last day.

C   Philippians 3:20   124

Our true home is in heaven,
  and Jesus Christ whose return we long for
  will come from heaven to save us.

D   Apocalypse 1:5-6   126

Jesus Christ is the first-born of the dead;
  glory and kingship be his for ever and ever. Amen.

Prayer over the Place of Committal

245 The minister says one of the following prayers.

A   All praise to you, Lord of all creation.
Praise to you, holy and living God.
We praise and bless you for your mercy,
we praise and bless you for your kindness.
Blessed is the Lord, our God.

R. Blessed is the Lord, our God.

You sanctify the homes of the living
and make holy the places of the dead.
You alone open the gates of righteousness
and lead us to the dwellings of the saints.
Blessed is the Lord, our God.

R. Blessed is the Lord, our God.

We praise you, our refuge and strength.
We bless you, our God and Redeemer.
Your praise is always in our hearts and on our lips.
We remember the mighty deeds of the covenant.
Blessed is the Lord, our God.

R. Blessed is the Lord, our God.

Almighty and ever-living God,
remember the mercy with which you graced
    your servant N. in life.
Receive him/her, we pray, into the mansions of the saints.
As we make ready our brother's/sister's resting place,
look also with favour on those who mourn
and comfort them in their loss.

Grant this through Christ our Lord.

R. Amen.

B   If the place of committal is to be blessed

Lord Jesus Christ,   53
by your own three days in the tomb,
you hallowed the graves of all who believe in you
and so made the grave a sign of hope
that promises resurrection
even as it claims our mortal bodies.

Grant that our brother/sister may sleep here in peace
until you awaken him/her to glory,
for you are the resurrection and the life.
Then he/she will see you face to face
and in your light will see light
and know the splendour of God,
for you live and reign for ever and ever.

R. Amen.

C   If the place of committal is to be blessed

O God,   193
by whose mercy the faithful departed find rest,
bless this grave,
and send your holy angel to watch over it.

As we bury here the body of our brother/sister,
deliver his/her soul from every bond of sin,
that he/she may rejoice in you with your saints for ever.

We ask this through Christ our Lord.

R. Amen.

D   If the place of committal is to be blessed

Almighty God,   194
you created the earth and shaped the vault of heaven;
you fixed the stars in their places.
When we were caught in the snares of death
you set us free through baptism;
in obedience to your will
our Lord Jesus Christ
broke the fetters of hell and rose to life,
bringing deliverance and resurrection
to those who are his by faith.
In your mercy look upon this grave,
so that your servant may sleep here in peace;
and on the day of judgment raise him/her up
to dwell with your saints in paradise.

We ask this through Christ our Lord.

R. Amen.

E   If the place of committal is to be blessed

God of endless ages,   195
through disobedience to your law
we fell from grace
and death entered the world;
but through the obedience and resurrection of your Son
you revealed to us a new life.
You granted Abraham, our father in faith,
a burial place in the promised land;
you prompted Joseph of Arimathea
to offer his own tomb for the burial of the Lord.
In a spirit of repentance
we earnestly ask you
to look upon this grave and bless it,
so that, while we commit to [the earth/its resting place]
    the body of your servant N.
his/her soul may be taken into paradise.

We ask this through Christ our Lord.

R. Amen.

COMMITTAL

246 The minister then says the words of committal. One of the
following texts is used, during or after which the coffin is lowered.

A   Because God has chosen to call our brother/sister N.   55
     from this life to himself,
we commit his/her body to [the earth/its resting place],
for we are dust and unto dust we shall return.

But the Lord Jesus Christ will change our mortal bodies
     to be like his in glory,
for he is risen, the firstborn from the dead.

So let us commend our brother/sister to the Lord,
that the Lord may embrace him/her in peace
and raise up his/her body on the last day.

B   In sure and certain hope of the resurrection to eternal life
     through our Lord Jesus Christ,
we commend to Almighty God our brother/sister N.,
and we commit his/her body to [the ground/its resting place]:
earth to earth, ashes to ashes, dust to dust.

The Lord bless him/her and keep him/her,
the Lord make his face to shine upon him/her
     and be gracious to him/her,
the Lord lift up his countenance upon him/her
     and give him/her peace.

C   For burial at sea
Lord God,
by the power of your Word
you stilled the chaos of the primeval seas,
you made the raging waters of the Flood subside,
and calmed the storm on the sea of Galilee.
As we commit the body of our brother/sister N. to the deep,
grant him/her peace and tranquility
until that day when he/she and all who believe in you
will be raised to the glory of new life
promised in the waters of baptism.

We ask this through Christ our Lord.

R. Amen.

247 One of the following sets of intercessions may be used or adapted to the circumstances, or new intercessions may be composed.

A   The minister begins:

For our brother/sister, N., let us pray to our Lord Jesus Christ, who said, 'I am the resurrection and the life. Whoever believes in me shall live even in death and whoever lives and believes in me shall never die.'

56
75

A reader or the minister then continues:

Lord, you consoled Martha and Mary in their distress; draw near to us who mourn for N., and dry the tears of those who weep. We pray to the Lord:

R. Lord, have mercy.

You wept at the grave of Lazarus, your friend; comfort us in our sorrow.
We pray to the Lord:

R. Lord, have mercy.

You raised the dead to life; give to our brother/sister eternal life.
We pray to the Lord:

R. Lord, have mercy.

You promised paradise to the repentant thief; bring N. to the joys of heaven.
We pray to the Lord:

R. Lord, have mercy.

Our brother/sister was washed in baptism and anointed with the Holy Spirit; give him/her fellowship with all your saints.
We pray to the Lord:

R. Lord, have mercy.

He/she was nourished with your body and blood; grant him/her a place at the table in your heavenly kingdom.
We pray to the Lord:

R. Lord, have mercy.

Comfort us in our sorrow at the death of N.; let our faith be our consolation, and eternal life our hope.
We pray to the Lord:

R. Lord, have mercy.

B   The minister begins:

Dear friends, in reverence let us pray to God, the source of all mercies.   202

       A reader or the minister then continues:

Gracious Lord, forgive the sins of those who have died in Christ.
Lord, in your mercy:

R. Hear our prayer.

Remember all the good they have done.
Lord, in your mercy:

R. Hear our prayer.

Welcome them into eternal life.
Lord, in your mercy:

R. Hear our prayer.

Let us pray for those who mourn.
Comfort them in their grief.
Lord, in your mercy:

R. Hear our prayer.

Lighten their sense of loss with your presence.
Lord, in your mercy:

R. Hear our prayer.

Increase their faith and strengthen their hope.
Lord, in your mercy:

R. Hear our prayer.

Let us pray also for ourselves on our pilgrimage through life.
Keep us faithful in your service.
Lord, in your mercy:

R. Hear our prayer.

Kindle in our hearts a longing for heaven.
Lord, in your mercy:

R. Hear our prayer.

C The minister begins:

Dear friends, our Lord comes to raise the dead and comforts us with the solace of his love. Let us praise the Lord Jesus Christ.

A reader or the minister then continues:

Word of God, Creator of the earth to which N. now returns: in baptism you called him/her to eternal life to praise your Father for ever:
Lord, have mercy.

R. Lord, have mercy.

Son of God, you raise up the just and clothe them with the glory of your kingdom:
Lord, have mercy.

R. Lord, have mercy.

Crucified Lord, you protect the soul of N. by the power of your cross, and on the day of your coming you will show mercy to all the faithful departed:
Lord, have mercy.

R. Lord, have mercy.

Judge of the living and the dead, at your voice the tombs will open and all the just who sleep in your peace will rise and sing the glory of God:
Lord, have mercy.

R. Lord, have mercy.

All praise to you, Jesus our Saviour, death is in your hands and all the living depend on you alone:
Lord, have mercy.

R. Lord, have mercy.

THE LORD'S PRAYER

248 Using one of the following invitations, or in similar words,
the minister invites those present to pray the Lord's Prayer.

A   Now let us pray as Christ the Lord has taught us:

B   With longing for the coming of God's kingdom, let us offer our
      prayer to the Father:

C   As sons and daughters of a loving God, we pray in the confi-
      dent words of his Son:

D   When Jesus gathered his disciples around him, he taught them
      to pray:

      All say:

Our Father . . .

249 The minister says one of the following prayers or one of those
provided in no. 580, p. 407.

A God of holiness and power, 56
accept our prayers on behalf of your servant N.;
do not count his/her deeds against him/her,
for in his/her heart he/she desired to do your will.
As his/her faith united him/her to your people on earth,
so may your mercy join him/her to the angels in heaven.

We ask this through Christ our Lord.

R. Amen.

B Almighty God, 199
through the death of your Son on the cross
you destroyed our death;
through his rest in the tomb
you hallowed the graves of all who believe in you;
and through his rising again
you restored us to eternal life.

God of the living and the dead,
accept our prayers
for those who have died in Christ
and are buried with him in the hope of rising again.
Since they were true to your name on earth,
let them praise you for ever in the joy of heaven.

We ask this through Christ our Lord.

R. Amen.

C Listen, O God, to the prayers of your Church 196
on behalf of the faithful departed,
and grant to your servant N.,
whose funeral we have celebrated today,
the inheritance promised to all your saints.

We ask this through Christ our Lord.

R. Amen.

D   Loving God, from whom all life proceeds   197
    and by whose hand the dead are raised again,
    though we are sinners, you wish always to hear us.
    Accept the prayers we offer in sadness for your servant N.:
    deliver his/her soul from death,
    number him/her among your saints
    and clothe him/her with the robe of salvation
    to enjoy for ever the delights of your kingdom.

    We ask this through Christ our Lord.

    R. Amen.

E   Lord God,   198
    whose days are without end
    and whose mercies beyond counting,
    keep us mindful
    that life is short and the hour of death unknown.
    Let your Spirit guide our days on earth
    in the ways of holiness and justice,
    that we may serve you
    in union with the whole Church,
    sure in faith, strong in hope, perfected in love.
    And when our earthly journey is ended,
    lead us rejoicing into your kingdom,
    where you live for ever and ever.

    R. Amen.

Prayer over the People

250 The assisting minister or the minister says:

Bow your heads and pray for God's blessing.

All pray silently. The minister, with hands outstretched over the people, says the following prayer.

Merciful Lord,
you know the anguish of the sorrowful,
you are attentive to the prayers of the humble.
Hear your people
who cry out to you in their need,
and strengthen their hope in your lasting goodness.
We ask this through Christ our Lord.

R. Amen.

The minister then says the following:

Eternal rest grant unto him/her, O Lord.

R. And let perpetual light shine upon him/her.

May he/she rest in peace.

R. Amen.

May his/her soul and the souls of all the faithful departed,
through the mercy of God, rest in peace.

R. Amen.

A *A minister who is a priest or deacon says:*

May the peace of God,
which is beyond all understanding,
keep your hearts and minds
in the knowledge and love of God
and of his Son, our Lord Jesus Christ.

R. Amen.

May almighty God bless you,
the Father, and the Son, ✠ and the Holy Spirit.

R. Amen.

B   A minister who is a priest or deacon says:

May the love of God and the peace of the Lord Jesus Christ
console you
and gently wipe every tear from your eyes.

R. Amen.

May almighty God bless you,
the Father, and the Son, ✠ and the Holy Spirit.

R. Amen.

C   A lay minister invokes God's blessing and signs himself or her-
              self with the sign of the cross, saying:

May the love of God and the peace of the Lord Jesus Christ
bless and console us
and gently wipe every tear from our eyes:
in the name of the Father,
and of the Son, and of the Holy Spirit.

R. Amen.

         The minister then concludes:

Go in the peace of Christ.

R.   Thanks be to God.

         A hymn or song may conclude the rite. Some sign or gesture
         of leave-taking may be made.

OUTLINE OF THE RITE

Greeting
Invitation
Scripture Verse
Prayer over the Place of Committal

Invitation to Prayer
Silence
Signs of Farewell
Song of Farewell
Prayer of Commendation
  and the Committal

Prayer over the People

7 RITE OF COMMITTAL AT A CEMETERY WITH FINAL COMMENDATION
[INCLUDING BURIAL OF ASHES AND BURIAL AT SEA]
WHEN A FUNERAL LITURGY HAS NOT IMMEDIATELY PRECEDED

GREETING

251   When all have gathered at the place of committal, the minister welcomes the funeral party and, using one of the following greetings, or in similar words, greets them.

A   May the God of hope give you the fullness of peace, and may the Lord of life be always with you.

R. And also with you.

B   The grace and peace of God our Father and the Lord Jesus Christ be with you.

R. And also with you.

C   The grace and peace of God our Father, who raised Jesus from the dead, be always with you.

R. And also with you.

D   May the Father of mercies, the God of all consolation, be with you.

R. And also with you.

Invitation

252 The minister then says one of the following or a similar invitation.

A   We gather here to commend our brother/sister N. to God our Father and to commit his/her body to the earth. In the spirit of faith in the resurrection of Jesus Christ from the dead, let us [raise our voices in song and] offer our prayers for N.

B   As we gather to commend our brother/sister N. to God our Father and to commit his/her body to the earth, let us express in [song and] prayer our common faith in the resurrection. As Jesus Christ was raised from the dead, we too are called to follow him through death to the glory where God will be all in all.

A hymn or song may be sung.

Scripture Verse

253 One of the following or another brief Scripture verse is read. The minister first says:

We read in sacred Scripture:

A   Matthew 25:34   119
Come, you whom my Father has blessed, says the Lord;
inherit the kingdom prepared for you since the foundation
    of the world.

B   John 6:39   121
This is the will of my Father, says the Lord,
that I should lose nothing of all that he has given to me,
and that I should raise it up on the last day.

C   Philippians 3:20   124
Our true home is in heaven,
and Jesus Christ whose return we long for
will come from heaven to save us.

D   Apocalypse 1:5-6   126
Jesus Christ is the first-born of the dead;
glory and kingship be his for ever and ever. Amen.

Prayer over the Place of Committal

254 The minister says one of the following prayers.

A All praise to you, Lord of all creation.
Praise to you, holy and living God.
We praise and bless you for your mercy,
we praise and bless you for your kindness.
Blessed is the Lord, our God.

R. Blessed is the Lord, our God.

You sanctify the homes of the living
and make holy the places of the dead.
You alone open the gates of righteousness
and lead us to the dwellings of the saints.
Blessed is the Lord, our God.

R. Blessed is the Lord, our God.

We praise you, our refuge and strength.
We bless you, our God and Redeemer.
Your praise is always in our hearts and on our lips.
We remember the mighty deeds of the covenant.
Blessed is the Lord, our God.

R. Blessed is the Lord, our God.

Almighty and ever-living God,
remember the mercy with which you graced
    your servant N. in life.
Receive him/her, we pray, into the mansions of the saints.
As we make ready our brother's/sister's resting place,
look also with favour on those who mourn
and comfort them in their loss.

Grant this through Christ our Lord.

R. Amen.

If the place of committal is to be blessed

Lord Jesus Christ,   53
by your own three days in the tomb,
you hallowed the graves of all who believe in you
and so made the grave a sign of hope
that promises resurrection
even as it claims our mortal bodies.

Grant that our brother/sister may sleep here in peace
until you awaken him/her to glory,
for you are the resurrection and the life.
Then he/she will see you face to face
and in your light will see light
and know the splendour of God,
for you live and reign for ever and ever.

R. Amen.

C   If the place of committal is to be blessed

O God,   193
by whose mercy the faithful departed find rest,
bless this grave,
and send your holy angel to watch over it.

As we bury here the body/ashes of our brother/sister,
deliver his/her soul from every bond of sin,
that he/she may rejoice in you with your saints for ever.

We ask this through Christ our Lord.

R. Amen.

If the place of committal is to be blessed

Almighty God,   194
you created the earth and shaped the vault of heaven;
you fixed the stars in their places.
When we were caught in the snares of death
you set us free through baptism;
in obedience to your will
our Lord Jesus Christ
broke the fetters of hell and rose to life,
bringing deliverance and resurrection
to those who are his by faith.
In your mercy look upon this grave,
so that your servant may sleep here in peace;
and on the day of judgment raise him/her up
to dwell with your saints in paradise.

We ask this through Christ our Lord.

R. Amen.

E   If the place of committal is to be blessed

God of endless ages,   195
through disobedience to your law
we fell from grace
and death entered the world;
but through the obedience and resurrection of your Son
you revealed to us a new life.
You granted Abraham, our father in faith,
a burial place in the promised land;
you prompted Joseph of Arimathea
to offer his own tomb for the burial of the Lord.
In a spirit of repentance
we earnestly ask you
to look upon this grave and bless it,
so that, while we commit to [the earth/its resting place]
   the body/ashes of your servant N.
his/her soul may be taken into paradise.

We ask this through Christ our Lord.

R. Amen.

255 Using one of the following invitations, or in similar words, the minister begins the final commendation.

A   Before we go our separate ways, let us take leave of our brother/ sister. May our farewell express our affection for him/her; may it ease our sadness and strengthen our hope. One day we shall joyfully greet him/her again when the love of Christ, which conquers all things, destroys even death itself.   185

B   Trusting in God, we have prayed together for N. and now we come to the last farewell. There is sadness in parting, but we take comfort in the hope that one day we shall see N. again and enjoy his/her friendship. Although this congregation will disperse in sorrow, the mercy of God will gather us together again in the joy of his kingdom. Therefore let us console one another in the faith of Jesus Christ.   186

C   With faith in Jesus Christ, we must reverently bury the body/ ashes of our brother/sister.   46 65

Let us pray with confidence to God, in whose sight all creation lives, that he will raise up in holiness and power the mortal body of our brother/sister and command his/her soul to be numbered among the blessed.

May God grant him/her a merciful judgment, deliverance from death, and pardon of sin. May Christ the Good Shepherd carry him/her home to be at peace with the Father. May he/she rejoice for ever in the presence of the eternal King and in the company of all the saints.

D   Our brother/sister N. has fallen asleep in Christ. Confident in our hope of eternal life, let us commend him/her to the loving mercy of our Father and let our prayers go with him/her. He/she was adopted as God's son/daughter in baptism and was nourished at the table of the Lord; may he/she now inherit the promise of eternal life and take his/her place at the table of God's children in heaven.   183

Let us pray also on our own behalf, that we who now mourn and are saddened may one day go forth with our brother/sister to meet the Lord of life when he appears in glory.

E   Because God has chosen to call our brother/sister N. from this ₁₈₄ life to himself, we commit his/her body/ashes to [the earth/its resting place/the deep], for we are dust and unto dust we shall return.

But the Lord Jesus Christ will change our mortal bodies to be like his in glory, for he is risen, the first-born from the dead.

So let us commend our brother/sister to the Lord, that the Lord may embrace him/her in peace and raise up his/her body on the last day.

F   For burial of ashes

My friends, as we prepare to bury/entomb the ashes of our brother/sister, we recall that our bodies bear the imprint of the first creation when they were fashioned from dust; but in faith we remember, too, that by the new creation we also bear the image of Jesus who was raised to glory.

In confident hope that one day God will raise us and transform our mortal bodies, let us pray.

Silence

256 All pray in silence.

Signs of Farewell

257 The coffin may now be sprinkled with holy water and incensed, or this may take place during or after the song of farewell.

Song of Farewell

258 The song of farewell is then sung. One of the following texts or another suitable hymn or song may be used.

A   I know that my Redeemer lives,   189
    And on that final day of days,
    His voice shall bid me rise again:
    Unending joy, unceasing praise!

    This hope I cherish in my heart:
    To stand on earth, my flesh restored,
    And, not a stranger but a friend,
    Behold my Saviour and my Lord.
       Tune: LM, for example, Duke Street

B   Saints of God, come to his/her aid!
Hasten to meet him/her, angels of the Lord!
R. Receive his/her soul and present him/her
to God the Most High.

May Christ, who called you, take you to himself;
may angels lead you to the bosom of Abraham.
R. Receive his/her soul and present him/her
to God the Most High.

Eternal rest grant unto him/her, O Lord,
and let perpetual light shine upon him/her.
R. Receive his/her soul and present him/her
to God the Most High.

Prayer of Commendation and the Committal

259 The minister then says one of the following prayers, during or after which the coffin is lowered.

A   Into your hands, Father of mercies,
we commend our brother/sister N.
in the sure and certain hope
that, together with all who have died in Christ,
he/she will rise with him on the last day.

[We give you thanks for the blessings
which you bestowed upon N. in this life:
they are signs to us of your goodness
and of our fellowship with the saints in Christ.]

Merciful Lord,
turn toward us and listen to our prayers:
open the gates of paradise to your servant
and help us who remain
to comfort one another with assurances of faith,
until we all meet in Christ
and are with you and with our brother/sister for ever.

We ask this through Christ our Lord.

R. Amen.

B   To you, O Lord, we commend the soul of N., your servant; 192
in the sight of this world he/she is now dead;
in your sight may he/she live for ever.

Forgive whatever sins he/she committed through human
    weakness
and in your goodness grant him/her everlasting peace.

We ask this through Christ our Lord.

R. Amen.

C   For burial of ashes

Faithful God,
Lord of all creation,
you desire that nothing redeemed by your Son
will ever be lost,
and that the just will be raised up on the last day.

Comfort us today with the word of your promise
as we return the ashes of our brother/sister to the earth.

Grant N. a place of rest and peace
where the world of dust and ashes has no dominion.
Confirm us in our hope that he/she will be created anew
on the day when you will raise him/her up in glory
to live with you and all the saints
for ever and ever.

R. Amen.

D   For burial at sea

Lord God,
by the power of your Word
you stilled the chaos of the primeval seas,
you made the raging waters of the Flood subside,
and calmed the storm on the sea of Galilee.
As we commit the body of our brother/sister N. to the deep,
grant him/her peace and tranquility
until that day when he/she and all who believe in you
will be raised to the glory of new life
promised in the waters of baptism.

We ask this through Christ our Lord.

R. Amen.

Prayer over the People

260 The assisting minister or the minister says:

Bow your heads and pray for God's blessing.

All pray silently. The minister, with hands outstretched over the
people, says the following prayer.

Merciful Lord,
you know the anguish of the sorrowful,
you are attentive to the prayers of the humble.
Hear your people
who cry out to you in their need,
and strengthen their hope in your lasting goodness.
We ask this through Christ our Lord.

R. Amen.

The minister then says the following:

Eternal rest grant unto him/her, O Lord.

R. And let perpetual light shine upon him/her.

May he/she rest in peace.

R. Amen.

May his/her soul and the souls of all the faithful departed,
through the mercy of God, rest in peace.

R. Amen.

A   A minister who is a priest or deacon says:

May the peace of God,
which is beyond all understanding,
keep your hearts and minds
in the knowledge and love of God
and of his Son, our Lord Jesus Christ.

R. Amen.

May almighty God bless you,
the Father, and the Son, ✠ and the Holy Spirit.

R. Amen.

B   A minister who is a priest or deacon says:

May the love of God and the peace of the Lord Jesus Christ
console you
and gently wipe every tear from your eyes.

R. Amen.

May almighty God bless you,
the Father, and the Son, ✠ and the Holy Spirit.

R. Amen.

C   A lay minister invokes God's blessing and signs himself or herself with the sign of the cross, saying:

May the love of God and the peace of the Lord Jesus Christ
bless and console us
and gently wipe every tear from our eyes:
in the name of the Father,
and of the Son, and of the Holy Spirit.

R. Amen.

The minister then concludes:

Go in the peace of Christ.

R. Thanks be to God.

A hymn or song may conclude the rite. Some sign or gesture
of leave-taking may be made.

OUTLINE OF THE RITE

INTRODUCTORY RITES

Greeting
Sprinkling with Holy Water
Entrance Procession
[Placing of the Pall]
[Placing of Christian Symbols]
Invitation to Prayer
Opening Prayer

LITURGY OF THE WORD

Readings
Homily
General Intercessions
    Intercessions
    The Lord's Prayer
    Concluding Prayer

FINAL COMMENDATION

Invitation to Prayer
Silence
Signs of Farewell
Song of Farewell
Prayer of Commendation

PROCESSION TO
THE PLACE OF COMMITTAL

RITE OF COMMITTAL

Invitation
Scripture Verse
Prayer over the Place of Committal
Committal

CONCLUDING RITE

Prayer over the People

8 RITE OF COMMITTAL FOR BURIAL

[INCLUDING BURIAL OF ASHES AND BURIAL AT SEA]
WHEN NO OTHER LITURGY HAS TAKEN PLACE

INTRODUCTORY RITES

GREETING

> 261 At or near the entrance to the chapel, the minister welcomes
> the funeral party and, using one of the following greetings, or
> in similar words, greets them.

A The grace of our Lord Jesus Christ and the love of God and
the fellowship of the Holy Spirit be with you all.

R. And also with you.

B The grace and peace of God our Father and the Lord Jesus
Christ be with you.

R. And also with you.

C The grace and peace of God our Father, who raised Jesus from
the dead, be always with you.

R. And also with you.

D May the Father of mercies, the God of all consolation, be with
you.

R. And also with you.

Sprinkling with Holy Water

> 262 Using one of the following texts, the minister then sprinkles the coffin with holy water.

A   In the waters of baptism
N. died with Christ and rose with him to new life.
May he/she now share with him eternal glory.

B   The Lord is our shepherd
and leads us to streams of living water.

C   Let this water call to mind our baptism into Christ,
who by his death and resurrection has redeemed us.

D   The Lord God lives in his holy temple yet abides in our midst.
Since in baptism N. became God's temple
and the Spirit of God lived in him/her,
with reverence we bless his/her mortal body.

Entrance Procession

> 263 The Easter candle may be placed beforehand near the position the coffin will occupy at the conclusion of the procession. The minister precedes the coffin and the mourners into the chapel. During the procession a psalm, a hymn, or a song may be sung.

Placing of the Pall

> 264 If it is the custom in the local community, the pall is then placed on the coffin by family members, friends, or the minister.

Placing of Christian Symbols

> 265 A symbol of the Christian life, such as a Book of the Gospels, a Bible, or a cross, may be carried in procession, then placed on the coffin, either in silence or as one of the following texts is said.

A   Book of the Gospels or Bible

In life N. cherished the Gospel of Christ.
May Christ now greet him/her with these words of eternal life:
Come, blessed of my Father!

B   Cross

In baptism N. received the sign of the cross.
May he/she now share
in Christ's victory over sin and death.

INVITATION TO PRAYER

266 Using one of the following texts, or in similar words, the
minister invites those present to pray.

A   My brothers and sisters, we believe that all the ties of friendship and affection which knit us as one throughout our lives
do not unravel with death.

Confident that God always remembers the good we have done
and forgives our sins, let us pray, asking God to gather N. to
himself.

B   Dear friends in Christ, in the name of Jesus and of his Church,
we gather to pray for N., that God may bring him/her to everlasting peace and rest.

We share the pain of loss, but the promise of eternal life gives
us hope. Let us comfort one another as we turn to God in prayer.

C   My brothers and sisters, we have come together to renew our
trust in Christ who, by dying on the cross, has freed us from
eternal death and, by rising, has opened for us the gates of
heaven.

Let us pray for our brother/sister, that he/she may share in
Christ's victory, and let us pray for ourselves, that the Lord may
grant us the gift of his loving consolation.

267 After a brief period of silent prayer, the minister says one
of the following prayers or one of those provided in no. 580,
p. 407.

A   Lord our God,
the death of our brother/sister N.
recalls our human condition
and the brevity of our lives on earth.
But for those who believe in your love
death is not the end,
nor does it destroy the bonds
that you forge in our lives.
We share the faith of your Son's disciples
and the hope of the children of God.
Bring the light of Christ's resurrection
to this time of testing and pain
as we pray for N. and for those who love him/her,
through Christ our Lord.

R. Amen.

B   O God,   171
glory of believers and life of the just,
by the death and resurrection of your Son, we are redeemed:
have mercy on your servant N.,
and make him/her worthy to share the joys of paradise,
for he/she believed in the resurrection of the dead.

We ask this through Christ our Lord.

R. Amen.

C   Lord, in our grief we turn to you.   33
Are you not the God of love
always ready to hear our cries?

Listen to our prayers for your servant N.,
whom you have called out of this world:
lead him/her to your kingdom of light and peace
and count him/her among the saints in glory.

We ask this through Christ our Lord.

R. Amen.

D   Lord Jesus, our Redeemer,
you willingly gave yourself up to death,
so that all might be saved and pass from death to life.
We humbly ask you to comfort your servants in their grief
and to receive N. into the arms of your mercy.
You alone are the Holy One,
you are mercy itself;
by dying you unlocked the gates of life
    for those who believe in you.
Forgive N. his/her sins,
and grant him/her a place of happiness, light, and peace
in the kingdom of your glory for ever.

R. Amen.

E   Almighty God and Father,
it is our certain faith
that your Son, who died on the cross, was raised from the dead,
the firstfruits of all who have fallen asleep.
Grant that through this mystery
your servant N., who has gone to his/her rest in Christ,
may share in the joy of his resurrection.

We ask this through our Lord Jesus Christ, your Son,
who lives and reigns with you and the Holy Spirit,
one God, for ever and ever.

R. Amen.

F   O God,
to whom mercy and forgiveness belong,
hear our prayers on behalf of your servant N.,
whom you have called out of this world;
and because he/she put his/her hope and trust in you,
command that he/she be carried safely home to heaven
and come to enjoy your eternal reward.

We ask this through our Lord Jesus Christ, your Son,
who lives and reigns with you and the Holy Spirit,
one God, for ever and ever.

R. Amen.

G   O God,
in whom sinners find mercy and the saints find joy,
we pray to you for our brother/sister N.,
whose body we honour with Christian burial,
that he/she may be delivered from the bonds of death.
Admit him/her to the joyful company of your saints
and raise him/her on the last day
to rejoice in your presence for ever.

We ask this through our Lord Jesus Christ, your Son,
who lives and reigns with you and the Holy Spirit,
one God, for ever and ever.

R. Amen.

H   During the Easter season   173

God of loving kindness,
listen favourably to our prayers:
strengthen our belief that your Son has risen from the dead
and our hope that your servant N. will also rise again.

We ask this through our Lord Jesus Christ, your Son,
who lives and reigns with you and the Holy Spirit,
one God, for ever and ever.

R. Amen.

LITURGY OF THE WORD

READINGS

268 After the introductory rites, the liturgy of the word is celebrated. Depending upon pastoral circumstances, either one or
two readings may be read before the gospel. If only one reading
is possible it should be the gospel. Between the readings a psalm
or suitable song may be used.

HOMILY

269 A brief homily is given after the gospel reading.

General Intercessions

270 The general intercessions then take place.

Intercessions

271 One of the following sets of intercessions may be used or adapted to the circumstances, or new intercessions may be composed.

A

The minister begins:

God, the almighty Father, raised Christ his Son from the dead; 200 with confidence we ask him to save all his people, living and dead:

A reader or the minister then continues:

For N. who in baptism was given the pledge of eternal life, that he/she may now be admitted to the company of the saints. Lord, in your mercy:

R. Hear our prayer.

For our brother/sister who ate the body of Christ, the bread of life, that he/she may be raised up on the last day. Lord, in your mercy:

R. Hear our prayer.

For our deceased relatives and friends and for all who have helped us, that they may have the reward of their goodness. Lord, in your mercy:

R. Hear our prayer.

For those who have fallen asleep in the hope of rising again, that they may see God face to face. Lord, in your mercy:

R. Hear our prayer.

For the family and friends of our brother/sister N., that they may be consoled in their grief by the Lord, who wept at the death of his friend Lazarus. Lord, in your mercy:

R. Hear our prayer.

For all of us assembled here to worship in faith, that we may be gathered together again in God's kingdom.
Lord, in your mercy:

R. Hear our prayer.

B   The minister begins:
Brothers and sisters, Jesus Christ is risen from the dead and sits at the right hand of the Father, where he intercedes for his Church. Confident that God hears the voices of those who trust in the Lord Jesus, we join our prayers to his:

A reader or the minister then continues:
In baptism N. received the light of Christ. Scatter the darkness now and lead him/her over the waters of death.
Lord, in your mercy:

R. Hear our prayer.

Our brother/sister N. was nourished at the table of the Saviour. Welcome him/her into the halls of the heavenly banquet.
Lord, in your mercy:

R. Hear our prayer.

Many friends and members of our families have gone before us and await the kingdom. Grant them an everlasting home with your Son.
Lord, in your mercy:

R. Hear our prayer.

Many people die by violence, war, and famine each day. Show your mercy to those who suffer so unjustly these sins against your love, and gather them to the eternal kingdom of peace.
Lord, in your mercy:

R. Hear our prayer.

Those who trusted in the Lord now sleep in the Lord. Give refreshment, rest, and peace to all whose faith is known to you alone.
Lord, in your mercy:

R. Hear our prayer.

The family and friends of N. seek comfort and consolation. Heal their pain and dispel the darkness and doubt that come from grief. Lord, in your mercy:

R. Hear our prayer.

We are assembled here in faith and confidence to pray for our brother/sister N. Strengthen our hope so that we may live in the expectation of your Son's coming.
Lord, in your mercy:

R. Hear our prayer.

C   The minister begins: 201

My dear friends, let us join with one another in praying to God, not only for our departed brother/sister, but also for the Church, for peace in the world, and for ourselves.

A reader or the minister then continues:

That the bishops and priests of the Church, and all who preach the Gospel, may be given the strength to express in action the word they proclaim.
We pray to the Lord:

R. Lord, hear our prayer.

That those in public office may promote justice and peace.
We pray to the Lord:

R. Lord, hear our prayer.

That those who bear the cross of pain in mind or body may never feel forsaken by God.
We pray to the Lord:

R. Lord, hear our prayer.

That God may deliver the soul of his servant N. from punishment and from the powers of darkness.
We pray to the Lord:

R. Lord, hear our prayer.

That God in his mercy may blot out all his/her offences.
We pray to the Lord:

R. Lord, hear our prayer.

That God may establish him/her in light and peace.
We pray to the Lord:

R. Lord, hear our prayer.

That God may call him/her to happiness in the company of all
the saints.
We pray to the Lord:

R. Lord, hear our prayer.

That God may welcome into his glory those of our family and
friends who have departed this life.
We pray to the Lord:

R. Lord, hear our prayer.

That God may give a place in the kingdom of heaven to all the
faithful departed.
We pray to the Lord:

R. Lord, hear our prayer.

THE LORD'S PRAYER

272 Using one of the following invitations, or in similar words,
the minister invites those present to pray the Lord's Prayer.

A   Now let us pray as Christ the Lord has taught us:

B   With longing for the coming of God's kingdom, let us offer our
prayer to the Father:

C   As sons and daughters of a loving God, we pray in the confident words of his Son:

D   When Jesus gathered his disciples around him, he taught them
to pray:

All say:
Our Father . . .

CONCLUDING PRAYER

273 The minister says one of the following prayers or one of those provided in no. 580, p. 407.

A   God, our shelter and our strength,
you listen in love to the cry of your people:
hear the prayers we offer for our departed brother/sister N.
Cleanse him/her and all the faithful departed of their sins
and grant them the fullness of redemption.

We ask this through Christ our Lord.

R. Amen.

B   Lord God,
giver of peace and healer of souls,
hear the prayers of the Redeemer, Jesus Christ,
and the voices of your people,
whose lives were purchased by the blood of the Lamb.
Forgive the sins of all who sleep in Christ
and grant them a place in the kingdom.

We ask this through Christ our Lord.

R. Amen.

C   O God,
Creator and Redeemer of all the faithful,
grant to the souls of your departed servants
release from all their sins.
Hear our prayers for those we love
and give them the pardon they have always desired.

We ask this through Christ our Lord.

R. Amen.

FINAL COMMENDATION

274 The minister then goes to a place near the coffin. If incense and holy water are to be used, they are carried by the assisting ministers.

A member or a friend of the family may speak in remembrance of the deceased before the final commendation begins.

275 Using one of the following invitations, or in similar words, the minister begins the final commendation.

A   Before we go our separate ways, let us take leave of our brother/   185
sister. May our farewell express our affection for him/her; may
it ease our sadness and strengthen our hope. One day we shall
joyfully greet him/her again when the love of Christ, which conquers all things, destroys even death itself.

B   Trusting in God, we have prayed together for N. and now we   186
come to the last farewell. There is sadness in parting, but we
take comfort in the hope that one day we shall see N. again
and enjoy his/her friendship. Although this congregation will
disperse in sorrow, the mercy of God will gather us together
again in the joy of his kingdom. Therefore let us console one
another in the faith of Jesus Christ.

C   With faith in Jesus Christ, we must reverently bury the body/   46
ashes of our brother/sister.   65

Let us pray with confidence to God, in whose sight all creation
lives, that he will raise up in holiness and power the mortal
body of our brother/sister and command his/her soul to be numbered among the blessed.

May God grant him/her a merciful judgment, deliverance from
death, and pardon of sin. May Christ the Good Shepherd carry
him/her home to be at peace with the Father. May he/she rejoice for ever in the presence of the eternal King and in the
company of all the saints.

D   Our brother/sister N. has fallen asleep in Christ. Confident in   183
our hope of eternal life, let us commend him/her to the loving
mercy of our Father and let our prayers go with him/her. He/she
was adopted as God's son/daughter in baptism and was
nourished at the table of the Lord; may he/she now inherit the
promise of eternal life and take his/her place at the table of God's
children in heaven.

Let us pray also on our own behalf, that we who now mourn
and are saddened may one day go forth with our brother/sister
to meet the Lord of life when he appears in glory.

E Because God has chosen to call our brother/sister N. from this life to himself, we commit his/her body/ashes [to the earth/its resting place/the deep], for we are dust and unto dust we shall return.

184

But the Lord Jesus Christ will change our mortal bodies to be like his in glory, for he is risen, the first-born from the dead.

So let us commend our brother/sister to the Lord, that the Lord may embrace him/her in peace and raise up his/her body on the last day.

SILENCE

276 All pray in silence.

SIGNS OF FAREWELL

277 The coffin may now be sprinkled with holy water and in-censed, or this may take place during or after the song of farewell.

SONG OF FAREWELL

278 The song of farewell is then sung. One of the following texts or another suitable hymn or song may be sung.

A I know that my Redeemer lives,
And on that final day of days,
His voice shall bid me rise again:
Unending joy, unceasing praise!

189

This hope I cherish in my heart:
To stand on earth, my flesh restored,
And, not a stranger but a friend,
Behold my Saviour and my Lord.
    Tune: LM, for example, Duke Street

B Saints of God, come to his/her aid!
Hasten to meet him/her, angels of the Lord!
R. Receive his/her soul and present him/her
to God the Most High.

47
66

May Christ, who called you, take you to himself;
may angels lead you to the bosom of Abraham.
R. Receive his/her soul and present him/her
to God the Most High.

Eternal rest grant unto him/her, O Lord,
and let perpetual light shine upon him/her.
R. Receive his/her soul and present him/her
to God the Most High.

Prayer of Commendation

279 The minister then says one of the following prayers.

A   Into your hands, Father of mercies,   48
we commend our brother/sister N.
in the sure and certain hope
that, together with all who have died in Christ,
he/she will rise with him on the last day.

[We give you thanks for the blessings
which you bestowed upon N. in this life:
they are signs to us of your goodness
and of our fellowship with the saints in Christ.]

Merciful Lord,
turn toward us and listen to our prayers:
open the gates of paradise to your servant
and help us who remain
to comfort one another with assurances of faith,
until we all meet in Christ
and are with you and with our brother/sister for ever.

We ask this through Christ our Lord.

R. Amen.

B   To you, O Lord, we commend the soul of N. your servant;   192
in the sight of this world he/she is now dead;
in your sight may he/she live for ever.
Forgive whatever sins he/she committed through human
    weakness
and in your goodness grant him/her everlasting peace.

We ask this through Christ our Lord.

R. Amen.

PROCESSION TO THE
PLACE OF COMMITTAL

280 The assisting minister or the minister says:

In peace let us take N. to his/her place of rest.

If a symbol of the Christian life has been placed on the coffin, it should be removed at this time.

The procession then begins: the minister and assisting ministers precede the coffin; the family and mourners follow.

One or more of the following texts or other suitable songs may be sung during the procession to the entrance of the chapel. The singing may continue during the journey to the place of committal.

A   The following antiphon may be sung with verses from Psalm 24 (25), p. 429.

May the angels lead you into paradise;   50
may the martyrs come to welcome you
and take you to the holy city,
the new and eternal Jerusalem.

B   The following antiphon may be sung with verses from Psalm 114 (116), p. 430, or separately.

May choirs of angels welcome you   50
and lead you to the bosom of Abraham;
and where Lazarus is poor no longer
may you find eternal rest.

C   May saints and angels lead you on,
Escorting you where Christ has gone.
Now he has called you, come to him
Who sits above the seraphim.

Come to the peace of Abraham
And to the supper of the Lamb:
Come to the glory of the blessed,
And to perpetual light and rest.

D   Another suitable psalm may also be used.

RITE OF COMMITTAL

Invitation

281 When the funeral procession arrives at the place of committal, the minister says one of the following or a similar invitation.

A   Our brother/sister N. has gone to his/her rest in the peace of Christ. May the Lord now welcome him/her to the table of God's children in heaven. With faith and hope in eternal life, let us assist him/her with our prayers.

Let us pray to the Lord also for ourselves. May we who mourn be reunited one day with our brother/sister; together may we meet Christ Jesus when he who is our life appears in glory.

B   For burial of ashes

My friends, as we prepare to bury/entomb the ashes of our brother/sister, we recall that our bodies bear the imprint of the first creation when they were fashioned from dust; but in faith we remember, too, that by the new creation we also bear the image of Jesus who was raised to glory.

Scripture Verse

282 One of the following or another brief Scripture verse is read. The minister first says:

We read in sacred Scripture:

A   Matthew 25:34   119

Come, you whom my Father has blessed, says the Lord;
inherit the kingdom prepared for you since the foundation
   of the world.

B   John 6:39   121

This is the will of my Father, says the Lord,
that I should lose nothing of all that he has given to me,
and that I should raise it up on the last day.

C   Philippians 3:20 124

Our true home is in heaven,
and Jesus Christ whose return we long for
will come from heaven to save us.

D   Apocalypse 1:5-6 126

Jesus Christ is the first-born of the dead;
glory and kingship be his for ever and ever. Amen.

Prayer over the Place of Committal

283 The minister says one of the following prayers.

A   All praise to you, Lord of all creation.
Praise to you, holy and living God.
We praise and bless you for your mercy,
we praise and bless you for your kindness.
Blessed is the Lord, our God.

R. Blessed is the Lord, our God.

You sanctify the homes of the living
and make holy the places of the dead.
You alone open the gates of righteousness
and lead us to the dwellings of the saints.
Blessed is the Lord, our God.

R. Blessed is the Lord, our God.

We praise you, our refuge and strength.
We bless you, our God and Redeemer.
Your praise is always in our hearts and on our lips.
We remember the mighty deeds of the covenant.
Blessed is the Lord, our God.

R. Blessed is the Lord, our God.

Almighty and ever-living God,
remember the mercy with which you graced
   your servant N. in life.
Receive him/her, we pray, into the mansions of the saints.
As we make ready our brother's/sister's resting place,
look also with favour on those who mourn
and comfort them in their loss.

Grant this through Christ our Lord.

R. Amen.

B   If the place of committal is to be blessed

Lord Jesus Christ,   53
by your own three days in the tomb,
you hallowed the graves of all who believe in you
and so made the grave a sign of hope
that promises resurrection
even as it claims our mortal bodies.

Grant that our brother/sister may sleep here in peace
until you awaken him/her to glory,
for you are the resurrection and the life.
Then he/she will see you face to face
and in your light will see light
and know the splendour of God,
for you live and reign for ever and ever.

R. Amen.

C   If the place of committal is to be blessed

O God,   193
by whose mercy the faithful departed find rest,
bless this grave,
and send your holy angel to watch over it.

As we bury here the body/ashes of our brother/sister,
deliver his/her soul from every bond of sin,
that he/she may rejoice in you with your saints for ever.

We ask this through Christ our Lord.

R. Amen.

D   If the place of committal is to be blessed

Almighty God,   194
you created the earth and shaped the vault of heaven;
you fixed the stars in their places.
When we were caught in the snares of death
you set us free through baptism;
in obedience to your will
our Lord Jesus Christ
broke the fetters of hell and rose to life,
bringing deliverance and resurrection
to those who are his by faith.
In your mercy look upon this grave,
so that your servant may sleep here in peace;
and on the day of judgment raise him/her up
to dwell with your saints in paradise.

We ask this through Christ our Lord.

R. Amen.

E   If the place of committal is to be blessed

God of endless ages,   195
through disobedience to your law
we fell from grace
and death entered the world;
but through the obedience and resurrection of your Son
you revealed to us a new life.
You granted Abraham, our father in faith,
a burial place in the promised land;
you prompted Joseph of Arimathea
to offer his own tomb for the burial of the Lord.
In a spirit of repentance
we earnestly ask you
to look upon this grave and bless it,
so that, while we commit to
  [the earth/its resting place/the deep]
 the body/ashes of your servant N.
his/her soul may be taken into paradise.

We ask this through Christ our Lord.

R. Amen.

Committal

284 284 The minister then says the words of committal. One of the
following texts is used, during or after which the coffin is lowered.

A   Because God has chosen to call our brother/sister N.   55
         from this life to himself,
     we commit his/her body to [the earth/its resting place],
     for we are dust and unto dust we shall return.

     But the Lord Jesus Christ will change our mortal bodies
         to be like his in glory,
     for he is risen, the firstborn from the dead.

     So let us commend our brother/sister to the Lord,
     that the Lord may embrace him/her in peace
     and raise up his/her body on the last day.

B   In sure and certain hope of the resurrection to eternal life
         through our Lord Jesus Christ,
     we commend to Almighty God our brother/sister N.,
     and we commit his/her body to [the ground/its resting place]:
     earth to earth, ashes to ashes, dust to dust.

     The Lord bless him/her and keep him/her,
     the Lord make his face to shine upon him/her
         and be gracious to him/her,
     the Lord lift up his countenance upon him/her
         and give him/her peace.

C   For burial of ashes

Faithful God,
Lord of all creation,
you desire that nothing redeemed by your Son
will ever be lost,
and that the just will be raised up on the last day.

Comfort us today with the word of your promise
as we return the ashes of our brother/sister to the earth.

Grant N. a place of rest and peace
where the world of dust and ashes has no dominion.
Confirm us in our hope that he/she will be created anew
on the day when you will raise him/her up in glory
to live with you and all the saints
for ever and ever.

R. Amen.

D   For burial at sea

Lord God,
by the power of your Word
you stilled the chaos of the primeval seas,
you made the raging waters of the Flood subside,
and calmed the storm on the sea of Galilee.
As we commit the body of our brother/sister N. to the deep,
grant him/her peace and tranquility
until that day when he/she and all who believe in you
will be raised to the glory of new life
promised in the waters of baptism.

We ask this through Christ our Lord.

R. Amen.

CONCLUDING RITE

PRAYER OVER THE PEOPLE

285 The assisting minister or the minister says:

Bow your heads and pray for God's blessing.

All pray silently. The minister, with hands outstretched over the
people, says the following prayer.

Merciful Lord,
you know the anguish of the sorrowful,
you are attentive to the prayers of the humble.
Hear your people
who cry out to you in their need,
and strengthen their hope in your lasting goodness.

We ask this through Christ our Lord.

R. Amen.

The minister then says the following:

Eternal rest grant unto him/her, O Lord.

R. And let perpetual light shine upon him/her.

May he/she rest in peace.

R. Amen.

May his/her soul and the souls of all the faithful departed,
through the mercy of God, rest in peace.

R. Amen.

A   A minister who is a priest or deacon says:

May the peace of God,
which is beyond all understanding,
keep your hearts and minds
in the knowledge and love of God
and of his Son, our Lord Jesus Christ.

R. Amen.

May almighty God bless you,
the Father, and the Son, ✠ and the Holy Spirit.

R. Amen.

B   A minister who is a priest or deacon says:

May the love of God and the peace of the Lord Jesus Christ
console you
and gently wipe every tear from your eyes.

R. Amen.

May almighty God bless you,
the Father, and the Son, ✠ and the Holy Spirit.

R. Amen.

C   A lay minister invokes God's blessing and signs himself or herself with the sign of the cross, saying:

May the love of God and the peace of the Lord Jesus Christ
bless and console us
and gently wipe every tear from our eyes:
in the name of the Father,
and of the Son, and of the Holy Spirit.

R. Amen.

      The minister then concludes:

Go in the peace of Christ.

R. Thanks be to God.

      A hymn or song may conclude the rite. Some sign or gesture
of leave-taking may be made.

OUTLINE OF THE RITE

Invitation
Scripture Verse
Prayer before Committal

Signs of Farewell
Committal
Intercessions
The Lord's Prayer
Concluding Prayer

Prayer over the People

9 RITE OF COMMITTAL AT A CREMATORIUM
WHEN A FUNERAL LITURGY HAS IMMEDIATELY PRECEDED

INVITATION

286 When all have gathered in the crematorium chapel, the minister then says one of the following or a similar invitation.

A We gather here to commend our brother/sister N. to God our Father and to commit his/her body to be cremated. In the spirit of faith in the resurrection of Jesus Christ from the dead, let us [raise our voices in song and] offer our prayers for N.

B As we gather to commend our brother/sister N. to God our Father and to commit his/her body to be cremated, let us express in [song and] prayer our common faith in the resurrection. As Jesus Christ was raised from the dead, we too are called to follow him through death to the glory where God will be all in all.

A hymn or song may be sung.

SCRIPTURE VERSE

287 One of the following or another brief Scripture verse is read. The minister first says:

We read in sacred Scripture:

A Matthew 25:34   119

Come, you whom my Father has blessed, says the Lord;
inherit the kingdom prepared for you since the foundation
of the world.

B John 6:39   121

This is the will of my Father, says the Lord,
that I should lose nothing of all that he has given to me,
and that I should raise it up on the last day.

C Philippians 3:20   124

Our true home is in heaven,
and Jesus Christ whose return we long for
will come from heaven to save us.

D Apocalypse 1:5-6   126

Jesus Christ is the first-born of the dead;
glory and kingship be his for ever and ever. Amen.

Prayer before Committal

288 The minister says one of the following prayers or one of those provided in no. 580, p. 407.

A   Almighty and ever-living God,
remember the love with which you graced
    your servant N. in life.
Receive him/her, we pray, into the mansions of the saints.
Look with favour on those who mourn
and comfort them in their loss.

Grant this through Christ our Lord.

R. Amen.

B   Almighty and ever-living God,
in you we place our trust and hope,
in you the dead whose bodies were temples of the Spirit
    find everlasting peace.

As we take leave of N.,
give our hearts peace in the firm hope
that one day he/she will live
in the mansion you have prepared for him/her in heaven.

We ask this through Christ our Lord.

R. Amen.

Signs of Farewell

289 The coffin may now be sprinkled with holy water and in-censed, or this may take place at the end of the rite. The family and other mourners may also sprinkle the coffin with holy water now or at the end of the rite if the coffin remains in view.

COMMITTAL

290 The minister then says the words of committal. One of the following texts is used, during or after which the coffin may be removed from view.

A Because God has chosen to call our brother/sister N.   55
from this life to himself,
we commit his/her body to be cremated,
for we are dust and unto dust we shall return.

But the Lord Jesus Christ will change our mortal bodies
to be like his in glory,
for he is risen, the firstborn from the dead.

So let us commend our brother/sister to the Lord,
that the Lord may embrace him/her in peace
and raise up his/her body on the last day.

B In sure and certain hope of the resurrection to eternal life
through our Lord Jesus Christ,
we commend to Almighty God our brother/sister N.,
and we commit his/her body to be cremated:
earth to earth, ashes to ashes, dust to dust.

The Lord bless him/her and keep him/her,
the Lord make his face to shine upon him/her
and be gracious to him/her,
the Lord lift up his countenance upon him/her
and give him/her peace.

INTERCESSIONS

291 One of the following sets of intercessions may be used or adapted to the circumstances, or new intercessions may be composed.

A The minister begins:

For our brother/sister, N., let us pray to our Lord Jesus Christ,   56
who said, 'I am the resurrection and the life. Whoever believes   75
in me shall live even in death and whoever lives and believes
in me shall never die.'

Lord, you consoled Martha and Mary in their distress; draw near to us who mourn for N., and dry the tears of those who weep. We pray to the Lord:

R. Lord, have mercy.

You wept at the grave of Lazarus, your friend; comfort us in our sorrow.
We pray to the Lord:

R. Lord, have mercy.

You raised the dead to life; give to our brother/sister eternal life.
We pray to the Lord:

R. Lord, have mercy.

You promised paradise to the repentant thief; bring N. to the joys of heaven.
We pray to the Lord:

R. Lord, have mercy.

Our brother/sister was washed in baptism and anointed with the Holy Spirit; give him/her fellowship with all your saints.
We pray to the Lord:

R. Lord, have mercy.

He/she was nourished with your body and blood; grant him/her a place at the table in your heavenly kingdom.
We pray to the Lord:

R. Lord, have mercy.

Comfort us in our sorrow at the death of N.; let our faith be our consolation, and eternal life our hope.
We pray to the Lord:

R. Lord, have mercy.

B   The minister begins:

Dear friends, in reverence let us pray to God, the source of all mercies.

A reader or the minister then continues:

Gracious Lord, forgive the sins of those who have died in Christ.
Lord, in your mercy:

R. Hear our prayer.

Remember all the good they have done.
Lord, in your mercy:

R. Hear our prayer.

Welcome them into eternal life.
Lord, in your mercy:

R. Hear our prayer.

Let us pray for those who mourn.
Comfort them in their grief.
Lord, in your mercy:

R. Hear our prayer.

Lighten their sense of loss with your presence.
Lord, in your mercy:

R. Hear our prayer.

Increase their faith and strengthen their hope.
Lord, in your mercy:

R. Hear our prayer.

Let us pray also for ourselves on our pilgrimage through life.
Keep us faithful in your service.
Lord, in your mercy:

R. Hear our prayer.

Kindle in our hearts a longing for heaven.
Lord, in your mercy:

R. Hear our prayer.

C   The minister begins:
Dear friends, our Lord comes to raise the dead and comforts
us with the solace of his love. Let us praise the Lord Jesus Christ.

A reader or the minister then continues:
Lifegiving Word of God, in baptism you called N. to eternal
life to praise your Father for ever:
Lord, have mercy.

R. Lord, have mercy.

Son of God, you raise up the just and clothe them with the glory
of your kingdom:
Lord, have mercy.

R. Lord, have mercy.

Crucified Lord, you protect the soul of N. by the power of your cross, and on the day of your coming you will show mercy to all the faithful departed:
Lord, have mercy.

R. Lord, have mercy.

All praise to you, Jesus our Saviour, death is in your hands and all the living depend on you alone:
Lord, have mercy.

R. Lord, have mercy.

The Lord's Prayer

292 Using one of the following invitations, or in similar words, the minister invites those present to pray the Lord's Prayer.

A   Now let us pray as Christ the Lord has taught us:

B   With longing for the coming of God's kingdom, let us offer our prayer to the Father:

C   As sons and daughters of a loving God, we pray in the confident words of his Son:

D   When Jesus gathered his disciples around him, he taught them to pray:

      All say:
Our Father . . .

Concluding Prayer

293 The minister says one of the following prayers or one of those provided in no. 580, p. 407.

A   God of holiness and power,
accept our prayers on behalf of your servant N.;
do not count his/her deeds against him/her,
for in his/her heart he/she desired to do your will.
As his/her faith united him/her to your people on earth,
so may your mercy join him/her to the angels in heaven.

We ask this through Christ our Lord.

R. Amen.

B   Listen, O God, to the prayers of your Church 196
on behalf of the faithful departed,
and grant to your servant N.,
whose funeral we have celebrated today,
the inheritance promised to all your saints.

We ask this through Christ our Lord.

R. Amen.

C   Loving God, from whom all life proceeds 197
and by whose hand the dead are raised again,
though we are sinners, you wish always to hear us.
Accept the prayers we offer in sadness for your servant N.:
deliver his/her soul from death,
number him/her among your saints
and clothe him/her with the robe of salvation
to enjoy for ever the delights of your kingdom.

We ask this through Christ our Lord.

R. Amen.

D   Lord God, 198
whose days are without end
and whose mercies beyond counting,
keep us mindful
that life is short and the hour of death unknown.
Let your Spirit guide our days on earth
in the ways of holiness and justice,
that we may serve you
in union with the whole Church,
sure in faith, strong in hope, perfected in love.
And when our earthly journey is ended,
lead us rejoicing into your kingdom,
where you live for ever and ever.

R. Amen.

Prayer over the People

294 The assisting minister or the minister says:

Bow your heads and pray for God's blessing.

All pray silently. The minister, with hands outstretched over the people, says the following prayer:

Merciful Lord,
you know the anguish of the sorrowful,
you are attentive to the prayers of the humble.
Hear your people
who cry out to you in their need,
and strengthen their hope in your lasting goodness.
We ask this through Christ our Lord.

R. Amen.

The minister then says the following:

Eternal rest grant unto him/her, O Lord.

R. And let perpetual light shine upon him/her.

May he/she rest in peace.

R. Amen.

May his/her soul and the souls of all the faithful departed,
through the mercy of God, rest in peace.

R. Amen.

A   A minister who is a priest or deacon says:

May the peace of God,
which is beyond all understanding,
keep your hearts and minds
in the knowledge and love of God
and of his Son, our Lord Jesus Christ.

R. Amen.

May almighty God bless you,
the Father, and the Son, ✠ and the Holy Spirit.

R. Amen.

B   A minister who is a priest or deacon says:

May the love of God and the peace of the Lord Jesus Christ
console you
and gently wipe every tear from your eyes.

R. Amen.

May almighty God bless you,
the Father, and the Son, ✠ and the Holy Spirit.

R. Amen.

C   A lay minister invokes God's blessing and signs himself or herself with the sign of the cross, saying:

May the love of God and the peace of the Lord Jesus Christ
bless and console us
and gently wipe every tear from our eyes:
in the name of the Father,
and of the Son, and of the Holy Spirit.

R. Amen.

The minister then concludes:

Go in the peace of Christ.

R. Thanks be to God.

A hymn or song may conclude the rite. Some sign or gesture
of leave-taking may be made, if this has not taken place earlier,
and if the coffin remains in view.

OUTLINE OF THE RITE

Greeting
Invitation
Scripture Verse

Invitation to Prayer
Silence
Signs of Farewell
Song of Farewell
Prayer of Commendation
  and the Committal

Prayer over the People

10 RITE OF COMMITTAL AT A CREMATORIUM WITH FINAL COMMENDATION

WHEN A FUNERAL LITURGY HAS NOT IMMEDIATELY PRECEDED

GREETING

295 When all have gathered in the crematorium chapel, the minister welcomes the funeral party and, using one of the following greetings, or in similar words, greets them.

A   May the God of hope give you the fullness of peace, and may the Lord of life be always with you.

    R. And also with you.

B   The grace and peace of God our Father and the Lord Jesus Christ be with you.

    R. And also with you.

C   The grace and peace of God our Father, who raised Jesus from the dead, be always with you.

    R. And also with you.

D   May the Father of mercies, the God of all consolation, be with you.

    R. And also with you.

296 The minister then says one of the following or a similar invitation.

A　We gather here to commend our brother/sister N. to God our Father and to commit his/her body to be cremated. In the spirit of faith in the resurrection of Jesus Christ from the dead, let us [raise our voices in song and] offer our prayers for N.

B　As we gather to commend our brother/sister N. to God our Father and to commit his/her body to be cremated, let us express in [song and] prayer our common faith in the resurrection. As Jesus Christ was raised from the dead, we too are called to follow him through death to the glory where God will be all in all.

A hymn or song may be sung.

SCRIPTURE VERSE

297 One of the following or another brief Scripture verse is read. The minister first says:

We read in sacred Scripture:

A　　　Matthew 25:34　　　　　　　　　　　　　　　　　119
Come, you whom my Father has blessed, says the Lord;
inherit the kingdom prepared for you since the foundation
　of the world.

B　　　John 6:39　　　　　　　　　　　　　　　　　　　121
This is the will of my Father, says the Lord,
that I should lose nothing of all that he has given to me,
and that I should raise it up on the last day.

C　　　Philippians 3:20　　　　　　　　　　　　　　　　124
Our true home is in heaven,
and Jesus Christ whose return we long for
will come from heaven to save us.

D　　　Apocalypse 1:5-6　　　　　　　　　　　　　　　　126
Jesus Christ is the first-born of the dead;
glory and kingship be his for ever and ever. Amen.

Invitation to Prayer

298 Using one of the following invitations, or in similar words, the minister begins the final commendation.

A Before we go our separate ways, let us take leave of our brother/ 185
sister. May our farewell express our affection for him/her; may it ease our sadness and strengthen our hope. One day we shall joyfully greet him/her again when the love of Christ, which conquers all things, destroys even death itself.

B Trusting in God, we have prayed together for N. and now we 186
come to the last farewell. There is sadness in parting, but we take comfort in the hope that one day we shall see N. again and enjoy his/her friendship. Although this congregation will disperse in sorrow, the mercy of God will gather us together again in the joy of his kingdom. Therefore let us console one another in the faith of Jesus Christ.

C Our brother/sister N. has fallen asleep in Christ. Confident in 183
our hope of eternal life, let us commend him/her to the loving mercy of our Father and let our prayers go with him/her. He/she was adopted as God's son/daughter in baptism and was nourished at the table of the Lord; may he/she now inherit the promise of eternal life and take his/her place at the table of God's children in heaven.

Let us pray also on our own behalf, that we who now mourn and are saddened may one day go forth with our brother/sister to meet the Lord of life when he appears in glory.

Silence

299 All pray in silence.

Signs of Farewell

300 The coffin may now be sprinkled with holy water and incensed, or this may take place during or after the song of farewell.

301 The song of farewell is then sung. One of the following texts or another suitable hymn or song may be sung.

A   I know that my Redeemer lives,   189
And on that final day of days,
His voice shall bid me rise again:
Unending joy, unceasing praise!

This hope I cherish in my heart:
To stand on earth, my flesh restored,
And, not a stranger but a friend,
Behold my Saviour and my Lord.

Tune: LM, for example, Duke Street

B   Saints of God, come to his/her aid!   47
Hasten to meet him/her, angels of the Lord!   66
R. Receive his/her soul and present him/her
to God the Most High.

May Christ, who called you, take you to himself;
may angels lead you to the bosom of Abraham.
R. Receive his/her soul and present him/her
to God the Most High.

Eternal rest grant unto him/her, O Lord,
and let perpetual light shine upon him/her.
R. Receive his/her soul and present him/her
to God the Most High.

Prayer of Commendation and the Committal

302 The minister then says one of the following prayers, during or after which the coffin may be removed from view.

A Into your hands, Father of mercies,   48
we commend our brother/sister N.
in the sure and certain hope
that, together with all who have died in Christ,
he/she will rise with him on the last day.

[We give you thanks for the blessings
which you bestowed upon N. in this life:
they are signs to us of your goodness
and of our fellowship with the saints in Christ.]

Merciful Lord,
turn toward us and listen to our prayers:
open the gates of paradise to your servant
and help us who remain
to comfort one another with assurances of faith,
until we all meet in Christ
and are with you and with our brother/sister for ever.

We ask this through Christ our Lord.

R. Amen.

B To you, O Lord, we commend the soul of N. your servant;   192
in the sight of this world he/she is now dead;
in your sight may he/she live for ever.

Forgive whatever sins he/she committed through human
    weakness
and in your goodness grant him/her everlasting peace.

We ask this through Christ our Lord.

R. Amen.

303 The assisting minister or the minister says:

Bow your heads and pray for God's blessing.

All pray silently. The minister, with hands outstretched over the
people, says the following prayer.

Merciful Lord,
you know the anguish of the sorrowful,
you are attentive to the prayers of the humble.
Hear your people
who cry out to you in their need,
and strengthen their hope in your lasting goodness.
We ask this through Christ our Lord.

R. Amen.

The minister then says the following:

Eternal rest grant unto him/her, O Lord.

R. And let perpetual light shine upon him/her.

May he/she rest in peace.

R. Amen.

May his/her soul and the souls of all the faithful departed,
through the mercy of God, rest in peace.

R. Amen.

A   A minister who is a priest or deacon says:

May the peace of God,
which is beyond all understanding,
keep your hearts and minds
in the knowledge and love of God
and of his Son, our Lord Jesus Christ.

R. Amen.

May almighty God bless you,
the Father, and the Son, ✠ and the Holy Spirit.

R. Amen.

A minister who is a priest or deacon says:

May the love of God and the peace of the Lord Jesus Christ
console you
and gently wipe every tear from your eyes.

R. Amen.

May almighty God bless you,
the Father, and the Son, ✠ and the Holy Spirit.

R. Amen.

C

A lay minister invokes God's blessing and signs himself or herself with the sign of the cross, saying:

May the love of God and the peace of the Lord Jesus Christ
bless and console us
and gently wipe every tear from our eyes:
in the name of the Father,
and of the Son, and of the Holy Spirit.

R. Amen.

The minister then concludes:

Go in the peace of Christ.

R. Thanks be to God.

A hymn or song may conclude the rite. Some sign or gesture
of leave-taking may be made, if this has not taken place earlier,
and if the coffin remains in view.

OUTLINE OF THE RITE

INTRODUCTORY RITES

Greeting
Sprinkling with Holy Water
Entrance Procession
[Placing of the Pall]
[Placing of Christian Symbols]
Invitation to Prayer
Opening Prayer

LITURGY OF THE WORD

Readings
Homily
General Intercessions
    Intercessions
    The Lord's Prayer
    Concluding Prayer

FINAL COMMENDATION

Invitation to Prayer
Silence
Signs of Farewell
Song of Farewell
Prayer of Commendation
  and the Committal

CONCLUDING RITE

Prayer over the People

11 RITE OF COMMITTAL FOR CREMATION
WHEN NO OTHER LITURGY HAS TAKEN PLACE

INTRODUCTORY RITES

GREETING

> 304 At or near the entrance to the crematorium chapel, the minister welcomes the funeral party and, using one of the following greetings, or in similar words, greets them.

A   The grace of our Lord Jesus Christ and the love of God and the fellowship of the Holy Spirit be with you all.

R. And also with you.

B   The grace and peace of God our Father and the Lord Jesus Christ be with you.

R. And also with you.

C   The grace and peace of God our Father, who raised Jesus from the dead, be always with you.

R. And also with you.

D   May the Father of mercies, the God of all consolation, be with you.

R. And also with you.

Sprinkling with Holy Water

305 Using one of the following texts, the minister then sprinkles the coffin with holy water.

A   In the waters of baptism
N. died with Christ and rose with him to new life.
May he/she now share with him eternal glory.

B   The Lord is our shepherd
and leads us to streams of living water.

C   Let this water call to mind our baptism into Christ,
who by his death and resurrection has redeemed us.

D   The Lord God lives in his holy temple yet abides in our midst.
Since in baptism N. became God's temple
and the Spirit of God lived in him/her,
with reverence we bless his/her mortal body.

Entrance Procession

The Easter candle may be placed beforehand near the position the coffin will occupy at the conclusion of the procession. The minister precedes the coffin and the mourners into the chapel. During the procession a hymn or song may be sung.

Placing of the Pall

307 If it is the custom in the local community, the pall is then placed on the coffin by family members, friends, or the minister.

Placing of Christian Symbols

308 A symbol of the Christian life, such as a Book of the Gospels, a Bible, or a cross, may be carried in procession, then placed on the coffin, either in silence or as one of the following texts is said.

A   Book of the Gospels or Bible

In life N. cherished the Gospel of Christ.
May Christ now greet him/her with these words of eternal life:
Come, blessed of my Father!

B   Cross

In baptism N. received the sign of the cross.
May he/she now share
in Christ's victory over sin and death.

INVITATION TO PRAYER

309 Using one of the following texts, or in similar words, the
minister invites those present to pray.

A   My brothers and sisters, we believe that all the ties of friendship and affection which knit us as one throughout our lives
do not unravel with death.

Confident that God always remembers the good we have done
and forgives our sins, let us pray, asking God to gather N. to
himself.

B   Dear friends in Christ, in the name of Jesus and of his Church,
we gather to pray for N., that God may bring him/her to everlasting peace and rest.

We share the pain of loss, but the promise of eternal life gives
us hope. Let us comfort one another as we turn to God in prayer.

C   My brothers and sisters, we have come together to renew our
trust in Christ who, by dying on the cross, has freed us from
eternal death and, by rising, has opened for us the gates of
heaven.

Let us pray for our brother/sister, that he/she may share in
Christ's victory, and let us pray for ourselves, that the Lord may
grant us the gift of his loving consolation.

OPENING PRAYER

310 After a brief period of silent prayer, the minister says one
of the following prayers or one of those provided in no. 580, p.
407.

A   Lord our God,
the death of our brother/sister N.
recalls our human condition
and the brevity of our lives on earth.
But for those who believe in your love
death is not the end,
nor does it destroy the bonds
that you forge in our lives.
We share the faith of your Son's disciples
and the hope of the children of God.
Bring the light of Christ's resurrection
to this time of testing and pain
as we pray for N. and for those who love him/her,
through Christ our Lord.

R. Amen.

B   O God,   171
glory of believers and life of the just,
by the death and resurrection of your Son, we are redeemed:
have mercy on your servant N.,
and make him/her worthy to share the joys of paradise,
for he/she believed in the resurrection of the dead.

We ask this through Christ our Lord.

R. Amen.

C   Lord, in our grief we turn to you.   33
Are you not the God of love
always ready to hear our cries?

Listen to our prayers for your servant N.,
whom you have called out of this world:
lead him/her to your kingdom of light and peace
and count him/her among the saints in glory.

We ask this through Christ our Lord.

R. Amen.

D   Lord Jesus, our Redeemer,   169
you willingly gave yourself up to death,
so that all might be saved and pass from death to life.
We humbly ask you to comfort your servants in their grief
and to receive N. into the arms of your mercy.
You alone are the Holy One,
you are mercy itself;
by dying you unlocked the gates of life
   for those who believe in you.
Forgive N. his/her sins,
and grant him/her a place of happiness, light, and peace
in the kingdom of your glory for ever.

R. Amen.

E   Almighty God and Father,   170
it is our certain faith
that your Son, who died on the cross, was raised from the dead,
the firstfruits of all who have fallen asleep.
Grant that through this mystery
your servant N., who has gone to his/her rest in Christ,
may share in the joy of his resurrection.

We ask this through our Lord Jesus Christ, your Son,
who lives and reigns with you and the Holy Spirit,
one God, for ever and ever.

R. Amen.

F   O God,
to whom mercy and forgiveness belong,
hear our prayers on behalf of your servant N.,
whom you have called out of this world;
and because he/she put his/her hope and trust in you,
command that he/she be carried safely home to heaven
and come to enjoy your eternal reward.

We ask this through our Lord Jesus Christ, your Son,
who lives and reigns with you and the Holy Spirit,
one God, for ever and ever.

R. Amen.

G   O God,
in whom sinners find mercy and the saints find joy,
we pray to you for our brother/sister N.,
whose body is to be cremated
that he/she may be delivered from the bonds of death.
Admit him/her to the joyful company of your saints
and raise him/her on the last day
to rejoice in your presence for ever.

We ask this through our Lord Jesus Christ, your Son,
who lives and reigns with you and the Holy Spirit,
one God, for ever and ever.

R. Amen.

H   During the Easter season   173

God of loving kindness,
listen favourably to our prayers:
strengthen our belief that your Son has risen from the dead
and our hope that your servant N. will also rise again.

We ask this through our Lord Jesus Christ, your Son,
who lives and reigns with you and the Holy Spirit,
one God, for ever and ever.

R. Amen.

LITURGY OF THE WORD

READINGS

> 311 After the introductory rites, the liturgy of the word is cele-
> brated. Depending upon pastoral circumstances, either one or
> two readings may be read before the gospel. If only one reading
> is possible it should be the gospel. Between the readings a psalm
> or suitable song may be used.

HOMILY

> 312 A brief homily is given after the gospel reading.

General Intercessions

313 The general intercessions then take place.

Intercessions

314 One of the following sets of intercessions may be used or
adapted to the circumstances, or new intercessions may be
composed.

A   The minister begins:

God, the almighty Father, raised Christ his Son from the dead;   200
with confidence we ask him to save all his people, living and dead:

A reader or the minister then continues:

For N. who in baptism was given the pledge of eternal life, that
he/she may now be admitted to the company of the saints.
Lord, in your mercy:

R. Hear our prayer.

For our brother/sister who ate the body of Christ, the bread
of life, that he/she may be raised up on the last day.
Lord, in your mercy:

R. Hear our prayer.

For our deceased relatives and friends and for all who have
helped us, that they may have the reward of their goodness.
Lord, in your mercy:

R. Hear our prayer.

For those who have fallen asleep in the hope of rising again,
that they may see God face to face.
Lord, in your mercy:

R. Hear our prayer.

For the family and friends of our brother/sister N., that they
may be consoled in their grief by the Lord, who wept at the
death of his friend Lazarus.
Lord, in your mercy:

R. Hear our prayer.

For all of us assembled here to worship in faith, that we may be gathered together again in God's kingdom.
Lord, in your mercy:

R. Hear our prayer.

B The minister begins:

Brothers and sisters, Jesus Christ is risen from the dead and sits at the right hand of the Father, where he intercedes for his Church. Confident that God hears the voices of those who trust in the Lord Jesus, we join our prayers to his:

A reader or the minister then continues:

In baptism N. received the light of Christ. Scatter the darkness now and lead him/her over the waters of death.
Lord, in your mercy:

R. Hear our prayer.

Our brother/sister N. was nourished at the table of the Saviour. Welcome him/her into the halls of the heavenly banquet.
Lord, in your mercy:

R. Hear our prayer.

Many friends and members of our families have gone before us and await the kingdom. Grant them an everlasting home with your Son.
Lord, in your mercy:

R. Hear our prayer.

Many people die by violence, war, and famine each day. Show your mercy to those who suffer so unjustly these sins against your love, and gather them to the eternal kingdom of peace.
Lord, in your mercy:

R. Hear our prayer.

Those who trusted in the Lord now sleep in the Lord. Give refreshment, rest, and peace to all whose faith is known to you alone.
Lord, in your mercy:

R. Hear our prayer.

The family and friends of N. seek comfort and consolation. Heal their pain and dispel the darkness and doubt that come from grief. Lord, in your mercy:

R. Hear our prayer.

We are assembled here in faith and confidence to pray for our brother/sister N. Strengthen our hope so that we may live in the expectation of your Son's coming.
Lord, in your mercy:

R. Hear our prayer.

C   *The minister begins:*
My dear friends, let us join with one another in praying to God, not only for our departed brother/sister, but also for the Church, for peace in the world, and for ourselves.

A reader or the minister then continues:
That the bishops and priests of the Church, and all who preach the Gospel, may be given the strength to express in action the word they proclaim.
We pray to the Lord:

R. Lord, hear our prayer.

That those in public office may promote justice and peace.
We pray to the Lord:

R. Lord, hear our prayer.

That those who bear the cross of pain in mind or body may never feel forsaken by God.
We pray to the Lord:

R. Lord, hear our prayer.

That God may deliver the soul of his servant N. from punishment and from the powers of darkness.
We pray to the Lord:

R. Lord, hear our prayer.

That God in his mercy may blot out all his/her offences.
We pray to the Lord: ·

R. Lord, hear our prayer.

That God may establish him/her in light and peace.
We pray to the Lord:

R. Lord, hear our prayer.

That God may call him/her to happiness in the company of all
the saints.
We pray to the Lord:

R. Lord, hear our prayer.

That God may welcome into his glory those of our family and
friends who have departed this life.
We pray to the Lord:

R. Lord, hear our prayer.

That God may give a place in the kingdom of heaven to all the
faithful departed.
We pray to the Lord:

R. Lord, hear our prayer.

The Lord's Prayer

315 Using one of the following invitations, or in similar words,
the minister invites those present to pray the Lord's Prayer.

A Now let us pray as Christ the Lord has taught us:

B With longing for the coming of God's kingdom, let us offer our
prayer to the Father:

C As sons and daughters of a loving God, we pray in the confident words of his Son:

D When Jesus gathered his disciples around him, he taught them
to pray:

All say:
Our Father . . .

CONCLUDING PRAYER

316 The minister says one of the following prayers or one of those
provided in no. 580, p. 407.

A God, our shelter and our strength,
you listen in love to the cry of your people:
hear the prayers we offer for our departed brother/sister N.
Cleanse him/her and all the faithful departed of their sins
and grant them the fullness of redemption.

We ask this through Christ our Lord.

R. Amen.

B Lord God,
giver of peace and healer of souls,
hear the prayers of the Redeemer, Jesus Christ,
and the voices of your people,
whose lives were purchased by the blood of the Lamb.
Forgive the sins of all who sleep in Christ
and grant them a place in the kingdom.

We ask this through Christ our Lord.

R. Amen.

C O God,
Creator and Redeemer of all the faithful,
grant to the souls of your departed servants
release from all their sins.
Hear our prayers for those we love
and give them the pardon they have always desired.

We ask this through Christ our Lord.

R. Amen.

FINAL COMMENDATION

> 317 The minister then goes to a place near the coffin. If incense and holy water are to be used, they are carried by the assisting ministers.
>
> A member or a friend of the family may speak in remembrance of the deceased before the final commendation begins.

INVITATION TO PRAYER

> 318 Using one of the following invitations, or in similar words, the minister begins the final commendation.

A   Before we go our separate ways, let us take leave of our brother/sister. May our farewell express our affection for him/her; may it ease our sadness and strengthen our hope. One day we shall joyfully greet him/her again when the love of Christ, which conquers all things, destroys even death itself.   185

B   Trusting in God, we have prayed together for N. and now we come to the last farewell. There is sadness in parting, but we take comfort in the hope that one day we shall see N. again and enjoy his/her friendship. Although this congregation will disperse in sorrow, the mercy of God will gather us together again in the joy of his kingdom. Therefore let us console one another in the faith of Jesus Christ.   186

C   Our brother/sister N. has fallen asleep in Christ. Confident in our hope of eternal life, let us commend him/her to the loving mercy of our Father and let our prayers go with him/her. He/she was adopted as God's son/daughter in baptism and was nourished at the table of the Lord; may he/she now inherit the promise of eternal life and take his/her place at the table of God's children in heaven.   183

Let us pray also on our own behalf, that we who now mourn and are saddened may one day go forth with our brother/sister to meet the Lord of life when he appears in glory.

SILENCE

> 319 All pray in silence.

Signs of Farewell

320 The coffin may now be sprinkled with holy water and incensed, or this may take place during or after the song of farewell. At this point the mourners may be invited to sprinkle the coffin, or it may be done at the end of the rite if the coffin remains in view.

Song of Farewell

321 The song of farewell is then sung. One of the following texts or another suitable hymn or song may be sung.

A
I know that my Redeemer lives,
And on that final day of days,
His voice shall bid me rise again:
Unending joy, unceasing praise!

This hope I cherish in my heart:
To stand on earth, my flesh restored,
And, not a stranger but a friend,
Behold my Saviour and my Lord.

Tune: LM, for example, Duke Street

189

B
Saints of God, come to his/her aid!
Hasten to meet him/her, angels of the Lord!
R. Receive his/her soul and present him/her
to God the Most High.

May Christ, who called you, take you to himself;
may angels lead you to the bosom of Abraham.
R. Receive his/her soul and present him/her
to God the Most High.

Eternal rest grant unto him/her, O Lord,
and let perpetual light shine upon him/her.
R. Receive his/her soul and present him/her
to God the Most High.

47
66

Prayer of Commendation and the Committal

322 The minister then says one of the following prayers, during or after which the coffin may be removed from view.

A Into your hands, Father of mercies,   48
we commend our brother/sister N.
in the sure and certain hope
that, together with all who have died in Christ,
he/she will rise with him on the last day.

[We give you thanks for the blessings
which you bestowed upon N. in this life:
they are signs to us of your goodness
and of our fellowship with the saints in Christ.]

Merciful Lord,
turn toward us and listen to our prayers:
open the gates of paradise to your servant
and help us who remain
to comfort one another with assurances of faith,
until we all meet in Christ
and are with you and with our brother/sister for ever.

We ask this through Christ our Lord.

R. Amen.

B To you, O Lord, we commend the soul of N. your servant;   192
in the sight of this world he/she is now dead;
in your sight may he/she live for ever.
Forgive whatever sins he/she committed through human
    weakness
and in your goodness grant him/her everlasting peace.

We ask this through Christ our Lord.

R. Amen.

CONCLUDING RITE

323 The assisting minister or the minister says:

Bow your heads and pray for God's blessing.

All pray silently. The minister, with hands outstretched over the
people, says the following prayer.

Merciful Lord,
you know the anguish of the sorrowful,
you are attentive to the prayers of the humble.
Hear your people
who cry out to you in their need,
and strengthen their hope in your lasting goodness.

We ask this through Christ our Lord.

R. Amen.

The minister then says the following:

Eternal rest grant unto him/her, O Lord.

R. And let perpetual light shine upon him/her.

May he/she rest in peace.

R. Amen.

May his/her soul and the souls of all the faithful departed,
through the mercy of God, rest in peace.

R. Amen.

A minister who is a priest or deacon says:

May the peace of God,
which is beyond all understanding,
keep your hearts and minds
in the knowledge and love of God
and of his Son, our Lord Jesus Christ.

R. Amen.

May almighty God bless you,
the Father, and the Son, ✠ and the Holy Spirit.

R. Amen.

B   A minister who is a priest or deacon says:

May the love of God and the peace of the Lord Jesus Christ
console you
and gently wipe every tear from your eyes.

R. Amen.

May almighty God bless you,
the Father, and the Son, ✠ and the Holy Spirit.

R. Amen.

C   A lay minister invokes God's blessing and signs himself or her-
           self with the sign of the cross, saying:

May the love of God and the peace of the Lord Jesus Christ
bless and console us
and gently wipe every tear from our eyes:
in the name of the Father,
and of the Son, and of the Holy Spirit.

R. Amen.

The minister then concludes:

Go in the peace of Christ.

R. Thanks be to God.

A hymn or song may conclude the rite. Some sign or gesture
of leave-taking may be made, if this has not taken place earlier,
and if the coffin remains in view.

OUTLINE OF THE RITE

Invitation
Scripture Verse
Prayer of Committal
The Lord's Prayer
Blessing

12 RITE FOR THE BURIAL OF ASHES

324 This rite may be used when the family and friends of the
deceased ask for the ashes to be buried shortly after the funeral.

INVITATION

325 The minister begins:

My friends, we have come together to bury/entomb the ashes
of our brother/sister N. In doing this we recall that our bodies
bear the imprint of the first creation when they were fashioned
from dust; but in faith we remember, too, that by the new creation we also bear the image of Jesus who was raised to glory.

In confident hope that one day God will raise us and transform
our mortal bodies:

SCRIPTURE VERSE

326 One of the following or another brief Scripture verse is read.
The minister first says:

Let us listen to the words of Scripture:

A   John 14:1-3

Jesus says:
'Do not let your hearts be troubled.
Trust in God still and trust in me.
There are many rooms in my Father's house;
if there were not, I should have told you.
I am going now to prepare a place for you,
and after I have gone and prepared you a place,
I shall return to take you with me,
so that where I am
you may be too.'

B   Colossians 3:3-4

You have died, and now the life you have is hidden with Christ
in God. But when Christ is revealed — and he is your life — you
too will be revealed in all your glory with him.

C   Romans 6:8-9

We believe that having died with Christ we shall return to life with him: Christ, as we know, having been raised from the dead will never die again. Death has no power over him any more.

PRAYER OF COMMITTAL

327 The minister then says the following prayer, during or after which the ashes are buried or entombed.

Let us pray.

Faithful God,
Lord of all creation,
you desire that nothing redeemed by your Son
will ever be lost,
and that the just will be raised up on the last day.

Comfort us today with the word of your promise
as we return the ashes of our brother/sister to the earth.

Grant N. a place of rest and peace
where the world of dust and ashes has no dominion.
Confirm us in our hope that he/she will be created anew
on the day when you will raise him/her up in glory
to live with you and all the saints
for ever and ever.

R. Amen.

A brief period of silent prayer or informal intercessions may follow.

THE LORD'S PRAYER

328 Using the following or similar words, the minister invites those present to pray the Lord's Prayer.

Now let us pray as Christ the Lord has taught us:

All say:

Our Father . . .

329 The minister then says the following:

Eternal rest grant unto him/her, O Lord.

R. And let perpetual light shine upon him/her.

May he/she rest in peace.

R. Amen.

May his/her soul and the souls of all the faithful departed, through the mercy of God, rest in peace.

R. Amen.

A   A minister who is a priest or deacon says:

May the peace of God,
which is beyond all understanding,
keep your hearts and minds
in the knowledge and love of God
and of his Son, our Lord Jesus Christ.

R. Amen.

May almighty God bless you,
the Father, and the Son, ✠ and the Holy Spirit.

R. Amen.

B   A lay minister invokes God's blessing and signs himself or herself with the sign of the cross, saying:

May the love of God and the peace of the Lord Jesus Christ
bless and console us
and gently wipe every tear from our eyes:
in the name of the Father,
and of the Son, and of the Holy Spirit.

R. Amen.

The minister then concludes:

Go in the peace of Christ.

R. Thanks be to God.

A sign or gesture of leave-taking may be made, for instance, sprinkling the place of burial or entombment with holy water.

Part II
FUNERAL RITES
FOR CHILDREN

Let the little children come to me;
it is to such as these that the kingdom of God belongs

Part II
FUNERAL RITES
FOR CHILDREN

330 Part II of the *Order of Christian Funerals* provides rites that are used in the funerals of infants and young children, including those of early school age. It includes 'Vigil for a Deceased Child,' 'Funeral Liturgy,' and 'Rite of Committal.'

Part II does not contain 'Prayers' and 'Related Rites' from 'Vigil and Related Rites and Prayers', nos. 54-71 and nos. 116-136, which are brief rites for prayer with the family and friends before the funeral liturgy. The rites as they are presented in Part I are models and should be adapted by the minister to the circumstances of the funeral for a child.

331 The minister, in consultation with those concerned, chooses those rites that best correspond to the particular needs and customs of the mourners. In some instances, for example, the death of an infant, only the rite of committal and perhaps one of the forms of prayer with the family may be desirable.

332 In the celebration of the funeral of a child the Church offers worship to God, the author of life, commends the child to God's love, and prays for the consolation of the family and close friends.

333 Funeral rites may be celebrated for children whose parents intended them to be baptized but who died before baptism.[1] In these celebrations the Christian community entrusts the child to God's all-embracing love and finds strength in this love and in Jesus' affirmation that the kingdom of God belongs to little children (see Matthew 19:14).

334 In its pastoral ministry to the bereaved the Christian community is challenged in a particular way by the death of an infant or child. The bewilderment and pain that death causes can be overwhelming in this situation, especially for the parents and the brothers and sisters of the deceased child. The community seeks to offer support and consolation to the family during and after the time of the funeral rites.

335 Through prayer and words of comfort the minister and others can help the mourners to understand that their child has gone before them into the kingdom of the Lord and that one day they will all be reunited there

---

[1] In the general catechesis of the faithful, priests and other ministers should explain that the celebration of the funeral rites for children who die before baptism is not intended to weaken the Church's teaching on the necessity of baptism.

in joy. The participation of the community in the funeral rites is a sign of the compassionate presence of Christ, who embraced little children, wept at the death of a friend, and endured the pain and separation of death in order to render it powerless over those he loves. Christ still sorrows with those who sorrow and longs with them for the fulfilment of the Father's plan in a new creation where tears and death will have no place.

336 The minister should invite members of the community to use their individual gifts in this ministry of consolation. Those who have lost children of their own may be able in a special way to help the family as they struggle to accept the death of the child.

337 Those involved in planning the funeral rites for a deceased child should take into account the age of the child, the circumstances of death, the grief of the family, and the needs and customs of those taking part in the rites. In choosing the texts and elements of celebration, the minister should bear in mind whether the child was baptized or died before baptism. Thus, for instance, the pall and holy water which are both reminders of baptism, should not be used in funerals of children who have died before baptism.

338 At its highest level of symbolism, the Easter candle is baptismal, since it reminds the faithful of their share in Christ's victory over sin and death by virtue of their initiation. But there are also other levels of meaning associated with the Easter candle in the funeral rites of the Church. For example, it reminds the faithful of Christ's undying presence among them. It recalls the Easter Vigil, the night when the Church awaits the Lord's resurrection and when new light for the living and the dead is kindled.

For these reasons, during the funeral liturgy of a child who died before baptism or a catechumen, and also during the vigil service, when celebrated in the church, the Easter candle may be placed beforehand near the position the coffin will occupy at the conclusion of the procession.

According to local custom, other candles may also be placed near the coffin during the funeral liturgy as a sign of reverence and solemnity.

339 Special consideration should be given to any sisters, brothers, friends, or classmates of the deceased child who may be present at the funeral rites. Children will be better able to take part in the celebration if the various elements are planned and selected with them in mind: texts, readings, music, gesture, processions, silence. The minister may wish to offer brief remarks for the children's benefit at suitable points during the celebration.

If children will be present at the funeral rites, those with requisite ability should be asked to exercise some of the liturgical roles. During the funeral Mass, for example, children may serve as readers, acolytes, or musicians, or assist in the reading of the general intercessions and in the procession with the gifts. Depending upon the age and number of children taking part, adaptations recommended in the *Directory for Masses with Children* may be appropriate.

VIGIL

It is good to wait in silence for the Lord

13 VIGIL FOR A DECEASED CHILD

340 The vigil for the deceased is the principal celebration of the Christian community during the time before the funeral liturgy or, if there is no funeral liturgy, before the rite of committal. The vigil may take the form of a liturgy of the word, as described in Part I, nos. 75-81, or of some part of the office for the dead (see Part IV, p. 378).

341 The vigil may be celebrated at a convenient time in the home of the deceased child, in the funeral home, parlour or chapel of rest, or in some other suitable place. The vigil may also be celebrated in the church, but at a time well before the funeral liturgy, so that the funeral liturgy will not be lengthy and the liturgy of the word repetitious. When the body is brought to the church for the celebration of the vigil, the vigil begins with the rite of reception (see no. 76). Otherwise the vigil begins with a greeting, followed by an opening song, an invitation to prayer, and an opening prayer.

342 After the opening prayer, the vigil continues with the liturgy of the word, which usually includes a first reading, responsorial psalm, gospel reading, and homily. If there is to be only one reading, however, it should be the gospel reading. The prayer of intercession, which includes a litany, the Lord's Prayer, and a concluding prayer, then follows. Alternative concluding prayers are provided for use in the case of a baptized child or of a child who died before baptism. The vigil concludes with a blessing, which may be followed by a song or a few moments of silent prayer or both.

343 The minister should adapt the vigil to the circumstances. If, for example, a large number of children are present or if the vigil is held in the home of the deceased child, elements of the rite may be simplified or shortened and other elements or symbols that have special meaning for those taking part may be incorporated into the celebration. If custom and circumstances suggest, a member or a friend of the family may speak in remembrance of the deceased child.

OUTLINE OF THE RITE

INTRODUCTORY RITES

Greeting
Sprinkling with Holy Water
  or Brief Address
Entrance Procession
[Placing of the Pall]
[Placing of Christian Symbols]
Invitation to Prayer
Opening Prayer

LITURGY OF THE WORD

First Reading
Responsorial Psalm
Gospel
Homily

PRAYER OF INTERCESSION

Litany
The Lord's Prayer
Concluding Prayer

CONCLUDING RITE

Blessing

VIGIL FOR A DECEASED CHILD

344 The vigil celebrated at the church may begin with the rite of reception (nos. 345-349) which then serves as the introductory rite. Otherwise the vigil may begin with an opening song followed by a greeting (no. 345) and the invitation to prayer (no. 350).

INTRODUCTORY RITES

GREETING

345 The minister, with assisting ministers, goes to the door of the church and, using one of the following greetings, or in similar words, greets those present.

A   May Christ Jesus, who welcomed children and laid his hands in blessing upon them, comfort you with his peace and be always with you.

R. And also with you.

B   May the God of hope give you the fullness of peace, and may the Lord of life be always with you.

R. And also with you.

C   The grace and peace of God our Father, who raised Jesus from the dead, be always with you.

R. And also with you.

D   May the Father of mercies, the God of all consolation, be with you.

R. And also with you.

Sprinkling with Holy Water or Brief Address

346 If the child was baptized, the minister sprinkles the coffin with holy water (option A). If the child died before baptism, the sprinkling with holy water is omitted and a brief address is given (option B).

A   Sprinkling with Holy Water—If the child was baptized, the minister then sprinkles the coffin with holy water, saying:

In the waters of baptism
N. died with Christ and rose with him to new life.
May he/she now share with him eternal glory.

B   Brief Address—If the child died before baptism, the minister may address the mourners using the following or similar words.

My brothers and sisters, the Lord is a faithful God who created us all after his own image. All things are of his making, all creation awaits the day of salvation. We now entrust the soul of N. to the abundant mercy of God, that our beloved child may find a home in his kingdom.

Entrance Procession

347 The Easter candle may be placed beforehand near the position the coffin will occupy at the conclusion of the procession. The minister and assisting ministers precede the coffin and the mourners into the church. During the procession a psalm, song, or responsory is sung.

Placing of the Pall

348 If it is the custom in the local community and the child was baptized, the pall is then placed on the coffin by family members, friends, or the minister.

Placing of Christian Symbols

349 A symbol of the Christian life, such as a Book of the Gospels, a Bible, or a cross, may be carried in procession, then placed on the coffin, either in silence or as one of the following texts is said.

A   Book of the Gospels or Bible

May Christ greet N. with these words of eternal life:
Come, blessed of my Father!

B   Cross, for a baptized child

In baptism N. received the sign of the cross.
May he/she now share
in Christ's victory over sin and death.

C   Cross, for a child who died before baptism

The cross we have brought here today was carried by the Lord Jesus in the hour of his suffering.

We place it now on/near this coffin as a sign of our hope for N.

As the cross is placed on or near the coffin, the minister says:

Lord Jesus Christ,
you loved us unto death.
Let this cross be a sign of your love for N.
and for the people you have gathered here today.

Invitation to Prayer

350 In the following or similar words, the minister invites those present to pray.

Let us pray for this child and entrust him/her to the care of our loving God.

Pause for silent prayer.

351 The minister says one of the following prayers or one of those provided in nos. 580-581, p. 407.

A   A baptized child

To you, O Lord,   224
we humbly entrust this child,
so precious in your sight.
Take him/her into your arms
and welcome him/her into paradise,
where there will be no sorrow, no weeping nor pain,
but the fullness of peace and joy
with your Son and the Holy Spirit
for ever and ever.

R. Amen.

B   A baptized child

Lord, in our grief we call upon your mercy: 223
open your ears to our prayers,
and one day unite us again with N.,
who, we firmly trust,
already enjoys eternal life in your kingdom.

We ask this through Christ our Lord.

R. Amen.

C   A child who died before baptism

God of all consolation,   236
searcher of mind and heart,
the faith of these parents [N. and N.] is known to you.

Comfort them with the knowledge
that the child for whom they grieve
is entrusted now to your loving care.

We ask this through Christ our Lord.

R. Amen.

LITURGY OF THE WORD

352 The celebration continues with the liturgy of the word. Other readings, psalms, and gospel readings are found in the Lectionary, Volume III, 'For the Burial of Children'.

FIRST READING

353 A reader proclaims the first reading.

A reading from the first letter of Saint John   3:1-2   103

We shall see God as he really is.

Think of the love that the Father has lavished on us,
by letting us be called God's children;
and that is what we are.
Because the world refused to acknowledge him,
therefore it does not acknowledge us.
My dear people, we are already the children of God
but what we are to be in the future has not yet been revealed;
all we know is, that when it is revealed
we shall be like him
because we shall see him as he really is.

This is the Word of the Lord.

RESPONSORIAL PSALM

354 The following or another suitable psalm is sung or said.

R. The Lord is my shepherd; there is nothing I shall want.

Psalm 22 (23)

The Lord is my shepherd;
there is nothing I shall want.
Fresh and green are the pastures
where he gives me repose.
Near restful waters he leads me,
to revive my drooping spirit. R.

He guides me along the right path;
he is true to his name.
If I should walk in the valley of darkness
no evil would I fear.
You are there with your crook and your staff;
with these you give me comfort.

R. The Lord is my shepherd; there is nothing I shall want.

You have prepared a banquet for me
in the sight of my foes.
My head you have anointed with oil;
my cup is overflowing. R.

Surely goodness and kindness shall follow me
all the days of my life.
In the Lord's own house shall I dwell
for ever and ever. R.

GOSPEL

355 The gospel reading is then proclaimed.

A reading from the holy gospel according to Mark   10:13-16

The kingdom of God belongs to little children.

People were bringing little children to Jesus, for him to touch
them. The disciples turned them away, but when Jesus saw this
he was indignant and said to them, 'Let the little children come
to me; do not stop them; for it is to such as these that the kingdom of God belongs. I tell you solemnly, anyone who does not
welcome the kingdom of God like a little child will never enter
it.' Then he put his arms around them, laid his hands on them
and gave them his blessing.

This is the Gospel of the Lord.

HOMILY

356 A brief homily on the readings is then given.

PRAYER OF INTERCESSION

Litany

357 The minister leads those present in the following litany.

The Lord Jesus is the lover of his people and our only sure hope.
Let us ask him to deepen our faith and sustain us in this dark
hour.

A reader or the minister then continues:

You became a little child for our sake, sharing our human life.
To you we pray:

R. Bless us and keep us, O Lord.

You grew in wisdom, age, and grace and learned obedience
through suffering.
To you we pray:

R. Bless us and keep us, O Lord.

You welcomed children, promising them your kingdom.
To you we pray:

R. Bless us and keep us, O Lord.

You comforted those who mourned the loss of children and
friends.
To you we pray:

R. Bless us and keep us, O Lord.

You took upon yourself the suffering and death of us all.
To you we pray:

R. Bless us and keep us, O Lord.

You promised to raise up those who believe in you, just as you
were raised up in glory by the Father.
To you we pray:

R. Bless us and keep us, O Lord.

The Lord's Prayer

358 Using one of the following invitations, or in similar words, the minister invites those present to pray the Lord's Prayer.

A   Together let us pray for strength, for acceptance, and for the coming of the kingdom in the words our Saviour taught us:

B   In love, God calls us his children, for that indeed is what we are. We ask for the strength we need by praying in the words Jesus gave us:

All say:

Our Father . . .

Concluding Prayer

The minister says one of the following prayers or one of those provided in nos. 580-581, p. 407.

A   A baptized child

Lord of all gentleness,   225
surround us with your care
and comfort us in our sorrow,
for we grieve at the loss of this [little] child.

As you washed N. in the waters of baptism
and welcomed him/her into the life of heaven,
so call us one day
to be united with him/her
and share for ever the joy of your kingdom.

We ask this through Christ our Lord.

R.   Amen.

Lord Jesus,
whose Mother stood grieving at the foot of the cross,
look kindly on these parents
who have suffered the loss of their child [N.].
Listen to the prayers of Mary on their behalf,
that their faith may be strong like hers
and find its promised reward,
for you live for ever and ever.

R. Amen.

CONCLUDING RITE

BLESSING

360 The minister says:

Jesus said: 'Let the children come to me. Do not keep them from me. The kingdom of God belongs to such as these.'

A gesture, for example, signing the forehead of the deceased child with the sign of the cross, may accompany the following words.

Eternal rest grant unto him/her, O Lord.

R. And let perpetual light shine upon him/her.

May he/she rest in peace.

R. Amen.

May his/her soul and the souls of all the faithful departed, through the mercy of God, rest in peace.

R. Amen.

A   A minister who is a priest or deacon says:

May the peace of God,
which is beyond all understanding,
keep your hearts and minds
in the knowledge and love of God
and of his Son, our Lord Jesus Christ.

R. Amen.

May almighty God bless you,
the Father, and the Son, ✠ and the Holy Spirit.

R. Amen.

B   A minister who is a priest or deacon says:

May the love of God and the peace of the Lord Jesus Christ
console you
and gently wipe every tear from your eyes:

R. Amen.

May almighty God bless you,
the Father, and the Son, ✠ and the Holy Spirit.

R. Amen.

C   A lay minister invokes God's blessing and signs himself or her-
           self with the sign of the cross, saying:

May the love of God and the peace of the Lord Jesus Christ
bless and console us
and gently wipe every tear from our eyes:
in the name of the Father,
and of the Son, and of the Holy Spirit.

R. Amen.

The vigil may conclude with a song or a few moments of silent
prayer or both.

FUNERAL LITURGY

The Lord will wipe away the tears from every cheek

FUNERAL LITURGY

361 The funeral liturgy, as described in nos. 128-153, is the central liturgical celebration of the Christian community for the deceased. Two forms of the funeral liturgy are provided: 'Funeral Mass' and 'Funeral Liturgy outside Mass.' If the second form is used, Mass may be celebrated at a later date.

362 The funeral Mass includes the reception of the body, if this has not already occurred, the celebration of the liturgy of the word, the liturgy of the eucharist, and the final commendation and farewell. The funeral liturgy outside Mass includes all these elements except the liturgy of the eucharist. Both the funeral Mass and the funeral liturgy outside Mass may be followed by the procession to the place of committal.

363 The rite of reception of the body begins with a greeting of the family and others who have accompanied the body to the door of the church. The minister may give brief explanations of the symbols in this rite for the benefit of any children who may be present for the celebration. In the case of a baptized child, the minister sprinkles the coffin in remembrance of the deceased child's acceptance into the community of faith. In the case of a child who died before baptism, the minister addresses the community with a few words. The entrance procession follows. The minister precedes the coffin and the mourners into the church, as all sing an entrance song. If the Easter candle is used on this occasion, it may be placed beforehand near the position the coffin will occupy at the conclusion of the procession. If it is the custom and the child was baptized, a funeral pall, a reminder of the garment given at baptism and therefore signifying life in Christ, may then be placed on the coffin by family members, friends, or the minister.

If in this rite a symbol of the Christian life is to be placed on the coffin, it is carried in the procession and is placed on the coffin by a family member, friend, or the minister at the conclusion of the procession.

364 The rite of final commendation and farewell is celebrated at the conclusion of the funeral liturgy unless it is deferred for celebration at the place of committal. The rite begins with the invitation to prayer, followed by a pause for silent prayer. In the case of a baptized child, the body may then be sprinkled with holy water and incensed. Or this may be done during or after the song of farewell. The song of farewell is then sung and the rite concludes with the prayer of commendation.

FUNERAL MASS

365 The funeral Mass is ordinarily celebrated in the parish church, but, at the discretion of the local Ordinary, it may be celebrated in the home of the deceased child or some other place.

366 The Mass texts are those of the Roman Missal and the Lectionary for Mass, 'Masses for the Dead'. The intercessions should be adapted to the circumstances; models are given in place.

367 In the choice of music for the funeral Mass, preference should be given to the singing of the acclamations, the responsorial psalm, the entrance and communion songs, and especially the song of farewell at the final commendation.

FUNERAL LITURGY OUTSIDE MASS

368 The funeral liturgy outside Mass may be celebrated for various reasons:
1. when the funeral Mass is not permitted, namely, on solemnities of obligation, on Holy Thursday and the Easter Triduum, and on the Sundays of Advent, Lent, and the Easter season;[1]
2. when in some places or circumstances it is not possible to celebrate the funeral Mass before the committal, for example, if a priest is not available;
3. when for pastoral reasons the priest and the family decide that the funeral liturgy outside Mass is a more suitable form of celebration for the deceased child.

369 The funeral liturgy outside Mass is ordinarily celebrated in the parish church, but may also be celebrated in the home of the deceased, a funeral home, parlour, chapel of rest, or cemetery chapel.

370 The readings are those of the Lectionary for Mass, 'Masses for the Dead'. The intercessions should be adapted to the circumstances; models are given in place. The celebration may include holy communion.

371 In the choice of music for the funeral liturgy, preference should be given to the singing of the entrance song, the responsorial psalm, the gospel acclamation, and especially the song of farewell at the final commendation.

372 The minister who is a priest or deacon wears an alb or surplice with stole (a cope may be used, if desired); a layperson who presides wears the liturgical vestments approved for the region.

---

[1] See General Instruction of the Roman Missal, no. 336.

OUTLINE OF THE RITE

INTRODUCTORY RITES

Greeting
Sprinkling with Holy Water
   or Brief Address
Entrance Procession
[Placing of the Pall]
[Placing of Christian Symbols]
Opening Prayer

LITURGY OF THE WORD

Readings
Homily
General Intercessions
   Intercessions
   Concluding Prayer

LITURGY OF THE EUCHARIST

FINAL COMMENDATION

Invitation to Prayer
Silence
Signs of Farewell
Song of Farewell
Prayer of Commendation

PROCESSION TO
THE PLACE OF COMMITTAL

14 FUNERAL MASS

373 If the rite of reception of the body takes place at the beginning of the funeral Mass, the introductory rites are those given here and the usual introductory rites for Mass, including the penitential rite, are omitted.

If the rite of reception of the body has already taken place, the Mass begins in the usual way, with the entrance procession, the greeting, and the penitential rite.

INTRODUCTORY RITES

GREETING

374 The priest, with assisting ministers, goes to the door of the church and, using one of the following greetings, or in similar words, greets those present.

A   The grace of our Lord Jesus Christ and the love of God and the fellowship of the Holy Spirit be with you all.

    R. And also with you.

B   The grace and peace of God our Father and the Lord Jesus Christ be with you.

    R. And also with you.

C   The grace and peace of God our Father, who raised Jesus from the dead, be always with you.

    R. And also with you.

D   May the Father of mercies, the God of all consolation, be with you.

    R. And also with you.

Sprinkling with Holy Water or Brief Address

375 If the child was baptized, the priest sprinkles the coffin with holy water (options A–D). If the child died before baptism, the sprinkling with holy water is omitted and a brief address is given (option E).

Sprinkling with Holy Water—If the child was baptized, the priest then sprinkles the coffin with holy water using one of the following texts.

A In the waters of baptism
N. died with Christ and rose with him to new life.
May he/she now share with him eternal glory.

B The Lord is our shepherd
and leads us to streams of living water.

C Let this water call to mind our baptism into Christ,
who by his death and resurrection has redeemed us.

D The Lord God lives in his holy temple yet abides in our midst.
Since in baptism N. became God's temple
and the Spirit of God lived in him/her,
with reverence we bless his/her mortal body.

E Brief Address—If the child died before baptism, the priest may address the mourners using the following or similar words.

My brothers and sisters, the Lord is a faithful God who created us all after his own image. All things are of his making, all creation awaits the day of salvation. We now entrust the soul of N. to the abundant mercy of God, that our beloved child may find a home in his kingdom.

Entrance Procession

376 The Easter candle may be placed beforehand near the position the coffin will occupy at the conclusion of the procession. The priest and assisting ministers precede the coffin and the mourners into the church. During the procession a hymn or song may be sung.

Placing of the Pall

> 377 If it is the custom in the local community and the child was baptized, the pall is then placed on the coffin by family members, friends, or the priest.

Placing of Christian Symbols

> 378 A symbol of the Christian life, such as a Book of the Gospels, a Bible, or a cross, may be carried in procession, then placed on the coffin, either in silence or as one of the following texts is said.

A   Book of the Gospels or Bible

May Christ greet N. with these words of eternal life:
Come, blessed of my Father!

B   Cross, for a baptized child

In baptism N. received the sign of the cross.
May he/she now share
in Christ's victory over sin and death.

C   Cross, for a child who died before baptism

The cross we have brought here today was carried by the Lord Jesus in the hour of his suffering.

We place it now on/near this coffin as a sign of our hope for N.

> As the cross is placed on or near the coffin, the priest says:

Lord Jesus Christ,
you loved us unto death.
Let this cross be a sign of your love for N.
and for the people you have gathered here today.

> On reaching the altar, the priest, with the assisting ministers, makes the customary reverence, kisses the altar, and (if incense is used) incenses it. Then he goes to the chair.

379 When all have reached their places, the priest invites the assembly to pray.

Let us pray.

After a brief period of silent prayer, the priest sings or says one of the following prayers or one of those provided in nos. 580-581, p. 407, or one from the Roman Missal.

A   A baptized child

To you, O Lord,   224
we humbly entrust this child,
so precious in your sight.
Take him/her into your arms
and welcome him/her into paradise,
where there will be no sorrow, no weeping nor pain,
but the fullness of peace and joy
with your Son and the Holy Spirit
for ever and ever.

R. Amen.

B   A baptized child

Lord, in our grief we call upon your mercy: 223
open your ears to our prayers,
and one day unite us again with N.,
who, we firmly trust,
already enjoys eternal life in your kingdom.

We ask this through Christ our Lord.

R. Amen.

C   A baptized child

Merciful Lord,
whose wisdom is beyond human understanding,
you adopted N. as your own in baptism
and have taken him/her to yourself
even as he/she stood on the threshold of life.
Listen to our prayers and extend to us your grace,
that one day we may share eternal life with N.,
for we firmly believe that he/she now rests with you.

We ask this through our Lord Jesus Christ, your Son,
who lives and reigns with you and the Holy Spirit,
one God, for ever and ever.

R. Amen.

D   A baptized child

Lord God,
from whom human sadness is never hidden,
you know the burden of grief
that we feel at the loss of this child.

As we mourn his/her passing from this life,
comfort us with the knowledge
that N. lives now in your loving embrace.

We make our prayer through our Lord Jesus Christ, your Son,
who lives and reigns with you and the Holy Spirit,
one God, for ever and ever.

R. Amen.

E   A child who died before baptism   236

God of all consolation,
searcher of mind and heart,
the faith of these parents [N. and N.] is known to you.

Comfort them with the knowledge
that the child for whom they grieve
is entrusted now to your loving care.

We ask this through our Lord Jesus Christ, your Son,
who lives and reigns with you and the Holy Spirit,
one God, for ever and ever.

R. Amen.

F   A child who died before baptism   235

O Lord, whose ways are beyond understanding,
listen to the prayers of your faithful people:
that those weighed down by grief
   at the loss of this [little] child
may find reassurance in your infinite goodness.

We ask this through our Lord Jesus Christ, your Son,
who lives and reigns with you and the Holy Spirit,
one God, for ever and ever.

R. Amen.

LITURGY OF THE WORD

READINGS

380 After the introductory rites, the liturgy of the word is celebrated. Depending upon pastoral circumstances, either one or two readings may be read before the gospel.

HOMILY

381 A brief homily is given after the gospel reading.

GENERAL INTERCESSIONS

382 The general intercessions then take place.

INTERCESSIONS

383 One of the following sets of intercessions may be used or adapted to the circumstances, or new intercessions may be composed.

A The priest begins:

Let us pray for N., his/her family and friends, and for all God's people.

A deacon or reader then continues:

For N., child of God [and heir to the kingdom], that he/she be held securely in God's loving embrace now and for all eternity.
We pray to the Lord.

R. Lord, hear our prayer.

For N.'s family, especially his/her mother and father, [his/her brother(s) and sister(s),] that they feel the healing power of Christ in the midst of their pain and grief.
We pray to the Lord.

R. Lord, hear our prayer.

For N.'s friends, those who played with him/her and those who cared for him/her, that they be consoled in their loss and strengthened in their love for one another.
We pray to the Lord.

R. Lord, hear our prayer.

For all parents who grieve over the death of their children, that they be comforted in the knowledge that their children dwell with God.
We pray to the Lord.

R. Lord, hear our prayer.

For children who have died of hunger and disease, that these little ones be seated close to the Lord at his heavenly table.
We pray to the Lord.

R. Lord, hear our prayer.

For the whole Church, that we prepare worthily for the hour of our death, when God will call us by name to pass from this world to the next.
We pray to the Lord.

R. Lord, hear our prayer.

B   A baptized child

The priest begins:

Jesus is the Son of God and the pattern for our own creation. His promise is that one day we shall truly be like him. With our hope founded on that promise, we pray:

A deacon or reader then continues:

That God will receive our praise and thanksgiving for the life of N.:
Let us pray to the Lord.

R. Lord, have mercy.

That God will bring to completion N.'s baptism into Christ:
Let us pray to the Lord.

R. Lord, have mercy.

That God will lead N. from death to life:
Let us pray to the Lord.

R. Lord, have mercy.

That all of us, N.'s family and friends, may be comforted in our grief:
Let us pray to the Lord.

R. Lord, have mercy.

That God will grant release to those who suffer:
Let us pray to the Lord.

R. Lord, have mercy.

That God will grant peace to all who have died in the faith of Christ:
Let us pray to the Lord.

R. Lord, have mercy.

That one day we may all share in the banquet of the Lord, praising God for victory over death:
Let us pray to the Lord.

R. Lord, have mercy.

CONCLUDING PRAYER

384 The priest then concludes:
Lord God,
you entrusted N. to our care
and now you embrace him/her in your love.

Take N. into your keeping
together with all children who have died.

Comfort us, your sorrowing servants,
who seek to do your will
and to know your saving peace.

We ask this through Christ our Lord.

R. Amen.

LITURGY OF THE EUCHARIST

385 The liturgy of the eucharist is celebrated in the usual manner and, if appropriate, one of the eucharistic prayers for children may be used.

386 If the final commendation is to be celebrated at the place of committal, the procession to the place of committal (no. 393) begins following the prayer after communion.

FINAL COMMENDATION

387 Following the prayer after communion, the priest goes to a place near the coffin. If incense and holy water are to be used, they are carried by the assisting ministers.

A member or a friend of the family may speak in remembrance of the deceased child before the final commendation begins.

INVITATION TO PRAYER

388 Using one of the following invitations, or in similar words, the priest begins the final commendation.

A   A baptized child

God in his wisdom knows the span of our days; he has chosen   227
to call to himself this child, whom he adopted as his own in
baptism. The body of N. will one day rise again to a new and
radiant life that will never end.

Our firm belief is that N., because he/she was baptized, has
already entered this new life; our firm hope is that we shall do
the same. Let us ask God to comfort his/her family and friends
and to increase our desire for the joys of heaven.

B   A baptized child

With faith in Jesus Christ, we bid farewell to N.   228

Let us pray with confidence to God, in whose sight all creation
lives, that he will raise up in holiness and power the mortal body
of this [little] child, for God has chosen to number him/her
among the blessed.

C   A child who died before baptism

Let us commend this child/baby to the Lord's merciful keep-   237
ing; and let us pray with all our hearts for N. and N. Even as
they grieve at the loss of their [little] child, they entrust him/her
to the loving embrace of God.

SILENCE

389 All pray in silence.

Signs of Farewell

390 The coffin of a baptized child may now be sprinkled with holy water and incensed, or this may take place during or after the song of farewell.

Song of Farewell

391 The song of farewell is then sung. One of the following texts or another suitable hymn or song may be sung.

A   I know that my Redeemer lives,   189
And on that final day of days,
His voice shall bid me rise again:
Unending joy, unceasing praise!

This hope I cherish in my heart:
To stand on earth, my flesh restored,
And, not a stranger but a friend,
Behold my Saviour and my Lord.

      Tune: LM, for example, Duke Street

B   Saints of God, come to his/her aid!   47
Hasten to meet him/her, angels of the Lord!   66
R. Receive his/her soul and present him/her
to God the Most High.

May Christ, who called you, take you to himself;
may angels lead you to the bosom of Abraham.
R. Receive his/her soul and present him/her
to God the Most High.

Eternal rest grant unto him/her, O Lord,
and let perpetual light shine upon him/her.
R. Receive his/her soul and present him/her
to God the Most High.

Prayer of Commendation

392 The priest then says one of the following prayers.

A   A baptized child

You are the author and sustainer of our lives, O God.
You are our final home.
We commend to you N., our child/baby.

In baptism he/she began his/her journey toward you.
Take him/her now to yourself
and give him/her the life
promised to those born again of water and the Spirit.

Turn also to us who have suffered this loss.
Strengthen the bonds of this family and our community.
Confirm us in faith, in hope, and in love,
so that we may bear your peace to one another
and one day stand together with all the saints
who praise you for your saving help.

We ask this in the name of your Son,
whom you raised from among the dead,
Jesus Christ, our Lord.

R. Amen.

B   A baptized child

Lord Jesus,
like a shepherd who gathers the lambs
to protect them from all harm,
you led N. to the waters of baptism
and shielded him/her in innocence.

Now carry this little one
on the path to your kingdom of light
where he/she will find happiness
and every tear will be wiped away.

To you be glory, now and for ever.

R. Amen.

C   A baptized child

Into your gentle keeping, O Lord,
we commend this child [N.].
Though our hearts are troubled,
we hope in your loving kindness.

By the sign of the cross
he/she was claimed for Christ,
and in the waters of baptism
he/she died with Christ to live in him for ever.

May the angels, our guardians,
lead N. now to paradise
where your saints will welcome him/her
and every tear will be wiped away.
There we shall join in songs of praise for ever.

We ask this through Christ our Lord.

R. Amen.

D   A child who died before baptism

You are the author and sustainer of our lives, O God,
you are our final home.
We commend to you N., our child/baby.

Trusting in your mercy
and in your all-embracing love,
we pray that you give him/her happiness for ever.

Turn also to us who have suffered this loss.
Strengthen the bonds of this family and our community.
Confirm us in faith, in hope, and in love,
so that we may bear your peace to one another
and one day stand together with all the saints
who praise you for your saving help.

We ask this in the name of your Son,
Jesus Christ, our Lord.

R. Amen.

PROCESSION TO THE
PLACE OF COMMITTAL

393 The deacon or, in the absence of a deacon, the priest says:

In peace let us take N. to his/her place of rest.

If a symbol of the Christian life has been placed on the coffin, it should be removed at this time.

The procession then begins: the priest and assisting ministers precede the coffin; the family and mourners follow.

One or more of the following texts or other suitable songs may be sung during the procession to the entrance of the church. The singing may continue during the journey to the place of committal.

A   The following antiphon may be sung with verses from Psalm 24 (25), p. 429.

May the angels lead you into paradise;   50
may the martyrs come to welcome you
and take you to the holy city,
the new and eternal Jerusalem.

B   The following antiphon may be sung with verses from Psalm 114 (116), p. 430, or separately.

May choirs of angels welcome you   50
and lead you to the bosom of Abraham;
and where Lazarus is poor no longer
may you find eternal rest.

C   May saints and angels lead you on,
Escorting you where Christ has gone.
Now he has called you, come to him
Who sits above the seraphim.

Come to the peace of Abraham
And to the supper of the Lamb:
Come to the glory of the blessed,
And to perpetual light and rest.

D   Another suitable psalm may also be used.

OUTLINE OF THE RITE

INTRODUCTORY RITES

Greeting
Sprinkling with Holy Water
  or Brief Address
Entrance Procession
[Placing of the Pall]
[Placing of Christian Symbols]
Invitation to Prayer
Opening Prayer

LITURGY OF THE WORD

Readings
Homily
General Intercessions
  Intercessions
  The Lord's Prayer
  [Concluding Prayer]

[LITURGY OF HOLY COMMUNION]

Communion
Silent Prayer
Prayer after Communion

FINAL COMMENDATION

Invitation to Prayer
Silence
Signs of Farewell
Song of Farewell
Prayer of Commendation

PROCESSION TO
THE PLACE OF COMMITTAL

15 FUNERAL LITURGY OUTSIDE MASS

394 If the rite of reception of the body takes place at the beginning of the funeral liturgy, the introductory rites are those given here.

If the rite of reception of the body has already taken place, the liturgy begins with an entrance song and the greeting (no. 395), followed by the invitation to prayer (no. 400).

GREETING

395 The presiding minister, with assisting ministers, goes to the door of the church and, using one of the following greetings, or in similar words, greets those present.

A   The grace of our Lord Jesus Christ and the love of God and the fellowship of the Holy Spirit be with you all.

R. And also with you.

B   The grace and peace of God our Father and the Lord Jesus Christ be with you.

R. And also with you.

C   The grace and peace of God our Father, who raised Jesus from the dead, be always with you.

R. And also with you.

D   May the Father of mercies, the God of all consolation, be with you.

R. And also with you.

Sprinkling with Holy Water or Brief Address

396 If the child was baptized, the presiding minister sprinkles the coffin with holy water (options A–D). If the child died before baptism, the sprinkling with holy water is omitted and a brief address is given (option E).

SPRINKLING WITH HOLY WATER—If the child was baptized, the presiding minister then sprinkles the coffin with holy water, using one of the following texts.

A   In the waters of baptism
N. died with Christ and rose with him to new life.
May he/she now share with him eternal glory.

B   The Lord is our shepherd
and leads us to streams of living water.

C   Let this water call to mind our baptism into Christ,
who by his death and resurrection has redeemed us.

D   The Lord God lives in his holy temple yet abides in our midst.
Since in baptism N. became God's temple
and the Spirit of God lived in him/her,
with reverence we bless his/her mortal body.

E   BRIEF ADDRESS—If the child died before baptism, the presiding minister may address the mourners using the following or similar words.

My brothers and sisters, the Lord is a faithful God who created us all after his own image. All things are of his making, all creation awaits the day of salvation. We now entrust the soul of N. to the abundant mercy of God, that our beloved child may find a home in his kingdom.

Entrance Procession

397 The Easter candle may be placed beforehand near the position the coffin will occupy at the conclusion of the procession. The presiding minister and assisting ministers precede the coffin and the mourners into the church. During the procession a hymn or song may be sung.

Placing of the Pall

398 If it is the custom in the local community and the child was baptized, the pall is then placed on the coffin by family members, friends, or the presiding minister.

Placing of Christian Symbols

399 A symbol of the Christian life, such as a Book of the Gospels, a Bible, or a cross, may be carried in procession, then placed on the coffin, either in silence or as one of the following texts is said.

A   Book of the Gospels or Bible

May Christ greet N. with these words of eternal life:
Come, blessed of my Father!

B   Cross, for a baptized child

In baptism N. received the sign of the cross.
May he/she now share
in Christ's victory over sin and death.

C   Cross, for a child who died before baptism

The cross we have brought here today was carried by the Lord Jesus in the hour of his suffering.

We place it now on/near this coffin as a sign of our hope for N.

As the cross is placed on or near the coffin, the presiding minister says:

Lord Jesus Christ,
you loved us unto death.
Let this cross be a sign of your love for N.
and for the people you have gathered here today.

On reaching the altar, the presiding minister, with the assisting ministers, makes the customary reverence and goes to the chair.

Invitation to Prayer

> 400 When all have reached their places, the presiding minister, using the following, or in similar words, invites the assembly to pray.

My brothers and sisters, we have come together to renew our trust in Christ who, by dying on the cross, has freed us from eternal death and, by rising, has opened for us the gates of heaven.

Let us pray that the Lord may grant us the gift of his loving consolation.

Opening Prayer

> 401 After a brief period of silent prayer, the presiding minister says one of the following prayers or one of those provided in nos. 580-581, p. 407.

A   A baptized child

To you, O Lord,   224
we humbly entrust this child,
so precious in your sight.
Take him/her into your arms
and welcome him/her into paradise,
where there will be no sorrow, no weeping nor pain,
but the fullness of peace and joy
with your Son and the Holy Spirit
for ever and ever.

R. Amen.

B   A baptized child

Lord, in our grief we call upon your mercy: 223
open your ears to our prayers,
and one day unite us again with N.,
who, we firmly trust,
already enjoys eternal life in your kingdom.

We ask this through Christ our Lord.

R. Amen.

C A baptized child

Merciful Lord,
whose wisdom is beyond human understanding,
you adopted N. as your own in baptism
and have taken him/her to yourself
even as he/she stood on the threshold of life.
Listen to our prayers and extend to us your grace,
that one day we may share eternal life with N.,
for we firmly believe that he/she now rests with you.

We ask this through our Lord Jesus Christ, your Son,
who lives and reigns with you and the Holy Spirit,
one God, for ever and ever.

R. Amen.

D A baptized child

Lord God,
from whom human sadness is never hidden,
you know the burden of grief
that we feel at the loss of this child.

As we mourn his/her passing from this life,
comfort us with the knowledge
that N. lives now in your loving embrace.

We make our prayer through our Lord Jesus Christ, your Son,
who lives and reigns with you and the Holy Spirit,
one God, for ever and ever.

R. Amen.

E A child who died before baptism 236

God of all consolation,
searcher of mind and heart,
the faith of these parents [N. and N.] is known to you.

Comfort them with the knowledge
that the child for whom they grieve
is entrusted now to your loving care.

We ask this through our Lord Jesus Christ, your Son,
who lives and reigns with you and the Holy Spirit,
one God, for ever and ever.

R. Amen.

O Lord, whose ways are beyond understanding,
listen to the prayers of your faithful people:
that those weighed down by grief
    at the loss of this [little] child
may find reassurance in your infinite goodness.

We ask this through our Lord Jesus Christ, your Son,
who lives and reigns with you and the Holy Spirit,
one God, for ever and ever.

R. Amen.

LITURGY OF THE WORD

READINGS

402 After the introductory rites, the liturgy of the word is celebrated. Depending upon pastoral circumstances, either one or
two readings may be read before the gospel.

HOMILY

403 A brief homily is given after the gospel reading.

GENERAL INTERCESSIONS

404 The general intercessions then take place.

INTERCESSIONS

405 One of the following sets of intercessions may be used or
adapted to the circumstances, or new intercessions may be
composed.

A   The presiding minister begins:

The Lord Jesus is the lover of his people and our only sure hope.
Let us ask him to deepen our faith and sustain us in this dark
hour.

You became a little child for our sake, sharing our human life.
To you we pray:

R. Bless us and keep us, O Lord.

You grew in wisdom, age and grace, and learned obedience
through suffering.
To you we pray:

R. Bless us and keep us, O Lord.

You welcomed children, promising them your kingdom.
To you we pray:

R. Bless us and keep us, O Lord.

You comforted those who mourned the loss of children and friends.
To you we pray:

R. Bless us and keep us, O Lord.

You took upon yourself the suffering and death of us all.
To you we pray:

R. Bless us and keep us, O Lord.

You promised to raise up those who believe in you, just as you
were raised up in glory by the Father.
To you we pray:

R. Bless us and keep us, O Lord.

B   The presiding minister begins:

Let us pray for N., his/her family and friends, and for all God's
people.

An assisting minister or reader then continues:

For N., child of God [and heir to the kingdom], that he/she be
held securely in God's loving embrace now and for all eternity.
We pray to the Lord.

R. Lord, hear our prayer.

For N.'s family, especially his/her mother and father, [his/her
brother(s) and sister(s),] that they feel the healing power of
Christ in the midst of their pain and grief.
We pray to the Lord.

R. Lord, hear our prayer.

For N.'s friends, those who played with him/her and those who cared for him/her, that they be consoled in their loss and strengthened in their love for one another.
We pray to the Lord.

R. Lord, hear our prayer.

For all parents who grieve over the death of their children, that they be comforted in the knowledge that their children dwell with God.
We pray to the Lord.

R. Lord, hear our prayer.

For children who have died of hunger and disease, that these little ones be seated close to the Lord at his heavenly table.
We pray to the Lord.

R. Lord, hear our prayer.

For the whole Church, that we prepare worthily for the hour of our death, when God will call us by name to pass from this world to the next.
We pray to the Lord.

R. Lord, hear our prayer.

C   The presiding minister begins:

Dear friends, let us turn to the Lord, the God of hope and consolation, who calls us to everlasting glory in Christ Jesus.

    An assisting minister or reader then continues:

For N., that he/she may now enjoy the place prepared for him/her in your great love.
Lord, in your mercy.

R. Hear our prayer.

For N.'s father and mother [and brother(s) and sister(s)], that they may know our love and support in their grief.
Lord, in your mercy.

R. Hear our prayer.

For his/her friends [and teachers], that they may love one another as you have loved us.
Lord, in your mercy.

R. Hear our prayer.

For this community, that we may bear one another's burdens.
Lord, in your mercy.

R. Hear our prayer.

For all those who mourn their children, that they may be comforted.
Lord, in your mercy.

R. Hear our prayer.

For all who are in need, that the fearful may find peace, the weary rest, and the oppressed freedom.
Lord, in your mercy.

R. Hear our prayer.

THE LORD'S PRAYER

406 Using one of the following invitations, or in similar words, the minister invites those present to pray the Lord's Prayer.

A   Now let us pray as Christ the Lord has taught us:

B   With longing for the coming of God's kingdom, let us offer our prayer to the Father:

All say:
Our Father . . .

CONCLUDING PRAYER

407 If there is no communion, the presiding minister then says one of the following prayers.

A   A baptized child

Lord God,
you entrusted N. to our care
and now you embrace him/her in your love.

Take N. into your keeping
together with all children who have died.

Comfort us, your sorrowing servants,
who seek to do your will
and to know your saving peace.

We ask this through Christ our Lord.

R. Amen.

B   A baptized child

Tender Shepherd of the flock,
N. has entered your kingdom
and now lies cradled in your love.
Soothe the hearts of his/her parents
and bring peace to their lives.
Enlighten their faith
and give hope to their hearts.

Loving God,
grant mercy to your entire family in this time of suffering.
Comfort us in the knowledge that this child [N.]
lives with you and your Son, Jesus Christ,
and the Holy Spirit,
for ever and ever.

R. Amen.

C   A baptized child   196

Listen, O God, to the prayers of your Church
on behalf of the faithful departed,
and grant to your child, N.,
whose funeral we have celebrated today,
the inheritance promised to all your saints.

We ask this through Christ our Lord.

R. Amen.

D   A child who died before baptism

God of mercy,
in the mystery of your wisdom
you have drawn this child [N.] to yourself.
In the midst of our pain and sorrow,
we acknowledge you as Lord of the living and the dead
and we search for our peace in your will.
In these final moments we stand together in prayer,
believing in your compassion and generous love.
Deliver this child [N.] out of death
and grant him/her a place in your kingdom of peace.

We ask this through Christ our Lord.

R. Amen.

LITURGY OF HOLY COMMUNION

Communion

408 If there is to be communion, the presiding minister shows
the eucharistic bread to those present, saying:

This is the Lamb of God
who takes away the sins of the world.
Happy are those who are called to his supper.

All then respond:

Lord, I am not worthy to receive you,
but only say the word and I shall be healed.

Those present then receive communion in the usual way.

Silent Prayer

409 A period of silence may be observed.

Prayer after Communion

410 When all have received communion, the presiding minister then says one of the following prayers.

Let us pray.

All pray in silence for a brief period, if this has not preceded.

A   A baptized child

Lord,
hear the prayers of those who share in the body and blood
   of your Son.
Comfort those who mourn for this child
and sustain them with the hope of eternal life.

We ask this through Christ our Lord.

R. Amen.

B   A baptized child

Lord,
you feed us with the gift of your eucharist.
May we rejoice with this child
at the feast of eternal life in your kingdom.

We ask this through Christ our Lord.

R. Amen.

C   A child who died before baptism

Lord,
hear the prayers of those who share in the body and blood
   of your Son.
By these sacred mysteries
you have filled them with hope of eternal life.
May they be comforted in the sorrows of this present life.

We ask this in the name of Jesus the Lord.

R. Amen.

FINAL COMMENDATION

412 The presiding minister goes to a place near the coffin. If
incense and holy water are to be used, they are carried by the
assisting ministers.

A member or a friend of the family may speak in remembrance
of the deceased child before the final commendation begins.

Invitation to Prayer

413 Using one of the following invitations, or in similar words,
the presiding minister begins the final commendation.

A   A baptized child

God in his wisdom knows the span of our days; he has chosen   227
to call to himself this child, whom he adopted as his own in
baptism. The body of N. will one day rise again to a new and
radiant life that will never end.

Our firm belief is that N., because he/she was baptized, has
already entered this new life; our firm hope is that we shall do
the same. Let us ask God to comfort his/her family and friends
and to increase our desire for the joys of heaven.

B   A baptized child

With faith in Jesus Christ, we bid farewell to N.   228

Let us pray with confidence to God, in whose sight all creation
lives, that he will raise up in holiness and power the mortal body
of this [little] child, for God has chosen to number him/her
among the blessed.

Let us commend this child/baby to the Lord's merciful keeping; and let us pray with all our hearts for N. and N. Even as
they grieve at the loss of their [little] child, they entrust him/her
to the loving embrace of God.

Silence

414 All pray in silence.

Signs of Farewell

415 The coffin of a baptized child may now be sprinkled with
holy water and incensed, or this may take place during or after
the song of farewell.

Song of Farewell

416 The song of farewell is then sung. One of the following texts
or another suitable hymn or song may be sung.

A   I know that my Redeemer lives,   189
     And on that final day of days,
     His voice shall bid me rise again:
     Unending joy, unceasing praise!

     This hope I cherish in my heart:
     To stand on earth, my flesh restored,
     And, not a stranger but a friend,
     Behold my Saviour and my Lord.

          Tune: LM, for example, Duke Street

B   Saints of God, come to his/her aid!   47
     Hasten to meet him/her, angels of the Lord!   66
     R. Receive his/her soul and present him/her
     to God the Most High.

May Christ, who called you, take you to himself;
may angels lead you to the bosom of Abraham.
R. Receive his/her soul and present him/her
to God the Most High.

Eternal rest grant unto him/her, O Lord,
and let perpetual light shine upon him/her.
R. Receive his/her soul and present him/her
to God the Most High.

PRAYER OF COMMENDATION

417 The presiding minister then says one of the following prayers.

A   A baptized child

You are the author and sustainer of our lives, O God.
You are our final home.
We commend to you N., our child/baby.

In baptism he/she began his/her journey toward you.
Take him/her now to yourself
and give him/her the life
promised to those born again of water and the Spirit.

Turn also to us who have suffered this loss.
Strengthen the bonds of this family and our community.
Confirm us in faith, in hope, and in love,
so that we may bear your peace to one another
and one day stand together with all the saints
who praise you for your saving help.

We ask this in the name of your Son,
whom you raised from among the dead,
Jesus Christ, our Lord.

R. Amen.

B   A baptized child

Lord Jesus,
like a shepherd who gathers the lambs
to protect them from all harm,
you led N. to the waters of baptism
and shielded him/her in innocence.

Now carry this little one
on the path to your kingdom of light
where he/she will find happiness
and every tear will be wiped away.

To you be glory, now and for ever.

R. Amen.

C   A baptized child

Into your gentle keeping, O Lord,
we commend this child [N.].
Though our hearts are troubled,
we hope in your loving kindness.

By the sign of the cross
he/she was claimed for Christ,
and in the waters of baptism
he/she died with Christ to live in him for ever.

May the angels, our guardians,
lead N. now to paradise
where your saints will welcome him/her
and every tear will be wiped away.
There we shall join in songs of praise for ever.

We ask this through Christ our Lord.

R. Amen.

D   A child who died before baptism

You are the author and sustainer of our lives, O God,
you are our final home.
We commend to you N., our child/baby.

Trusting in your mercy
and in your all-embracing love,
we pray that you give him/her happiness for ever.

Turn also to us who have suffered this loss.
Strengthen the bonds of this family and our community.
Confirm us in faith, in hope, and in love,
so that we may bear your peace to one another
and one day stand together with all the saints
who praise you for your saving help.

We ask this in the name of your Son,
Jesus Christ, our Lord.

R. Amen.

PROCESSION TO THE
PLACE OF COMMITTAL

418 The deacon or, in the absence of a deacon, the presiding
minister says:

In peace let us take N. to his/her place of rest.

If a symbol of the Christian life has been placed on the coffin,
it should be removed at this time.

The procession then begins: the presiding minister and assisting ministers precede the coffin; the family and mourners follow.

One or more of the following texts or other suitable songs may
be sung during the procession to the entrance of the church. The
singing may continue during the journey to the place of committal..

A   The following antiphon may be sung with verses from Psalm 24 (25), p. 429.

May the angels lead you into paradise;   50
may the martyrs come to welcome you
and take you to the holy city,
the new and eternal Jerusalem.

B   The following antiphon may be sung with verses from Psalm 114 (116), p. 430, or separately.

May choirs of angels welcome you   50
and lead you to the bosom of Abraham;
and where Lazarus is poor no longer
may you find eternal rest.

C   May saints and angels lead you on,
Escorting you where Christ has gone.
Now he has called you, come to him
Who sits above the seraphim.

Come to the peace of Abraham
And to the supper of the Lamb:
Come to the glory of the blessed,
And to perpetual light and rest.

D   Another suitable psalm may also be used.

RITE OF COMMITTAL

The Lord is my shepherd;
fresh and green are the pastures
where he gives me repose

RITE OF COMMITTAL

419 The rite of committal, the conclusion of the funeral rites (see nos. 219-242), is celebrated at the grave, tomb, or crematorium and may be used for burial at sea.

420 Seven forms of the rite of committal are provided here: The 'Rite of Committal at a Cemetery' and 'Rite of Committal at a Crematorium' are used when the final commendation is celebrated as part of the conclusion of the funeral liturgy. The 'Rite of Committal at a Cemetery with Final Commendation' and 'Rite of Committal at a Crematorium with Final Commendation' are used when the final commendation does not take place during the funeral liturgy, or when the funeral liturgy does not immediately precede the committal. The 'Rite of Committal for Burial' and 'Rite of Committal for Cremation' are intended for use at a cemetery or crematorium chapel when no other liturgical celebration at all has taken place, and they incorporate elements of the funeral liturgy itself. A seventh form is provided for the final commendation of an infant.

421 The 'Rite of Final Commendation for an Infant' may be used in the case of a stillbirth or a newborn infant who dies shortly after birth, or may be adapted for use with parents who have suffered a miscarriage. This short rite of prayer with the parents is celebrated to give them comfort and to commend and entrust the infant to God. This rite is a model and the minister should adapt it to the circumstances. It may be used in the hospital or place of birth or at the time of the committal of the body.

OUTLINE OF THE RITE

Invitation
Scripture Verse
Prayer over the Place of Committal

Committal
Intercessions
The Lord's Prayer
Concluding Prayer

Prayer over the People

16 RITE OF COMMITTAL AT A CEMETERY
WHEN A FUNERAL LITURGY HAS IMMEDIATELY PRECEDED

INVITATION

422 When the funeral procession arrives at the place of committal, the minister says the following or a similar invitation.

The life which this child/baby N. received from his/her parents is not destroyed by death. God has taken him/her into eternal life.

As we commit his/her body to the earth, let us comfort each other in our sorrow with the assurance of our faith, that one day we will be reunited with N.

SCRIPTURE VERSE

423 One of the following or another brief Scripture verse is read. The minister first says:

We read in sacred Scripture:

A

Matthew 25:34   119

Come, you whom my Father has blessed, says the Lord;
inherit the kingdom prepared for you since the foundation
   of the world.

B

John 6:39   121

This is the will of my Father, says the Lord,
that I should lose nothing of all that he has given to me,
and that I should raise it up on the last day.

C

Philippians 3:20   124

Our true home is in heaven,
and Jesus Christ whose return we long for
will come from heaven to save us.

D

Apocalypse 1:5-6   126

Jesus Christ is the first-born of the dead;
glory and kingship be his for ever and ever. Amen.

Prayer over the Place of Committal

424 The minister says one of the following prayers.

A All praise to you, Lord of all creation.
Praise to you, holy and living God.
We praise and bless you for your mercy,
we praise and bless you for your kindness.
Blessed is the Lord, our God.

R. Blessed is the Lord, our God.

You sanctify the homes of the living
and make holy the places of the dead.
You alone open the gates of righteousness
and lead us to the dwellings of the saints.
Blessed is the Lord, our God.

R. Blessed is the Lord, our God.

We praise you, our refuge and strength.
We bless you, our God and Redeemer.
Your praise is always in our hearts and on our lips.
We remember the mighty deeds of the covenant.
Blessed is the Lord, our God.

R. Blessed is the Lord, our God.

Almighty and ever-living God,
remember the love with which you graced
    your child N. in [his/her short] life.
Receive him/her, we pray, into the mansions of the saints.
As we make ready this resting place,
look also with favour on those who mourn
and comfort them in their loss.

Grant this through Christ our Lord.

R. Amen.

B   Almighty and ever-living God,
in you we place our trust and hope,
in you the dead, whose bodies were temples of the Spirit,
    find everlasting peace.

As we take leave of N.,
give our hearts peace in the firm hope
that one day he/she will live
in the mansion you have prepared for him/her in heaven.

We ask this through Christ our Lord.

R. Amen.

C   If the place of committal is to be blessed

O God,   193
by whose mercy the faithful departed find rest,
bless this grave,
and send your holy angel to watch over it.

As we bury here the body of N.,
welcome him/her into your presence,
that he/she may rejoice in you with your saints for ever.

We ask this through Christ our Lord.

R. Amen.

COMMITTAL

425 The minister then says the words of committal. One of the
following texts is used, during or after which the coffin is lowered.

A   A baptized child

Into your hands, O merciful Saviour, we commend N.
Acknowledge, we humbly beseech you,
a sheep of your own fold, a lamb of your own flock.
Receive him/her into the arms of your mercy,
into the blessed rest of everlasting peace,
and into the glorious company of the saints in light.

B   A child who died before baptism

Lord God,
ever-caring and gentle,
we commit to your love this little one [N.],
who brought joy to our lives for so short a time.
Enfold him/her in eternal life.

We pray for his/her parents
who are saddened by the loss of their child/baby.
Give them courage
and help them in their pain and grief.
May they all meet one day
in the joy and peace of your kingdom.

We ask this through Christ our Lord.

R. Amen.

INTERCESSIONS

426 The following intercessions may be used or adapted to the circumstances, or new intercessions may be composed.

The minister begins:

Dear friends, let us turn to the Lord, the God of hope and consolation, who calls us to everlasting glory in Christ Jesus.

A reader or the minister then continues:

For N., that he/she may now enjoy the place prepared for him/her in your great love.
Lord, in your mercy.

R. Hear our prayer.

For N.'s father and mother [and brother(s) and sister(s)], that they may know our love and support in their grief.
Lord, in your mercy.

R. Hear our prayer.

For his/her friends [and teachers], that they may love one another as you have loved us.
Lord, in your mercy.

R. Hear our prayer.

For this community, that we may bear one another's burdens.
Lord, in your mercy.

R. Hear our prayer.

For all those who mourn their children, that they may be comforted.
Lord, in your mercy.

R. Hear our prayer.

For all who are in need, that the fearful may find peace, the weary rest, and the oppressed freedom.
Lord, in your mercy.

R. Hear our prayer.

THE LORD'S PRAYER

427 Using one of the following invitations, or in similar words, the minister invites those present to pray the Lord's Prayer.

A   Now let us pray as Christ the Lord has taught us:

B   With longing for the coming of God's kingdom, let us offer our prayer to the Father:

C   As sons and daughters of a loving God, we pray in the confident words of his Son:

D   When Jesus gathered his disciples around him, he taught them to pray:

All say:

Our Father . . .

CONCLUDING PRAYER

428 The minister says one of the following prayers or one of those provided in nos. 580-581, p. 407.

A   A baptized child

Tender Shepherd of the flock,
N. has entered your kingdom
and now lies cradled in your love.
Soothe the hearts of his/her parents
and bring peace to their lives.
Enlighten their faith
and give hope to their hearts.

Loving God,
grant mercy to your entire family in this time of suffering.
Comfort us in the knowledge that this child [N.]
lives with you and your Son, Jesus Christ,
and the Holy Spirit,
for ever and ever.

R. Amen.

Listen, O God, to the prayers of your Church
on behalf of the faithful departed,
and grant to your child, N.,
whose funeral we have celebrated today,
the inheritance promised to all your saints.

We ask this through Christ our Lord.

R. Amen.

C   A child who died before baptism

God of mercy,
in the mystery of your wisdom
you have drawn this child [N.] to yourself.
In the midst of our pain and sorrow,
we acknowledge you as Lord of the living and the dead
and we search for our peace in your will.
In these final moments we stand together in prayer,
believing in your compassion and generous love.
Deliver this child [N.] out of death
and grant him/her a place in your kingdom of peace.

We ask this through Christ our Lord.

R. Amen.

429 The assisting minister or the minister says:

Bow your heads and pray for God's blessing.

All pray silently. The minister, with hands outstretched over the
people, says one of the following prayers.

A   Merciful Lord,
you know the anguish of the sorrowful,
you are attentive to the prayers of the humble.
Hear your people
who cry out to you in their need,
and strengthen their hope in your lasting goodness.
We ask this through Christ our Lord.

R. Amen.

B
Most merciful God,
whose wisdom is beyond our understanding,
surround the family of N. with your love,
that they may not be overwhelmed by their loss,
but have confidence in your goodness,
and strength to meet the days to come.
We ask this through Christ our Lord.

R. Amen.

The minister then says the following:

Eternal rest grant unto him/her, O Lord.

R. And let perpetual light shine upon him/her.

May he/she rest in peace.

R. Amen.

May his/her soul and the souls of all the faithful departed,
through the mercy of God, rest in peace.

R. Amen.

A   A minister who is a priest or deacon says:

May the peace of God,
which is beyond all understanding,
keep your hearts and minds
in the knowledge and love of God
and of his Son, our Lord Jesus Christ.

℞. Amen.

May almighty God bless you,
the Father, and the Son, ✠ and the Holy Spirit.

℞. Amen.

B   A minister who is a priest or deacon says:

May the love of God and the peace of the Lord Jesus Christ
console you
and gently wipe every tear from your eyes.

℞. Amen.

May almighty God bless you,
the Father, and the Son, ✠ and the Holy Spirit.

℞. Amen.

C   A lay minister invokes God's blessing and signs himself or her-
          self with the sign of the cross, saying:

May the love of God and the peace of the Lord Jesus Christ
bless and console us
and gently wipe every tear from our eyes:
in the name of the Father,
and of the Son, and of the Holy Spirit.

℞. Amen.

The minister then concludes:

Go in the peace of Christ.

℞. Thanks be to God.

A hymn or song may conclude the rite. Some sign or gesture
of leave-taking may be made.

OUTLINE OF THE RITE

Greeting
Invitation
Scripture Verse
Prayer over the Place of Committal

Invitation to Prayer
Silence
Signs of Farewell
Song of Farewell
Prayer of Commendation
  and the Committal

Prayer over the People

17 RITE OF COMMITTAL AT A CEMETERY WITH FINAL COMMENDATION
[INCLUDING BURIAL OF ASHES AND BURIAL AT SEA]
WHEN A FUNERAL LITURGY HAS NOT IMMEDIATELY PRECEDED

GREETING

430   When all have gathered at the place of committal, the minister welcomes the funeral party and, using one of the following greetings, or in similar words, greets them.

A   May Christ Jesus, who welcomed children and laid his hands in blessing upon them, comfort you with his peace and be always with you.

R. And also with you.

B   May the God of hope give you the fullness of peace, and may the Lord of life be always with you.

R. And also with you.

C   The grace and peace of God our Father, who raised Jesus from the dead, be always with you.

R. And also with you.

D   May the Father of mercies, the God of all consolation, be with you.

R. And also with you.

E   The grace of our Lord Jesus Christ, and the love of God, and the fellowship of the Holy Spirit be with you all.

R. And also with you.

INVITATION

431 The minister then says the following or a similar invitation.

The life which this child/baby N. received from his/her parents is not destroyed by death. God has taken him/her into eternal life.

As we commend N. to God and commit his/her body to the earth, let us express in [song and] prayer our common faith in the resurrection. As Jesus Christ was raised from the dead, we too are called to follow him through death to the glory where God will be all in all.

A hymn or song may be sung.

SCRIPTURE VERSE

432 One of the following or another brief Scripture verse is read. The minister first says:

We read in sacred Scripture:

A   Matthew 25:34   119

Come, you whom my Father has blessed, says the Lord;
inherit the kingdom prepared for you since the foundation
    of the world.

B   John 6:39   121

This is the will of my Father, says the Lord,
that I should lose nothing of all that he has given to me,
and that I should raise it up on the last day.

C   Philippians 3:20   124

Our true home is in heaven,
and Jesus Christ whose return we long for
will come from heaven to save us.

D   Apocalypse 1:5-6   126

Jesus Christ is the first-born of the dead;
glory and kingship be his for ever and ever. Amen.

Prayer over the Place of Committal

433 The minister says one of the following prayers.

A All praise to you, Lord of all creation.
Praise to you, holy and living God.
We praise and bless you for your mercy,
we praise and bless you for your kindness.
Blessed is the Lord, our God.

R. Blessed is the Lord, our God.

You sanctify the homes of the living
and make holy the places of the dead.
You alone open the gates of righteousness
and lead us to the dwellings of the saints.
Blessed is the Lord, our God.

R. Blessed is the Lord, our God.

We praise you, our refuge and strength.
We bless you, our God and Redeemer.
Your praise is always in our hearts and on our lips.
We remember the mighty deeds of the covenant.
Blessed is the Lord, our God.

R. Blessed is the Lord, our God.

Almighty and ever-living God,
remember the love with which you graced
    your child N. in [his/her short] life.
Receive him/her, we pray, into the mansions of the saints.
As we make ready this resting place,
look also with favour on those who mourn
and comfort them in their loss.

Grant this through Christ our Lord.

R. Amen.

B   Almighty and ever-living God,
     in you we place our trust and hope,
     in you the dead whose bodies were temples of the Spirit
          find everlasting peace.

     As we take leave of N.,
     give our hearts peace in the firm hope
     that one day he/she will live
     in the mansion you have prepared for him/her in heaven.

     We ask this through Christ our Lord.

     R. Amen.

C   If the place of committal is to be blessed

     O God,   193
     by whose mercy the faithful departed find rest,
     bless this grave,
     and send your holy angel to watch over it.

     As we bury here the body of N.,
     welcome him/her into your presence,
     that he/she may rejoice in you with your saints for ever.

     We ask this through Christ our Lord.

     R. Amen.

434 Using one of the following invitations, or in similar words, the minister begins the final commendation.

A   A baptized child

God in his wisdom knows the span of our days; he has chosen   227
to call to himself this child, whom he adopted as his own in
baptism. The body we must now bury will one day rise again
to a new and radiant life that will never end.

Our firm belief is that N., because he/she was baptized, has
already entered this new life; our firm hope is that we shall do
the same. Let us ask God to comfort his/her family and friends
and to increase our desire for the joys of heaven.

B   A baptized child

With faith in Jesus Christ, we must reverently bury the body   228
of N.

Let us pray with confidence to God, in whose sight all creation
lives, that he will raise up in holiness and power the mortal body
of this [little] child, for God has chosen to number his/her soul
among the blessed.

C   A child who died before baptism

Let us commend this child to the Lord's merciful keeping; and   237
let us pray with all our hearts for N. and N. Even as they grieve
at the loss of their [little] child, they entrust him/her to the loving embrace of God.

D   For burial of ashes

My friends, as we prepare to bury/entomb the ashes of this
child/baby, we recall that our bodies bear the imprint of the
first creation when they were fashioned from dust; but in faith
we remember, too, that by the new creation we also bear the
image of Jesus who was raised to glory.

In confident hope that one day God will raise us and transform
our mortal bodies, let us pray.

Silence

435 All pray in silence.

Signs of Farewell

436 The coffin of a baptized child may now be sprinkled with holy water and incensed, or this may take place during or after the song of farewell.

In the case of an unbaptized child a suitable sign may be used: for example, the minister may place his or her hand on the coffin during the song of farewell.

Song of Farewell

437 The song of farewell is then sung. One of the following texts or another suitable hymn or song may be used.

A   I know that my Redeemer lives,   189
And on that final day of days,
His voice shall bid me rise again:
Unending joy, unceasing praise!

This hope I cherish in my heart:
To stand on earth, my flesh restored,
And, not a stranger but a friend,
Behold my Saviour and my Lord.

Tune: LM, for example, Duke Street

B   Saints of God, come to his/her aid!   47
Hasten to meet him/her, angels of the Lord!   66
R. Receive his/her soul and present him/her
to God the Most High.

May Christ, who called you, take you to himself;
may angels lead you to the bosom of Abraham.
R. Receive his/her soul and present him/her
to God the Most High.

Eternal rest grant unto him/her, O Lord,
and let perpetual light shine upon him/her.
R. Receive his/her soul and present him/her
to God the Most High.

PRAYER OF COMMENDATION AND THE COMMITTAL

438 The minister then says one of the following prayers, during or after which the coffin is lowered.

A   A baptized child

You are the author and sustainer of our lives, O God.
You are our final home.
We commend to you N., our child/baby.

In baptism he/she began his/her journey toward you.
Take him/her now to yourself
and give him/her the life
promised to those born again of water and the Spirit.

Turn also to us who have suffered this loss.
Strengthen the bonds of this family and our community.
Confirm us in faith, in hope, and in love,
so that we may bear your peace to one another
and one day stand together with all the saints
who praise you for your saving help.

We ask this in the name of your Son,
whom you raised from among the dead,
Jesus Christ, our Lord.

R. Amen.

B   A baptized child

Lord Jesus,
like a shepherd who gathers the lambs
to protect them from all harm,
you led N. to the waters of baptism
and shielded him/her in innocence.

Now carry this little one
on the path to your kingdom of light
where he/she will find happiness
and every tear will be wiped away.

To you be glory, now and for ever.

R. Amen.

C A baptized child

Into your gentle keeping, O Lord,
we commend this child N.
Though our hearts are troubled,
we hope in your loving kindness.

By the sign of the cross
he/she was claimed for Christ,
and in the waters of baptism
he/she died with Christ to live in him for ever.

May the angels, our guardians,
lead him/her now to paradise
where your saints will welcome him/her
and every tear will be wiped away.
There we shall join in songs of praise for ever.

We ask this through Christ our Lord.

R. Amen.

D For burial of ashes

Faithful God,
Lord of all creation,
you desire that nothing redeemed by your Son
will ever be lost,
and that the just will be raised up on the last day.

Comfort us today with the word of your promise
as we return the ashes of N. to the earth.

Grant him/her a place of rest and peace
where the world of dust and ashes has no dominion.
Confirm us in our hope that he/she will be created anew
on the day when you will raise him/her up in glory
to live with you and all the saints
for ever and ever.

R. Amen.

E   A child who died before baptism

You are the author and sustainer of our lives, O God,
you are our final home.
We commend to you N., our child/baby.

Trusting in your mercy
and in your all-embracing love,
we pray that you give him/her happiness for ever.

Turn also to us who have suffered this loss.
Strengthen the bonds of this family and our community.
Confirm us in faith, in hope, and in love,
so that we may bear your peace to one another
and one day stand together with all the saints
who praise you for your saving help.

We ask this in the name of your Son,
Jesus Christ, our Lord.

R. Amen.

PRAYER OVER THE PEOPLE

439 The assisting minister or the minister says:

Bow your heads and pray for God's blessing.

All pray silently. The minister, with hands outstretched over the
people, says one of the following prayers.

A   Merciful Lord,
you know the anguish of the sorrowful,
you are attentive to the prayers of the humble.
Hear your people
who cry out to you in their need,
and strengthen their hope in your lasting goodness.

We ask this through Christ our Lord.

R. Amen.

B   Most merciful God,
    whose wisdom is beyond our understanding,
    surround the family of N. with your love,
    that they may not be overwhelmed by their loss,
    but have confidence in your goodness,
    and strength to meet the days to come.

    We ask this through Christ our Lord.

    R. Amen.

The minister then says the following:

Eternal rest grant unto him/her, O Lord.

R. And let perpetual light shine upon him/her.

May he/she rest in peace.

R. Amen.

May his/her soul and the souls of all the faithful departed,
through the mercy of God, rest in peace.

R. Amen.

A   A minister who is a priest or deacon says:

    May the peace of God,
    which is beyond all understanding,
    keep your hearts and minds
    in the knowledge and love of God
    and of his Son, our Lord Jesus Christ.

    R. Amen.

    May almighty God bless you,
    the Father, and the Son, ✠ and the Holy Spirit.

    R. Amen.

B   A minister who is a priest or deacon says:

May the love of God and the peace of the Lord Jesus Christ
console you
and gently wipe every tear from your eyes.

R. **Amen.**

May almighty God bless you,
the Father, and the Son, ✠ and the Holy Spirit.

R. **Amen.**

C   A lay minister invokes God's blessing and signs himself or her-
    self with the sign of the cross, saying:

May the love of God and the peace of the Lord Jesus Christ
bless and console us
and gently wipe every tear from our eyes:
in the name of the Father,
and of the Son, and of the Holy Spirit.

R. **Amen.**

The minister then concludes:

Go in the peace of Christ.

R. **Thanks be to God.**

A hymn or song may conclude the rite. Some sign or gesture
of leave-taking may be made.

OUTLINE OF THE RITE

INTRODUCTORY RITES

Greeting
Sprinkling with Holy Water
or Brief Address
Entrance Procession
[Placing of the Pall]
[Placing of Christian Symbols]
Invitation to Prayer
Opening Prayer

LITURGY OF THE WORD

Readings
Homily
General Intercessions
Intercessions
The Lord's Prayer
Concluding Prayer

FINAL COMMENDATION

Invitation to Prayer
Silence
Signs of Farewell
Song of Farewell
Prayer of Commendation

PROCESSION TO
THE PLACE OF COMMITTAL

RITE OF COMMITTAL

Invitation
Scripture Verse
Prayer over the Place of Committal
Committal

CONCLUDING RITE

Prayer over the People

18 RITE OF COMMITTAL FOR BURIAL
[INCLUDING BURIAL OF ASHES AND BURIAL AT SEA]
WHEN NO OTHER LITURGY HAS TAKEN PLACE

INTRODUCTORY RITES

GREETING

> 440 At or near the entrance to the chapel, the minister welcomes
> the funeral party and, using one of the following greetings, or
> in similar words, greets them.

A May Christ Jesus, who welcomed children and laid his hands
in blessing upon them, comfort you with his peace and be always with you.

 R. And also with you.

B May the God of hope give you the fullness of peace, and may
the Lord of life be always with you.

 R. And also with you.

C The grace and peace of God our Father, who raised Jesus from
the dead, be always with you.

 R. And also with you.

D May the Father of mercies, the God of all consolation, be with
you.

 R. And also with you.

E The grace of our Lord Jesus Christ, and the love of God, and
the fellowship of the Holy Spirit be with you all.

 R. And also with you.

Sprinkling with Holy Water or Brief Address

441 If the child was baptized, the minister sprinkles the coffin with holy water (option A). If the child died before baptism, the sprinkling with holy water is omitted and a brief address is given (option B).

A   Sprinkling with Holy Water—If the child was baptized, the minister then sprinkles the coffin with holy water, saying:

In the waters of baptism
N. died with Christ and rose with him to new life.
May he/she now share with him eternal glory.

B   Brief Address—If the child died before baptism, the minister may address the mourners using the following or similar words.

My brothers and sisters, the Lord is a faithful God who created us all after his own image. All things are of his making, all creation awaits the day of salvation. We now entrust the soul of N. to the abundant mercy of God, that our beloved child may find a home in his kingdom.

Entrance Procession

442 The Easter candle may be placed beforehand near the position the coffin will occupy at the conclusion of the procession. The minister precedes the coffin and the mourners into the chapel. During the procession a psalm, song, or responsory is sung.

Placing of the Pall

443 If it is the custom in the local community and the child was baptized, the pall is then placed on the coffin by family members, friends, or the minister.

Placing of Christian Symbols

444 A symbol of the Christian life, such as a Book of the Gospels, a Bible, or a cross, may be carried in procession, then placed on the coffin, either in silence or as one of the following texts is said.

A   Book of the Gospels or Bible

May Christ greet N. with these words of eternal life:
Come, blessed of my Father!

B   Cross, for a baptized child

In baptism N. received the sign of the cross.
May he/she now share
in Christ's victory over sin and death.

C   Cross, for a child who died before baptism

The cross we have brought here today was carried by the Lord
Jesus in the hour of his suffering.

We place it now on/near this coffin as a sign of our hope for N.

As the cross is placed on or near the coffin, the minister says:

Lord Jesus Christ,
you loved us unto death.
Let this cross be a sign of your love for N.
and for the people you have gathered here today.

INVITATION TO PRAYER

445 Using one of the following texts, or in similar words, the
minister invites those present to pray.

A   Let us pray for this child/baby and entrust him/her to the care
of our loving God.

B   My brothers and sisters, we have come together to renew our
trust in Christ who, by dying on the cross, has freed us from
eternal death and, by rising, has opened for us the gates of
heaven.

Let us pray that the Lord may grant us the gift of his loving
consolation.

Pause for silent prayer.

446 After a brief period of silent prayer, the minister says one of the following prayers or one of those provided in nos. 580-581, p. 407.

A   A baptized child

To you, O Lord,   224
we humbly entrust this child,
so precious in your sight.
Take him/her into your arms
and welcome him/her into paradise,.
where there will be no sorrow, no weeping nor pain,
but the fullness of peace and joy
with your Son and the Holy Spirit
for ever and ever.

R. Amen.

B   A baptized child

Lord, in our grief we call upon your mercy: 223
open your ears to our prayers,
and one day unite us again with N.,
who, we firmly trust,
already enjoys eternal life in your kingdom.

We ask this through our Lord Jesus Christ, your Son,
who lives and reigns with you and the Holy Spirit,
one God, for ever and ever.

R. Amen.

C   A baptized child

Lord God,
from whom human sadness is never hidden,
you know the burden of grief
that we feel at the loss of this child.

As we mourn his/her passing from this life,
comfort us with the knowledge
that N. lives now in your loving embrace.

We make our prayer through our Lord Jesus Christ, your Son,
who lives and reigns with you and the Holy Spirit,
one God, for ever and ever.

R. Amen.

D A baptized child

Merciful Lord,
whose wisdom is beyond human understanding,
you adopted N. as your own in baptism
and have taken him/her to yourself
even as he/she stood on the threshold of life.
Listen to our prayers and extend to us your grace,
that one day we may share eternal life with N.,
for we firmly believe that he/she now rests with you.

We ask this through our Lord Jesus Christ, your Son,
who lives and reigns with you and the Holy Spirit,
one God, for ever and ever.

R. Amen.

E A child who died before baptism   236

God of all consolation,
searcher of mind and heart,
the faith of these parents [N. and N.] is known to you.

Comfort them with the knowledge
that the child for whom they grieve
is entrusted now to your loving care.

We ask this through our Lord Jesus Christ, your Son,
who lives and reigns with you and the Holy Spirit,
one God, for ever and ever.

R. Amen.

F A child who died before baptism   235

O Lord, whose ways are beyond understanding,
listen to the prayers of your faithful people:
that those weighed down by grief
 at the loss of this [little] child
may find reassurance in your infinite goodness.

We ask this through our Lord Jesus Christ, your Son,
who lives and reigns with you and the Holy Spirit,
one God, for ever and ever.

R. Amen.

LITURGY OF THE WORD

READINGS

447 After the introductory rites, the liturgy of the word is celebrated. Depending upon pastoral circumstances, either one or
two readings may be read before the gospel. If only one reading
is possible it should be the gospel. Between the readings a psalm
or suitable song may be used.

HOMILY

448 A brief homily is given after the gospel reading.

GENERAL INTERCESSIONS

449 The general intercessions then take place.

INTERCESSIONS

450 One of the following sets of intercessions may be used or
adapted to the circumstances, or new intercessions may be
composed.

A   The minister begins:

The Lord Jesus is the lover of his people and our only sure hope.
Let us ask him to deepen our faith and sustain us in this dark
hour.

A reader or the minister then continues:

You became a little child for our sake, sharing our human life.
To you we pray:

R. Bless us and keep us, O Lord.

You grew in wisdom, age and grace, and learned obedience
through suffering.
To you we pray:

R. Bless us and keep us, O Lord.

You welcomed children, promising them your kingdom.
To you we pray:

R. Bless us and keep us, O Lord.

You comforted those who mourned the loss of children and friends.
To you we pray:

R. Bless us and keep us, O Lord.

You took upon yourself the suffering and death of us all.
To you we pray:

R. Bless us and keep us, O Lord.

You promised to raise up those who believe in you, just as you
were raised up in glory by the Father.
To you we pray:

R. Bless us and keep us, O Lord.

B   The minister begins:

Let us pray for N., his/her family and friends, and for all God's
people.

          A reader or the minister then continues:

For N., child of God [and heir to the kingdom], that he/she be
held securely in God's loving embrace now and for all eternity.
We pray to the Lord.

R. Lord, hear our prayer.

For N.'s family, especially his/her mother and father, [his/her
brother(s) and sister(s),] that they feel the healing power of
Christ in the midst of their pain and grief.
We pray to the Lord.

R. Lord, hear our prayer.

For N.'s friends, those who played with him/her and those who
cared for him/her, that they be consoled in their loss and
strengthened in their love for one another.
We pray to the Lord.

R. Lord, hear our prayer.

For all parents who grieve over the death of their children, that
they be comforted in the knowledge that their children dwell
with God.
We pray to the Lord.

R. Lord, hear our prayer.

For children who have died of hunger and disease, that these little ones be seated close to the Lord at his heavenly table. We pray to the Lord.

R. Lord, hear our prayer.

For the whole Church, that we prepare worthily for the hour of our death, when God will call us by name to pass from this world to the next.
We pray to the Lord.

R. Lord, hear our prayer.

C   The minister begins:

Dear friends, let us turn to the Lord, the God of hope and consolation, who calls us to everlasting glory in Christ Jesus.

A reader or the minister then continues:

For N., that he/she may now enjoy the place prepared for him/her in your great love.
Lord, in your mercy.

R. Hear our prayer.

For N.'s father and mother [and brother(s) and sister(s)], that they may know our love and support in their grief.
Lord, in your mercy.

R. Hear our prayer.

For his/her friends [and teachers], that they may love one another as you have loved us.
Lord, in your mercy.

R. Hear our prayer.

For this community, that we may bear one another's burdens.
Lord, in your mercy.

R. Hear our prayer.

For all those who mourn their children, that they may be comforted.
Lord, in your mercy.

R. Hear our prayer.

For all who are in need, that the fearful may find peace, the weary rest, and the oppressed freedom.
Lord, in your mercy.

R. Hear our prayer.

THE LORD'S PRAYER

> 451 Using one of the following invitations, or in similar words, the minister invites those present to pray the Lord's Prayer.

A Now let us pray as Christ the Lord has taught us:

B With longing for the coming of God's kingdom, let us offer our prayer to the Father:

C As sons and daughters of a loving God, we pray in the confident words of his Son:

D When Jesus gathered his disciples around him, he taught them to pray:

> All say:

Our Father . . .

CONCLUDING PRAYER

> 452 The minister says one of the following prayers or one of those provided in nos. 580-581, p. 407.

A   A baptized child

Lord God,
you entrusted N. to our care
and now you embrace him/her in your love.

Take N. into your keeping
together with all children who have died.

Comfort us, your sorrowing servants,
who seek to do your will
and to know your saving peace.

We ask this through Christ our Lord.

R. Amen.

B   A baptized child

Tender Shepherd of the flock,
N. has entered your kingdom
and now lies cradled in your love.
Soothe the hearts of his/her parents
and bring peace to their lives.
Enlighten their faith
and give hope to their hearts.

Loving God,
grant mercy to your entire family in this time of suffering.
Comfort us in the knowledge that this child [N.]
lives with you and your Son, Jesus Christ,
and the Holy Spirit,
for ever and ever.

R. Amen.

C   A baptized child   196

Listen, O God, to the prayers of your Church
on behalf of the faithful departed,
and grant to your child, N.,
whose funeral we celebrate today,
the inheritance promised to all your saints.

We ask this through Christ our Lord.

R. Amen.

D   A child who died before baptism

God of mercy,
in the mystery of your wisdom
you have drawn this child [N.] to yourself.
In the midst of our pain and sorrow,
we acknowledge you as Lord of the living and the dead
and we search for our peace in your will.
In these final moments we stand together in prayer,
believing in your compassion and generous love.
Deliver this child [N.] out of death
and grant him/her a place in your kingdom of peace.

We ask this through Christ our Lord.

R. Amen.

FINAL COMMENDATION

453 The minister then goes to a place near the coffin. If incense and holy water are to be used, they are carried by the assisting ministers.

A member or a friend of the family may speak in remembrance of the deceased child before the final commendation begins.

INVITATION TO PRAYER

454 Using one of the following invitations, or in similar words, the minister begins the final commendation.

A   A baptized child

God in his wisdom knows the span of our days; he has chosen   227
to call to himself this child, whom he adopted as his own in baptism. The body of N. will one day rise again to a new and radiant life that will never end.

Our firm belief is that N., because he/she was baptized, has already entered this new life; our firm hope is that we shall do the same. Let us ask God to comfort his/her family and friends and to increase our desire for the joys of heaven.

B   A baptized child

With faith in Jesus Christ, we bid farewell to N.   228

Let us pray with confidence to God, in whose sight all creation lives, that he will raise up in holiness and power the mortal body of this [little] child, for God has chosen to number his/her soul among the blessed.

C   A child who died before baptism   237

Let us commend this child/baby to the Lord's merciful keeping; and let us pray with all our hearts for N. and N. Even as they grieve at the loss of their [little] child, they entrust him/her to the loving embrace of God.

SILENCE

455 All pray in silence.

SIGNS OF FAREWELL

456 The coffin of a baptized child may now be sprinkled with holy water and incensed, or this may take place during or after the song of farewell.

In the case of an unbaptized child a suitable sign may be used: for example, the minister may place his or her hand on the coffin during the song of farewell and invite others to do the same.

SONG OF FAREWELL

457 The song of farewell is then sung. One of the following texts or another suitable hymn or song may be used.

A   I know that my Redeemer lives,   189
And on that final day of days,
His voice shall bid me rise again:
Unending joy, unceasing praise!

This hope I cherish in my heart:
To stand on earth, my flesh restored,
And, not a stranger but a friend,
Behold my Saviour and my Lord.

Tune: LM, for example, Duke Street

B   Saints of God, come to his/her aid!   47
Hasten to meet him/her, angels of the Lord!   66
R. Receive his/her soul and present him/her
to God the Most High.

May Christ, who called you, take you to himself;
may angels lead you to the bosom of Abraham.
R. Receive his/her soul and present him/her
to God the Most High.

Eternal rest grant unto him/her, O Lord,
and let perpetual light shine upon him/her.
R. Receive his/her soul and present him/her
to God the Most High.

Prayer of Commendation

458 The minister then says one of the following prayers.

A   A baptized child

You are the author and sustainer of our lives, O God.
You are our final home.
We commend to you N. our child/baby.

In baptism he/she began his/her journey toward you.
Take him/her now to yourself
and give him/her the life
promised to those born again of water and the Spirit.

Turn also to us who have suffered this loss.
Strengthen the bonds of this family and our community.
Confirm us in faith, in hope, and in love,
so that we may bear your peace to one another
and one day stand together with all the saints
who praise you for your saving help.

We ask this in the name of your Son,
whom you raised from among the dead,
Jesus Christ, our Lord.

R. Amen.

B   A baptized child

Lord Jesus,
like a shepherd who gathers the lambs
to protect them from all harm,
you led N. to the waters of baptism
and shielded him/her in innocence.

Now carry this little one
on the path to your kingdom of light
where he/she will find happiness
and every tear will be wiped away.

To you be glory, now and for ever.

R. Amen.

C   A baptized child

Into your gentle keeping, O Lord,
we commend this child N.
Though our hearts are troubled,
we hope in your loving kindness.

By the sign of the cross
he/she was claimed for Christ,
and in the waters of baptism
he/she died with Christ to live in him for ever.

May the angels, our guardians,
lead him/her now to paradise
where your saints will welcome him/her
and every tear will be wiped away.
There we shall join in songs of praise for ever.

We ask this through Christ our Lord.

R. Amen.

D   A child who died before baptism

You are the author and sustainer of our lives, O God,
you are our final home.
We commend to you N., our child/baby.

Trusting in your mercy
and in your all-embracing love,
we pray that you give him/her happiness for ever.

Turn also to us who have suffered this loss.
Strengthen the bonds of this family and our community.
Confirm us in faith, in hope, and in love,
so that we may bear your peace to one another
and one day stand together with all the saints
who praise you for your saving help.

We ask this in the name of your Son,
Jesus Christ, our Lord.

R. Amen.

PROCESSION TO THE
PLACE OF COMMITTAL

459 The assisting minister or the minister says:

In peace let us take N. to his/her place of rest.

If a symbol of the Christian life has been placed on the coffin, it should be removed at this time.

The procession then begins: the minister and assisting ministers precede the coffin; the family and mourners follow.

One or more of the following texts or other suitable songs may be sung during the procession to the entrance of the church. The singing may continue during the journey to the place of committal.

A   The following antiphon may be sung with verses from Psalm 24 (25), p. 429.

May the angels lead you into paradise;   50
may the martyrs come to welcome you
and take you to the holy city,
the new and eternal Jerusalem.

B   The following antiphon may be sung with verses from Psalm 114 (116), p. 430, or separately.

May choirs of angels welcome you   50
and lead you to the bosom of Abraham;
and where Lazarus is poor no longer
may you find eternal rest.

C   May saints and angels lead you on,
Escorting you where Christ has gone.
Now he has called you, come to him
Who sits above the seraphim.

Come to the peace of Abraham
And to the supper of the Lamb:
Come to the glory of the blessed,
And to perpetual light and rest.

D   Another suitable psalm may also be used.

RITE OF COMMITTAL

INVITATION

> 460 When the funeral procession arrives at the place of committal, the minister says one of the following, or a similar invitation.

A The life which this child N. received from his/her parents is not destroyed by death. God has taken him/her into eternal life.

As we commit his/her body to the earth, let us comfort each other in our sorrow with the assurance of our faith, that one day we will be reunited with N.

B For burial of ashes

My friends, as we prepare to bury/entomb the ashes of this child/baby, we recall that our bodies bear the imprint of the first creation when they were fashioned from dust; but in faith we remember, too, that by the new creation we also bear the image of Jesus who was raised to glory.

SCRIPTURE VERSE

> 461 One of the following or another brief Scripture verse is read. The minister first says:

We read in sacred Scripture:

A Matthew 25:34   119

Come, you whom my Father has blessed, says the Lord;
 inherit the kingdom prepared for you since the foundation
  of the world.

B John 6:39   121

This is the will of my Father, says the Lord,
that I should lose nothing of all that he has given to me,
and that I should raise it up on the last day.

C Philippians 3:20   124

Our true home is in heaven,
and Jesus Christ whose return we long for
will come from heaven to save us.

D Apocalypse 1:5-6   126

Jesus Christ is the first-born of the dead;
glory and kingship be his for ever and ever. Amen.

Prayer over the Place of Committal

462 The minister says one of the following prayers.

A   All praise to you, Lord of all creation.
      Praise to you, holy and living God.
      We praise and bless you for your mercy,
      we praise and bless you for your kindness.
      Blessed is the Lord, our God.

      R. Blessed is the Lord, our God.

      You sanctify the homes of the living
      and make holy the places of the dead.
      You alone open the gates of righteousness
      and lead us to the dwellings of the saints.
      Blessed is the Lord, our God.

      R. Blessed is the Lord, our God.

      We praise you, our refuge and strength.
      We bless you, our God and Redeemer.
      Your praise is always in our hearts and on our lips.
      We remember the mighty deeds of the covenant.
      Blessed is the Lord, our God.

      R. Blessed is the Lord, our God.

      Almighty and ever-living God,
      remember the love with which you graced
          your child N. in [his/her short] life.
      Receive him/her, we pray, into the mansions of the saints.
      As we make ready this resting place,
      look also with favour on those who mourn
      and comfort them in their loss.

      Grant this through Christ our Lord.

      R. Amen.

B   Almighty and ever-living God,
in you we place our trust and hope,
in you the dead whose bodies were temples of the Spirit
    find everlasting peace.

As we take leave of N.,
give our hearts peace in the firm hope
that one day he/she will live
in the mansion you have prepared for him/her in heaven.

We ask this through Christ our Lord.

R. Amen.

C   If the place of committal is to be blessed

O God,
by whose mercy the faithful departed find rest,
bless this grave,
and send your holy angel to watch over it.

As we bury here the body of N.,
welcome him/her into your presence,
that he/she may rejoice in you with your saints for ever.

We ask this through Christ our Lord.

R. Amen.

COMMITTAL

463 The minister then says the words of committal. One of the
following texts is used, during or after which the coffin is lowered.

A   A baptized child

Into your hands, O merciful Saviour, we commend N.
Acknowledge, we humbly beseech you,
a sheep of your own fold, a lamb of your own flock.
Receive him/her into the arms of your mercy,
into the blessed rest of everlasting peace,
and into the glorious company of the saints in light.

B   A child who died before baptism

Lord God,
ever-caring and gentle,
we commit to your love this little one [N.],
who brought joy to our lives for so short a time.
Enfold him/her in eternal life.

We pray for his/her parents
who are saddened by the loss of their child/baby.
Give them courage
and help them in their pain and grief.
May they all meet one day
in the joy and peace of your kingdom.

We ask this through Christ our Lord.

R. Amen.

C   For burial of ashes

Faithful God,
Lord of all creation,
you desire that nothing redeemed by your Son
will ever be lost,
and that the just will be raised up on the last day.

Comfort us today with the word of your promise
as we return the ashes of N. to the earth.

Grant him/her a place of rest and peace
where the world of dust and ashes has no dominion.
Confirm us in our hope that he/she will be created anew
on the day when you will raise him/her up in glory
to live with you and all the saints
for ever and ever.

R. Amen.

CONCLUDING RITE

PRAYER OVER THE PEOPLE

464 The assisting minister or the minister says:

Bow your heads and pray for God's blessing.

All pray silently. The minister, with hands outstretched over the people, says one of the following prayers.

A Merciful Lord,
you know the anguish of the sorrowful,
you are attentive to the prayers of the humble.
Hear your people
who cry out to you in their need,
and strengthen their hope in your lasting goodness.
We ask this through Christ our Lord.
R. Amen.

B

Most merciful God,
whose wisdom is beyond our understanding,
surround the family of N. with your love,
that they may not be overwhelmed by their loss,
but have confidence in your goodness,
and strength to meet the days to come.
We ask this through Christ our Lord.
R. Amen.

The minister then says the following:

Eternal rest grant unto him/her, O Lord.

R. And let perpetual light shine upon him/her.

May he/she rest in peace.

R. Amen.

May his/her soul and the souls of all the faithful departed,
through the mercy of God, rest in peace.

R. Amen.

A minister who is a priest or deacon says:

May the peace of God,
which is beyond all understanding,
keep your hearts and minds
in the knowledge and love of God
and of his Son, our Lord Jesus Christ.

R. Amen.

May almighty God bless you,
the Father, and the Son, ✠ and the Holy Spirit.

R. Amen.

A minister who is a priest or deacon says:

May the love of God and the peace of the Lord Jesus Christ
console you
and gently wipe every tear from your eyes.

R. Amen.

May almighty God bless you,
the Father, and the Son, ✠ and the Holy Spirit.

R. Amen.

A lay minister invokes God's blessing and signs himself or herself with the sign of the cross, saying:

May the love of God and the peace of the Lord Jesus Christ
bless and console us
and gently wipe every tear from our eyes:
in the name of the Father,
and of the Son, and of the Holy Spirit.

R. Amen.

The minister then concludes:

Go in the peace of Christ.

R. Thanks be to God.

A hymn or song may conclude the rite. Some sign or gesture
of leave-taking may be made.

OUTLINE OF THE RITE

Invitation
Scripture Verse
Prayer before Committal

Signs of Farewell
Committal
Intercessions
The Lord's Prayer
Concluding Prayer

Prayer over the People

19 RITE OF COMMITTAL AT A CREMATORIUM
WHEN A FUNERAL LITURGY HAS IMMEDIATELY PRECEDED

INVITATION

465 When all have gathered in the crematorium chapel, the minister says the following or a similar invitation.

The life which this child/baby N. received from his/her parents is not destroyed by death. God has taken him/her into eternal life.

As we commit his/her body to be cremated, let us comfort each other in our sorrow with the assurance of our faith, that one day we will be reunited with N.

SCRIPTURE VERSE

466 One of the following or another brief Scripture verse is read. The minister first says:

We read in sacred Scripture:

A   Matthew 25:34   119

Come, you whom my Father has blessed, says the Lord;
inherit the kingdom prepared for you since the foundation
    of the world.

B   John 6:39   121

This is the will of my Father, says the Lord,
that I should lose nothing of all that he has given to me,
and that I should raise it up on the last day.

C   Philippians 3:20   124

Our true home is in heaven,
and Jesus Christ whose return we long for
will come from heaven to save us.

D   Apocalypse 1:5-6   126

Jesus Christ is the first-born of the dead;
glory and kingship be his for ever and ever. Amen.

Prayer before Committal

467 The minister says one of the following prayers.

A Almighty and ever-living God,
   remember the love with which you graced
      your child N. in [his/her short] life.
   Receive him/her, we pray, into the mansions of the saints.
   Look with favour on those who mourn
   and comfort them in their loss.

   Grant this through Christ our Lord.

   R. Amen.

B Almighty and ever-living God,
   in you we place our trust and hope,
   in you the dead, whose bodies were temples of the Spirit,
      find everlasting peace.

   As we take leave of N.,
   give our hearts peace in the firm hope
   that one day he/she will live
   in the mansion you have prepared for him/her in heaven.

   We ask this through Christ our Lord.

   R. Amen.

Signs of Farewell

468 The coffin of a baptized child may now be sprinkled with holy water and incensed, or this may take place at the end of the rite. The family and other mourners may also sprinkle the coffin with holy water now or at the end of the rite, if the coffin remains in view.

In the case of an unbaptized child a suitable sign may be used: for example, the minister may place his or her hand on the coffin and invite others to do the same.

COMMITTAL

469 The minister then says the words of committal. One of the
following texts is used, during or after which the coffin may be
removed from view.

A A baptized child

Into your hands, O merciful Saviour, we commend N.
Acknowledge, we humbly beseech you,
a sheep of your own fold, a lamb of your own flock.
Receive him/her into the arms of your mercy,
into the blessed rest of everlasting peace,
and into the glorious company of the saints in light.

B A child who died before baptism

Lord God,
ever-caring and gentle,
we commit to your love this little one [N.],
who brought joy to our lives for so short a time.
Enfold him/her in eternal life.

We pray for his/her parents
who are saddened by the loss of their child/baby.
Give them courage
and help them in their pain and grief.
May they all meet one day
in the joy and peace of your kingdom.

We ask this through Christ our Lord.

R. Amen.

470 The following intercessions may be used or adapted to the circumstances, or new intercessions may be composed.

The minister begins:

Dear friends, let us turn to the Lord, the God of hope and consolation, who calls us to everlasting glory in Christ Jesus.

A reader or the minister then continues:

For N., that he/she may now enjoy the place prepared for him/her in your great love.
Lord, in your mercy.

R. Hear our prayer.

For N.'s father and mother [and brother(s) and sister(s)], that they may know our love and support in their grief.
Lord, in your mercy.

R. Hear our prayer.

For his/her friends [and teachers], that they may love one another as you have loved us.
Lord, in your mercy.

R. Hear our prayer.

For this community, that we may bear one another's burdens.
Lord, in your mercy.

R. Hear our prayer.

For all those who mourn their children, that they may be comforted.
Lord, in your mercy.

R. Hear our prayer.

For all who are in need, that the fearful may find peace, the weary rest, and the oppressed freedom.
Lord, in your mercy.

R. Hear our prayer.

The Lord's Prayer

471 Using one of the following invitations, or in similar words, the minister invites those present to pray the Lord's Prayer.

A   Now let us pray as Christ the Lord has taught us:

B   With longing for the coming of God's kingdom, let us offer our prayer to the Father:

C   As sons and daughters of a loving God, we pray in the confident words of his Son:

D   When Jesus gathered his disciples around him, he taught them to pray:

All say:

Our Father . . .

Concluding Prayer

472 The minister says one of the following prayers or one of those provided in nos. 580-581, p. 407.

A   A baptized child

Tender Shepherd of the flock,
N. has entered your kingdom
and now lies cradled in your love.
Soothe the hearts of his/her parents
and bring peace to their lives.
Enlighten their faith
and give hope to their hearts.

Loving God,
grant mercy to your entire family in this time of suffering.
Comfort us in the knowledge that this child [N.]
lives with you and your Son, Jesus Christ,
and the Holy Spirit,
for ever and ever.

R. Amen.

Listen, O God, to the prayers of your Church
on behalf of the faithful departed,
and grant to your child, N.,
whose funeral we have celebrated today,
the inheritance promised to all your saints.

We ask this through Christ our Lord.

R. Amen.

C   A child who died before baptism

God of mercy,
in the mystery of your wisdom
you have drawn this child [N.] to yourself.
In the midst of our pain and sorrow,
we acknowledge you as Lord of the living and the dead
and we search for our peace in your will.
In these final moments we stand together in prayer,
believing in your compassion and generous love.
Deliver this child [N.] out of death
and grant him/her a place in your kingdom of peace.

We ask this through Christ our Lord.

R. Amen.

Prayer over the People

473 The assisting minister or the minister says:

Bow your heads and pray for God's blessing.

All pray silently. The minister, with hands outstretched over the people, says one of the following prayers.

A   Merciful Lord,
     you know the anguish of the sorrowful,
     you are attentive to the prayers of the humble.
     Hear your people
     who cry out to you in their need,
     and strengthen their hope in your lasting goodness.

     We ask this through Christ our Lord.

     R. Amen.

B
     Most merciful God,
     whose wisdom is beyond our understanding,
     surround the family of N. with your love,
     that they may not be overwhelmed by their loss,
     but have confidence in your goodness,
     and strength to meet the days to come.

     We ask this through Christ our Lord.

     R. Amen.

The minister then says the following:

Eternal rest grant unto him/her, O Lord.

R. And let perpetual light shine upon him/her.

May he/she rest in peace.

R. Amen.

May his/her soul and the souls of all the faithful departed,
through the mercy of God, rest in peace.

R. Amen.

A   A minister who is a priest or deacon says:

May the peace of God,
which is beyond all understanding,
keep your hearts and minds
in the knowledge and love of God
and of his Son, our Lord Jesus Christ.

R. **Amen.**

May almighty God bless you,
the Father, and the Son, ✠ and the Holy Spirit.

R. **Amen.**

B   A minister who is a priest or deacon says:

May the love of God and the peace of the Lord Jesus Christ
console you
and gently wipe every tear from your eyes.

R. **Amen.**

May almighty God bless you,
the Father, and the Son, ✠ and the Holy Spirit.

R. **Amen.**

C   A lay minister invokes God's blessing and signs himself or her-
           self with the sign of the cross, saying:

May the love of God and the peace of the Lord Jesus Christ
bless and console us
and gently wipe every tear from our eyes:
in the name of the Father,
and of the Son, and of the Holy Spirit.

R. **Amen.**

The minister then concludes:

Go in the peace of Christ.

R. **Thanks be to God.**

A hymn or song may conclude the rite. Some sign or gesture
of leave-taking may be made, if this has not taken place earlier,
and if the coffin remains in view.

OUTLINE OF THE RITE

Greeting
Invitation
Scripture Verse

Invitation to Prayer
Silence
Signs of Farewell
Song of Farewell
Prayer of Commendation
   and the Committal

Prayer over the People

20 RITE OF COMMITTAL AT A CREMATORIUM WITH FINAL COMMENDATION

WHEN A FUNERAL LITURGY HAS NOT IMMEDIATELY PRECEDED

GREETING

474 When all have gathered in the crematorium chapel, the minister welcomes the funeral party and, using one of the following greetings, or in similar words, greets them.

A   May Christ Jesus, who welcomed children and laid his hands in blessing upon them, comfort you with his peace and be always with you.

    R. And also with you.

B   May the God of hope give you the fullness of peace, and may the Lord of life be always with you.

    R. And also with you.

C   The grace and peace of God our Father, who raised Jesus from the dead, be always with you.

    R. And also with you.

D   May the Father of mercies, the God of all consolation, be with you.

    R. And also with you.

E   The grace of our Lord Jesus Christ, and the love of God, and the fellowship of the Holy Spirit be with you all.

    R. And also with you.

Invitation

475 The minister then says the following or a similar invitation.

The life which this child/baby N. received from his/her parents is not destroyed by death. God has taken him/her into eternal life.

As we commend N. to God and commit his/her body to be cremated, let us express in [song and] prayer our common faith in the resurrection. As Jesus Christ was raised from the dead, we too are called to follow him through death to the glory where God will be all in all.

A hymn or song may be sung.

Scripture Verse

476 One of the following or another brief Scripture verse is read.
The minister first says:

We read in sacred Scripture:

A   Matthew 25:34   119

Come, you whom my Father has blessed, says the Lord;
inherit the kingdom prepared for you since the foundation
of the world.

B   John 6:39   121

This is the will of my Father, says the Lord,
that I should lose nothing of all that he has given to me,
and that I should raise it up on the last day.

C   Philippians 3:20   124

Our true home is in heaven,
and Jesus Christ whose return we long for
will come from heaven to save us.

D   Apocalypse 1:5-6   126

Jesus Christ is the first-born of the dead;
glory and kingship be his for ever and ever. Amen.

INVITATION TO PRAYER

477 Using one of the following invitations, or in similar words,
the minister begins the final commendation.

A   A baptized child

God in his wisdom knows the span of our days; he has chosen   227
to call to himself this child, whom he adopted as his own in
baptism. The body of N. will one day rise again to a new and
radiant life that will never end.

Our firm belief is that N., because he/she was baptized, has already entered this new life; our firm hope is that we shall do
the same. Let us ask God to comfort his/her family and friends
and to increase our desire for the joys of heaven.

B   A baptized child

With faith in Jesus Christ, we bid farewell to N.   228

Let us pray with confidence to God, in whose sight all creation
lives, that he will raise up in holiness and power the mortal body
of this [little] child, for God has chosen to number his/her soul
among the blessed.

C   A child who died before baptism

Let us commend this child/baby to the Lord's merciful keep-   237
ing; and let us pray with all our hearts for N. and N. Even as
they grieve at the loss of their [little] child, they entrust him/her
to the loving embrace of God.

SILENCE

478 All pray in silence.

Signs of Farewell

479 The coffin of a baptized child may now be sprinkled with holy water and incensed, or this may take place during or after the song of farewell. The family and other mourners may also sprinkle the coffin with holy water now or at the end of the rite, if the coffin remains in view.

In the case of an unbaptized child a suitable sign may be used: for example, the minister may place his or her hand on the coffin during the song of farewell and invite others to do the same.

Song of Farewell

480 The song of farewell is then sung. One of the following texts or another suitable hymn or song may be used.

A I know that my Redeemer lives,   189
And on that final day of days,
His voice shall bid me rise again:
Unending joy, unceasing praise!

This hope I cherish in my heart:
To stand on earth, my flesh restored,
And, not a stranger but a friend,
Behold my Saviour and my Lord.

Tune: LM, for example, Duke Street

B Saints of God, come to his/her aid!   47
Hasten to meet him/her, angels of the Lord!   66
R. Receive his/her soul and present him/her
to God the Most High.

May Christ, who called you, take you to himself;
may angels lead you to the bosom of Abraham.
R. Receive his/her soul and present him/her
to God the Most High.

Eternal rest grant unto him/her, O Lord,
and let perpetual light shine upon him/her.
R. Receive his/her soul and present him/her
to God the Most High.

Prayer of Commendation and the Committal

481 The minister then says one of the following prayers, during or after which the coffin may be removed from view.

A   A baptized child

You are the author and sustainer of our lives, O God.
You are our final home.
We commend to you N., our child/baby.

In baptism he/she began his/her journey toward you.
Take him/her now to yourself
and give him/her the life
promised to those born again of water and the Spirit.

Turn also to us who have suffered this loss.
Strengthen the bonds of this family and our community.
Confirm us in faith, in hope, and in love,
so that we may bear your peace to one another
and one day stand together with all the saints
who praise you for your saving help.

We ask this in the name of your Son,
whom you raised from among the dead,
Jesus Christ, our Lord.

R. Amen.

B   A baptized child

Lord Jesus,
like a shepherd who gathers the lambs
to protect them from all harm,
you led N. to the waters of baptism
and shielded him/her in innocence.

Now carry this little one
on the path to your kingdom of light
where he/she will find happiness
and every tear will be wiped away.

To you be glory, now and for ever.

R. Amen.

C   A baptized child

Into your gentle keeping, O Lord,
we commend this child N.
Though our hearts are troubled,
we hope in your loving kindness.

By the sign of the cross
he/she was claimed for Christ,
and in the waters of baptism
he/she died with Christ to live in him for ever.

May the angels, our guardians,
lead him/her now to paradise
where your saints will welcome him/her
and every tear will be wiped away.
There we shall join in songs of praise for ever.

We ask this through Christ our Lord.

R. Amen.

D   A child who died before baptism

You are the author and sustainer of our lives, O God,
you are our final home.
We commend to you N., our child/baby.

Trusting in your mercy
and in your all-embracing love,
we pray that you give him/her happiness for ever.

Turn also to us who have suffered this loss.
Strengthen the bonds of this family and our community.
Confirm us in faith, in hope, and in love,
so that we may bear your peace to one another
and one day stand together with all the saints
who praise you for your saving help.

We ask this in the name of your Son,
Jesus Christ, our Lord.

R. Amen.

Prayer over the People

482 The assisting minister or the minister says:

Bow your heads and pray for God's blessing.

All pray silently. The minister, with hands outstretched over the people, says one of the following prayers.

A Merciful Lord,
   you know the anguish of the sorrowful,
   you are attentive to the prayers of the humble.
   Hear your people
   who cry out to you in their need,
   and strengthen their hope in your lasting goodness.
   We ask this through Christ our Lord.
   R. Amen.

B Most merciful God,
   whose wisdom is beyond our understanding,
   surround the family of N. with your love,
   that they may not be overwhelmed by their loss,
   but have confidence in your goodness,
   and strength to meet the days to come.
   We ask this through Christ our Lord.
   R. Amen.

The minister then says the following:

Eternal rest grant unto him/her, O Lord.
R. And let perpetual light shine upon him/her.

May he/she rest in peace.
R. Amen.

May his/her soul and the souls of all the faithful departed,
through the mercy of God, rest in peace.
R. Amen.

A   A minister who is a priest or deacon says:

May the peace of God,
which is beyond all understanding,
keep your hearts and minds
in the knowledge and love of God
and of his Son, our Lord Jesus Christ.

R. Amen.

May almighty God bless you,
the Father, and the Son, ✠ and the Holy Spirit.

R. Amen.

B   A minister who is a priest or deacon says:

May the love of God and the peace of the Lord Jesus Christ
console you
and gently wipe every tear from your eyes.

R. Amen.

May almighty God bless you,
the Father, and the Son, ✠ and the Holy Spirit.

R. Amen.

C   A lay minister invokes God's blessing and signs himself or her-
         self with the sign of the cross, saying:

May the love of God and the peace of the Lord Jesus Christ
bless and console us
and gently wipe every tear from our eyes:
in the name of the Father,
and of the Son, and of the Holy Spirit.

R. Amen.

         The minister then concludes:

Go in the peace of Christ.

R. Thanks be to God.

         A hymn or song may conclude the rite. Some sign or gesture
         of leave-taking may be made, if this has not taken place earlier,
         and if the coffin remains in view.

OUTLINE OF THE RITE

INTRODUCTORY RITES

Greeting
Sprinkling with Holy Water
   or Brief Address
Entrance Procession
[Placing of the Pall]
[Placing of Christian Symbols]
Invitation to Prayer
Opening Prayer

LITURGY OF THE WORD

Readings
Homily
General Intercessions
   Intercessions
   The Lord's Prayer
   Concluding Prayer

FINAL COMMENDATION

Invitation to Prayer
Silence
Signs of Farewell
Song of Farewell
Prayer of Commendation
   and the Committal

CONCLUDING RITE

Prayer over the People

21 RITE OF COMMITTAL FOR CREMATION
WHEN NO OTHER LITURGY HAS TAKEN PLACE

INTRODUCTORY RITES

GREETING

483 At or near the entrance to the crematorium chapel, the minister welcomes the funeral party and, using one of the following greetings, or in similar words, greets them.

A May Christ Jesus, who welcomed children and laid his hands in blessing upon them, comfort you with his peace and be always with you.

R. And also with you.

B May the God of hope give you the fullness of peace, and may the Lord of life be always with you.

R. And also with you.

C The grace and peace of God our Father, who raised Jesus from the dead, be always with you.

R. And also with you.

D May the Father of mercies, the God of all consolation, be with you.

R. And also with you.

E The grace of our Lord Jesus Christ, and the love of God, and the fellowship of the Holy Spirit be with you all.

R. And also with you.

Sprinkling with Holy Water or Brief Address

484 If the child was baptized, the minister sprinkles the coffin with holy water (option A). If the child died before baptism, the sprinkling with holy water is omitted and a brief address is given (option B).

A   SPRINKLING WITH HOLY WATER—If the child was baptized, the minister then sprinkles the coffin with holy water, saying:

In the waters of baptism
N. died with Christ and rose with him to new life.
May he/she now share with him eternal glory.

B   BRIEF ADDRESS—If the child died before baptism, the minister may address the mourners using the following or similar words.

My brothers and sisters, the Lord is a faithful God who created us all after his own image. All things are of his making, all creation awaits the day of salvation. We now entrust the soul of N. to the abundant mercy of God, that our beloved child may find a home in his kingdom.

Entrance Procession

485 The Easter candle may be placed beforehand near the position the coffin will occupy at the conclusion of the procession. The minister precedes the coffin and the mourners into the chapel. During the procession a psalm, song, or responsory is sung.

Placing of the Pall

486 If it is the custom in the local community and the child was baptized, the pall is then placed on the coffin by family members, friends, or the minister.

Placing of Christian Symbols

487 A symbol of the Christian life, such as a Book of the Gospels, a Bible, or a cross, may be carried in procession, then placed on the coffin, either in silence or as one of the following texts is said.

A   Book of the Gospels or Bible

May Christ greet N. with these words of eternal life:
Come, blessed of my Father!

B   Cross, for a baptized child

In baptism N. received the sign of the cross.
May he/she now share
in Christ's victory over sin and death.

C   Cross, for a child who died before baptism

The cross we have brought here today was carried by the Lord
Jesus in the hour of his suffering.

We place it now on/near this coffin as a sign of our hope for N.

As the cross is placed on or near the coffin, the minister says:

Lord Jesus Christ,
you loved us unto death.
Let this cross be a sign of your love for N.
and for the people you have gathered here today.

INVITATION TO PRAYER

488 Using one of the following texts, or in similar words, the
minister invites those present to pray.

A   Let us pray for this child/baby and entrust him/her to the care
of our loving God.

B   My brothers and sisters, we have come together to renew our
trust in Christ who, by dying on the cross, has freed us from
eternal death and, by rising, has opened for us the gates of
heaven.

Let us pray that the Lord may grant us the gift of his loving
consolation.

489 After a brief period of silent prayer, the minister says one of the following prayers or one of those provided in nos. 580-581, p. 407.

A   A baptized child

To you, O Lord,   224
we humbly entrust this child,
so precious in your sight.
Take him/her into your arms
and welcome him/her into paradise,
where there will be no sorrow, no weeping nor pain,
but the fullness of peace and joy
with your Son and the Holy Spirit
for ever and ever.
R. Amen.

B   A baptized child

Lord, in our grief we call upon your mercy: 223
open your ears to our prayers,
and one day unite us again with N.,
who, we firmly trust,
already enjoys eternal life in your kingdom.

We ask this through our Lord Jesus Christ, your Son,
who lives and reigns with you and the Holy Spirit,
one God, for ever and ever.
R. Amen.

C   A baptized child

Lord God,
from whom human sadness is never hidden,
you know the burden of grief
that we feel at the loss of this child.

As we mourn his/her passing from this life,
comfort us with the knowledge
that N. lives now in your loving embrace.

We make our prayer through our Lord Jesus Christ, your Son,
who lives and reigns with you and the Holy Spirit,
one God, for ever and ever.
R. Amen.

D   A baptized child

Merciful Lord,
whose wisdom is beyond human understanding,
you adopted N. as your own in baptism
and have taken him/her to yourself
even as he/she stood on the threshold of life.
Listen to our prayers and extend to us your grace,
that one day we may share eternal life with N.,
for we firmly believe that he/she now rests with you.

We ask this through our Lord Jesus Christ, your Son,
who lives and reigns with you and the Holy Spirit,
one God, for ever and ever.

R. Amen.

E   A child who died before baptism   236

God of all consolation,
searcher of mind and heart,
the faith of these parents [N. and N.] is known to you.

Comfort them with the knowledge
that the child for whom they grieve
is entrusted now to your loving care.

We ask this through our Lord Jesus Christ, your Son,
who lives and reigns with you and the Holy Spirit,
one God, for ever and ever.

R. Amen.

F   A child who died before baptism   235

O Lord, whose ways are beyond understanding,
listen to the prayers of your faithful people:
that those weighed down by grief
    at the loss of this [little] child
may find reassurance in your infinite goodness.

We ask this through our Lord Jesus Christ, your Son,
who lives and reigns with you and the Holy Spirit,
one God, for ever and ever.

R. Amen.

LITURGY OF THE WORD

READINGS

490 After the introductory rites, the liturgy of the word is celebrated. Depending upon pastoral circumstances, either one or
two readings may be read before the gospel. If only one reading
is possible it should be the gospel. Between the readings a psalm
or suitable song may be used.

HOMILY

491 A brief homily is given after the gospel reading.

GENERAL INTERCESSIONS

492 The general intercessions are then said.

INTERCESSIONS

493 One of the following sets of intercessions may be used or
adapted to the circumstances, or new intercessions may be
composed.

A The minister begins:

The Lord Jesus is the lover of his people and our only sure hope.
Let us ask him to deepen our faith and sustain us in this dark
hour.

A reader or the minister then continues:

You became a little child for our sake, sharing our human life.
To you we pray:
R. Bless us and keep us, O Lord.

You grew in wisdom, age and grace, and learned obedience
through suffering.
To you we pray:
R. Bless us and keep us, O Lord.

You welcomed children, promising them your kingdom.
To you we pray:
R. Bless us and keep us, O Lord.

You comforted those who mourned the loss of children and friends. To you we pray:

R. Bless us and keep us, O Lord.

You took upon yourself the suffering and death of us all. To you we pray:

R. Bless us and keep us, O Lord.

You promised to raise up those who believe in you, just as you were raised up in glory by the Father. To you we pray:

R. Bless us and keep us, O Lord.

B   The minister begins:

Let us pray for N., his/her family and friends, and for all God's people.

A reader or the minister then continues:

For N., child of God [and heir to the kingdom], that he/she be held securely in God's loving embrace now and for all eternity. We pray to the Lord.

R. Lord, hear our prayer.

For N.'s family, especially his/her mother and father, [his/her brother(s) and sister(s),] that they feel the healing power of Christ in the midst of their pain and grief. We pray to the Lord.

R. Lord, hear our prayer.

For N.'s friends, those who played with him/her and those who cared for him/her, that they be consoled in their loss and strengthened in their love for one another. We pray to the Lord.

R. Lord, hear our prayer.

For all parents who grieve over the death of their children, that they be comforted in the knowledge that their children dwell with God. We pray to the Lord.

R. Lord, hear our prayer.

For children who have died of hunger and disease, that these little ones be seated close to the Lord at his heavenly table. We pray to the Lord.

R. Lord, hear our prayer.

For the whole Church, that we prepare worthily for the hour of our death, when God will call us by name to pass from this world to the next.
We pray to the Lord.

R. Lord, hear our prayer.

C   The minister begins:

Dear friends, let us turn to the Lord, the God of hope and consolation, who calls us to everlasting glory in Christ Jesus.

A reader or the minister then continues:

For N., that he/she may now enjoy the place prepared for him/her in your great love.
Lord, in your mercy.

R. Hear our prayer.

For N.'s father and mother [and brother(s) and sister(s)], that they may know our love and support in their grief.
Lord, in your mercy.

R. Hear our prayer.

For his/her friends [and teachers], that they may love one another as you have loved us.
Lord, in your mercy.

R. Hear our prayer.

For this community, that we may bear one another's burdens.
Lord, in your mercy.

R. Hear our prayer.

For all those who mourn their children, that they may be comforted.
Lord, in your mercy.

R. Hear our prayer.

For all who are in need, that the fearful may find peace, the weary rest, and the oppressed freedom.
Lord, in your mercy.

R. Hear our prayer.

The Lord's Prayer

494 Using one of the following invitations, or in similar words, the minister invites those present to pray the Lord's Prayer.

A Now let us pray as Christ the Lord has taught us:

B With longing for the coming of God's kingdom, let us offer our prayer to the Father:

C As sons and daughters of a loving God, we pray in the confident words of his Son:

D When Jesus gathered his disciples around him, he taught them to pray:

All say:
Our Father . . .

Concluding Prayer

495 The minister says one of the following prayers or one of those provided in nos. 580-581, p. 407.

A   A baptized child

Lord God,
you entrusted N. to our care
and now you embrace him/her in your love.

Take N. into your keeping
together with all children who have died.

Comfort us, your sorrowing servants,
who seek to do your will
and to know your saving peace.

We ask this through Christ our Lord.

R. Amen.

B   A baptized child

Tender Shepherd of the flock,
N. has entered your kingdom
and now lies cradled in your love.
Soothe the hearts of his/her parents
and bring peace to their lives.
Enlighten their faith
and give hope to their hearts.

Loving God,
grant mercy to your entire family in this time of suffering.
Comfort us in the knowledge that this child [N.]
lives with you and your Son, Jesus Christ,
and the Holy Spirit,
for ever and ever.

R. Amen.

C   A baptized child   196

Listen, O God, to the prayers of your Church
on behalf of the faithful departed,
and grant to your child, N.,
whose funeral we celebrate today,
the inheritance promised to all your saints.

We ask this through Christ our Lord.

R. Amen.

D   A child who died before baptism

God of mercy,
in the mystery of your wisdom
you have drawn this child [N.] to yourself.
In the midst of our pain and sorrow,
we acknowledge you as Lord of the living and the dead
and we search for our peace in your will.
In these final moments we stand together in prayer,
believing in your compassion and generous love.
Deliver this child [N.] out of death
and grant him/her a place in your kingdom of peace.

We ask this through Christ our Lord.

R. Amen.

FINAL COMMENDATION

496 The minister then goes to a place near the coffin. If incense and holy water are to be used, they are carried by the assisting ministers.

A member or a friend of the family may speak in remembrance of the deceased child before the final commendation begins.

INVITATION TO PRAYER

497 Using one of the following invitations, or in similar words, the minister begins the final commendation.

A   A baptized child

God in his wisdom knows the span of our days; he has chosen   227
to call to himself this child, whom he adopted as his own in baptism. The body of N. will one day rise again to a new and radiant life that will never end.

Our firm belief is that N., because he/she was baptized, has already entered this new life; our firm hope is that we shall do the same. Let us ask God to comfort his/her family and friends and to increase our desire for the joys of heaven.

B   A baptized child

With faith in Jesus Christ, we bid farewell to N.   228

Let us pray with confidence to God, in whose sight all creation lives, that he will raise up in holiness and power the mortal body of this [little] child, for God has chosen to number him/her among the blessed.

C   A child who died before baptism   237

Let us commend this child/baby to the Lord's merciful keeping; and let us pray with all our hearts for N. and N. Even as they grieve at the loss of their [little] child, they entrust him/her to the loving embrace of God.

SILENCE

498 All pray in silence.

Signs of Farewell

499 The coffin of a baptized child may now be sprinkled with holy water and incensed, or this may take place during or after the song of farewell. The family and other mourners may also sprinkle the coffin with holy water now or at the end of the rite, if the coffin remains in view.

In the case of an unbaptized child a suitable sign may be used: for example, the minister may place his or her hand on the coffin during the song of farewell and invite others to do the same.

Song of Farewell

500 The song of farewell is then sung. One of the following texts or another suitable hymn or song may be used.

A   I know that my Redeemer lives,   189
And on that final day of days,
His voice shall bid me rise again:
Unending joy, unceasing praise!

This hope I cherish in my heart:
To stand on earth, my flesh restored,
And, not a stranger but a friend,
Behold my Saviour and my Lord.

Tune: LM, for example, Duke Street

B   Saints of God, come to his/her aid!   47
Hasten to meet him/her, angels of the Lord!   66
R. Receive his/her soul and present him/her
to God the Most High.

May Christ, who called you, take you to himself;
may angels lead you to the bosom of Abraham.
R. Receive his/her soul and present him/her
to God the Most High.

Eternal rest grant unto him/her, O Lord,
and let perpetual light shine upon him/her.
R. Receive his/her soul and present him/her
to God the Most High.

PRAYER OF COMMENDATION AND THE COMMITTAL

501 The minister then says one of the following prayers, during or after which the coffin may be removed from view.

A   A baptized child

You are the author and sustainer of our lives, O God.
You are our final home.
We commend to you N., our child/baby.

In baptism he/she began his/her journey toward you.
Take him/her now to yourself
and give him/her the life
promised to those born again of water and the Spirit.

Turn also to us who have suffered this loss.
Strengthen the bonds of this family and our community.
Confirm us in faith, in hope, and in love,
so that we may bear your peace to one another
and one day stand together with all the saints
who praise you for your saving help.

We ask this in the name of your Son,
whom you raised from among the dead,
Jesus Christ, our Lord.

R. Amen.

B   A baptized child

Lord Jesus,
like a shepherd who gathers the lambs
to protect them from all harm,
you led N. to the waters of baptism
and shielded him/her in innocence.

Now carry this little one
on the path to your kingdom of light
where he/she will find happiness
and every tear will be wiped away.

To you be glory, now and for ever.

R. Amen.

C A baptized child

Into your gentle keeping, O Lord,
we commend this child N.
Though our hearts are troubled,
we hope in your loving kindness.

By the sign of the cross
he/she was claimed for Christ,
and in the waters of baptism
he/she died with Christ to live in him for ever.

May the angels, our guardians,
lead him/her now to paradise
where your saints will welcome him/her
and every tear will be wiped away.
There we shall join in songs of praise for ever.

We ask this through Christ our Lord.

R. Amen.

D A child who died before baptism

You are the author and sustainer of our lives, O God,
you are our final home.
We commend to you N., our child/baby.

Trusting in your mercy
and in your all-embracing love,
we pray that you give him/her happiness for ever.

Turn also to us who have suffered this loss.
Strengthen the bonds of this family and our community.
Confirm us in faith, in hope, and in love,
so that we may bear your peace to one another
and one day stand together with all the saints
who praise you for your saving help.

We ask this in the name of your Son,
Jesus Christ, our Lord.

R. Amen.

CONCLUDING RITE

PRAYER OVER THE PEOPLE

502 The assisting minister or the minister says:

Bow your heads and pray for God's blessing.

All pray silently. The minister, with hands outstretched over the people, says one of the following prayers.

A　Merciful Lord,
you know the anguish of the sorrowful,
you are attentive to the prayers of the humble.
Hear your people
who cry out to you in their need,
and strengthen their hope in your lasting goodness.

We ask this through Christ our Lord.

R.　Amen.

B

Most merciful God,
whose wisdom is beyond our understanding,
surround the family of N. with your love,
that they may not be overwhelmed by their loss,
but have confidence in your goodness,
and strength to meet the days to come.

We ask this through Christ our Lord.

R.　Amen.

The minister then says the following:

Eternal rest grant unto him/her, O Lord.

R.　And let perpetual light shine upon him/her.

May he/she rest in peace.

R.　Amen.

May his/her soul and the souls of all the faithful departed,
through the mercy of God, rest in peace.

R.　Amen.

A   A minister who is a priest or deacon says:

May the peace of God,
which is beyond all understanding,
keep your hearts and minds
in the knowledge and love of God
and of his Son, our Lord Jesus Christ.

R. Amen.

May almighty God bless you,
the Father, and the Son, ✠ and the Holy Spirit.

R. Amen.

B   A minister who is a priest or deacon says:

May the love of God and the peace of the Lord Jesus Christ
console you
and gently wipe every tear from your eyes.

R. Amen.

May almighty God bless you,
the Father, and the Son, ✠ and the Holy Spirit.

R. Amen.

C   A lay minister invokes God's blessing and signs himself or herself with the sign of the cross, saying:

May the love of God and the peace of the Lord Jesus Christ
bless and console us
and gently wipe every tear from our eyes:
in the name of the Father,
and of the Son, and of the Holy Spirit.

R. Amen.

The minister then concludes:

Go in the peace of Christ.

R. Thanks be to God.

A hymn or song may conclude the rite. Some sign or gesture
of leave-taking may be made, if this has not taken place earlier,
and if the coffin remains in view.

OUTLINE OF THE RITE

Brief Address
Scripture Verse
Blessing of the Body
The Lord's Prayer
Prayer of Commendation
Blessing

22 RITE OF FINAL COMMENDATION FOR AN INFANT

503 The 'Rite of Final Commendation for an Infant' may be used in the case of a stillbirth or a newborn infant who dies shortly after birth, or may be adapted for use with parents who have suffered a miscarriage. This short rite of prayer with the parents is celebrated to give them comfort and to commend and entrust the infant to God. This rite is a model and the minister should adapt it to the circumstances. It may be used in the hospital or place of birth or at the time of the committal of the body.

BRIEF ADDRESS

504 In the following or similar words, the minister addresses those who have assembled.

Dear friends, in the face of death all human wisdom fails. Yet the Lord Jesus teaches us, by the three days he spent in the tomb, that death has no hold over us. Christ has conquered death; his dying and rising have redeemed us. Even in our sorrow for the loss of this little child, we believe that, one short sleep past, he/she will wake eternally.

SCRIPTURE VERSE

505 The minister then introduces the Scripture verse.

The Lord speaks to us now of our hope for this child in these words of consolation.

A member of the family or one of those present reads one of the following verses.

A   Romans 5:5

Hope is not deceptive, because the love of God has been poured into our hearts by the Holy Spirit which has been given to us.

B   1 John 3:2

My dear people, we are already the children of God but what we are to be in the future has not yet been revealed; all we know is, that when it is revealed we shall be like him because we shall see him as he really is.

Blessing of the Body

506 If the body of the child is present, the minister blesses it using the following words.

Trusting in Jesus, the loving Saviour,
who gathered children into his arms
and blessed the little ones,
we now commend this infant [N.]
   to that same embrace of love,
in the hope that he/she will rejoice
and be happy in the presence of Christ.

Then all join the minister, saying:

May the angels and saints lead him/her
to the place of light and peace
where one day
we will be brought together again.

The minister continues:

Lord Jesus,
lovingly receive this little child;
bless him/her
and take him/her to your Father.
We ask this in hope,
and we pray:

Lord, have mercy.

R. Lord, have mercy.

Christ, have mercy.

R. Christ, have mercy.

Lord, have mercy.

R. Lord, have mercy.

The Lord's Prayer

507 Using one of the following invitations, or in similar words, the minister invites those present to pray the Lord's Prayer.

A   Now let us pray as Christ the Lord has taught us:

B   With longing for the coming of God's kingdom, let us offer our prayer to the Father:

C   As sons and daughters of a loving God, we pray in the confident words of his Son:

D   When Jesus gathered his disciples around him, he taught them to pray:

All say:

Our Father . . .

Prayer of Commendation

508 The minister then says one of the following prayers.

A   Tender Shepherd of the flock,
N. now lies cradled in your love.
Soothe the hearts of his/her parents
and bring peace to their lives.
Enlighten their faith
and give hope to their hearts.

Loving God,
grant mercy to your entire family in this time of suffering.
Comfort us with the hope that this infant/baby [N.]
lives with you and your Son, Jesus Christ,
and the Holy Spirit,
for ever and ever.

R. Amen.

B For parents who have suffered a miscarriage

  The section in brackets should be omitted unless the parents wish
  to name the child.

Lord God,
ever-caring and gentle,
we commit to your love this little one,
who brought joy to our lives for so short a time.
Enfold him/her in eternal life.

[Lord, you formed this child in the womb;
you have known it by name before time began.
We now wish to name this little one N.:
a name we shall treasure in our hearts for ever.]

We pray for these parents
who are saddened by the loss of their baby.
Give them courage
and help them in their pain and grief.
May they all meet one day
in the joy and peace of your kingdom.

We ask this through Christ our Lord.

R. Amen.

BLESSING

  509 Using one of the following blessings, the minister blesses
  those present.

A A minister who is a priest or deacon says:

May the God of all consolation
bring you comfort and peace,
in the name of the Father, ✠ and of the Son,
and of the Holy Spirit.

R. Amen.

B A lay minister invokes God's blessing and signs himself or herself with the sign of the cross, saying:

May the God of all consolation
bring us comfort and peace,
in the name of the Father, and of the Son,
and of the Holy Spirit.

R. Amen.

Part III
FUNERALS FOR CATECHUMENS: GUIDELINES AND TEXTS

We shall not live on bread alone,
but on every word that comes from God

PART III
FUNERALS FOR CATECHUMENS: GUIDELINES AND TEXTS

510 Part III of the *Order of Christian Funerals* provides for funerals of catechumens, including children of catechetical age who died before baptism, since the Church recognises them as part of the household of Christ.[1]

Part III does not contain detailed rites, but provides some pastoral guidelines and selected prayers and texts for use in the various rites as presented in Parts I, II, and IV.

511 The minister, in consultation with those concerned, chooses those rites that best correspond to the particular needs and customs of the mourners. In some instances, for example, a funeral liturgy outside Mass may be more appropriate (see 189:3).

512 In the celebration of the funeral of catechumens, the Church offers worship, praise, and thanksgiving to God who calls all people to salvation, commends the catechumens to God's merciful love, and pleads for the forgiveness of their sins.

513 Those involved in planning the funeral rites for a catechumen should take into account the circumstances of death, the grief of the family, and the needs and customs of those taking part in the rites. Where the family has not shared the catechumen's journey of faith, particular sensitivity will be required to help them find support and consolation in the Church's liturgy.

514 In choosing the texts and elements of celebration, the minister should bear in mind that the catechumen had not yet celebrated the sacraments of initiation.

THE WORD OF GOD

515 In every celebraton for the dead, the Church attaches great importance to the reading of the word of God. For catechumens, this word has nourished their faith. They heard it proclaimed in the assembly and shared it with those who accompanied them on their journey of faith.[2] Texts appropriate for the funeral of a catechumen may be chosen from those given in the Lectionary, Volume III.

---

[1] See *Rite of Christian Initiation of Adults*, no. 47; Vatican Council II, Dogmatic Constitution on the Church *Lumen gentium*, no. 14; Decree on the Church's Missionary Activity *Ad gentes*, no. 14.

[2] See *Rite of Christian Initiation of Adults*, nos. 81-84.

516 The homilist, mindful of the part the catechumen played in the life of the Church, should dwell on God's compassionate love and on the paschal mystery of the Lord proclaimed in the Scripture readings. Since the catechumen sought to make this mystery present in his or her life, the homilist will offer the family and community consolation and strength, with a hope nourished by the saving word of God.

PRAYERS AND INTERCESSIONS

517 From the variety of prayers provided, the minister in consultation with the family should carefully select texts that truly capture the unspoken prayers and hopes of the assembly and also respond to the needs of the mourners. Prayers which speak of or allude to the baptismal and eucharistic status of the deceased (for example, 'faithful departed') are inappropriate for catechumens, since they have not yet celebrated the sacraments of initiation. Appropriate prayers and a model of intercessions are provided in this part.

SYMBOLS

Cross

518 A cross may be placed on the coffin as a reminder that the catechumen was marked by the cross in the 'Rite of Acceptance into the Order of Catechumens'.

Book of the Gospels or Bible

519 A book of the Gospels or a Bible, which may have been presented to the catechumen, may be placed on the coffin as a sign that Christ's followers live by the word of God and that fidelity to that word leads to eternal life.

Easter Candle and Other Candles

520 At its highest level of symbolism, the Easter candle is baptismal, since it reminds the faithful of their share in Christ's victory over sin and death by virtue of their initiation. But there are also other levels of meaning associated with the Easter candle in the funeral rites of the Church. For example, it reminds the faithful of Christ's undying presence among them. It recalls the Easter Vigil, the night when the Church awaits the Lord's resurrection and when new light for the living and the dead is kindled.

For these reasons, during the funeral liturgy of a catechumen or a child who died before baptism, and also during the vigil service, when celebrated in the church, the Easter candle may be placed beforehand near the position the coffin will occupy at the conclusion of the procession.

According to local custom, other candles may also be placed near the coffin during the funeral liturgy as a sign of reverence and solemnity.

Holy Water

521 Blessed or holy water reminds the assembly of the saving waters of baptism. Consequently, this symbol is inappropriate for the catechumen.

Pall

522 The Pall, a reminder of the baptismal garment, is similarly unsuitable for the funeral of a catechumen.

Incense

523 Incense may be used during the funeral liturgy as a sign of the community's prayer for the deceased catechumen rising to the throne of God, but the coffin itself should not be incensed (see no. 37).

23 PRAYERS AND TEXTS FOR CATECHUMENS

PRAYERS FOR THE DEAD

524 The following prayers for the dead may be used in the various rites of Parts I and II and in Part IV. The prayers should be chosen taking the character of the text into account as well as the place in the rite where it will occur. All of the prayers in this section end with the shorter conclusion. When a prayer is used as the opening prayer at the funeral liturgy, the longer conclusion is used.

1   God of loving kindness, 173
listen favourably to our prayers:
strengthen our belief that your Son has risen from the dead
and our hope that your servant N. will also rise again.

We ask this through Christ our Lord.

R. Amen.

2   O God,
in whom sinners find mercy and the saints find joy,
we pray to you for our brother/sister N.,
whose body we honour with Christian burial,
that he/she may be delivered from the bonds of death.
Admit him/her to the joyful company of your saints
and raise him/her on the last day
to rejoice in your presence for ever.

We ask this through Christ our Lord.

R. Amen.

3   Almighty and faithful Creator,
        all things are of your making,
        all people are shaped in your image.
        We now entrust the soul of N. to your goodness.
        In your infinite wisdom and power,
        work in him/her your merciful purpose,
        known to you alone from the beginning of time.
        Console the hearts of those who love him/her
        in the hope that all who trust in you
        will find peace and rest in your kingdom.

        We ask this in the name of Jesus the Lord.

        R. Amen.

4   All-powerful God,
        whose mercy is never withheld
        from those who call upon you in hope,
        look kindly on your servants N. and N.,
        who departed this life confessing your name,
        and number them among your saints for evermore.

        We ask this through Christ our Lord.

        R. Amen.

525 The following texts may be used during the 'Reception at the Church' (or, if there is no liturgy in church, at the cemetery or crematorium chapel.

In Place of Sprinkling with Holy Water—The minister may address the mourners in the following or in similar words.

My brothers and sisters, the Lord is a faithful God who created us all after his own image. All things are of his making, all creation awaits the day of salvation. We now entrust the soul of N. to the abundant mercy of God, that he/she may find a home in his kingdom.

Book of the Gospels or Bible—While the Book of the Gospels or Bible is placed on the coffin, the minister may say the following or similar words.

In life N. cherished the Gospel of Christ.
May Christ now greet him/her with these words of eternal life:
Come, blessed of my Father!

Cross—While a cross is placed on the coffin, the minister may say the following or similar words.

N. received the sign of the cross when he/she entered
the household of Christ.
My he/she now share in Christ's victory over sin and death.

526 The following intercessions and litany may be used and should be adapted according to the circumstances. Only the first form is appropriate for use at Mass.

1   The minister begins:

My dear friends, let us join with one another in praying to God, not only for our departed brother/sister, but also for the Church, for peace in the world, and for ourselves.

201

An assisting minister or the reader then continues:

That the bishops and priests of the Church, and all who preach the Gospel, may be given the strength to express in action the word they proclaim.
We pray to the Lord:

R. Lord, hear our prayer.

That those in public office may promote justice and peace.
We pray to the Lord:

R. Lord, hear our prayer.

That those who bear the cross of pain in mind or body may never feel forsaken by God.
We pray to the Lord:

R. Lord, hear our prayer.

That God may deliver the soul of his servant N. from punishment and from the powers of darkness.
We pray to the Lord:

R. Lord, hear our prayer.

That God in his mercy may blot out all his/her offences.
We pray to the Lord:

R. Lord, hear our prayer.

That God may establish him/her in light and peace.
We pray to the Lord:

R. Lord, hear our prayer.

That God may call him/her to happiness in the company of all
the saints.
We pray to the Lord:

R. Lord, hear our prayer.

That God may welcome into his glory those of our family and
friends who have departed this life.
We pray to the Lord:

R. Lord, hear our prayer.

That God may give a place in the kingdom of heaven to all the
faithful departed, and to all catechumens and elect who have
died.
We pray to the Lord:

R. Lord, hear our prayer.

The minister concludes:

God, our shelter and our strength,
you listen in love to the cry of your people:
hear the prayers we offer for our departed brothers and sisters.
Cleanse them of their sins
and grant them the fullness of redemption.

We ask this through Christ our Lord.

R. Amen.

The minister begins:

Let us turn to Christ Jesus with confidence and faith in the
power of his cross and resurrection:

An assisting minister or reader then continues:

Risen Lord, pattern of our life for ever:
Lord, have mercy.

R. Lord, have mercy.

Promise and image of what we shall be:
Lord, have mercy.

R. Lord, have mercy.

Son of God who came to destroy sin and death:
Lord, have mercy.

R. Lord, have mercy.

Word of God who delivered us from the fear of death:
Lord, have mercy.

R. Lord, have mercy.

Crucified Lord, forsaken in death, raised in glory:
Lord, have mercy.

R. Lord, have mercy.

Lord Jesus, gentle Shepherd who bring rest to our souls, give
peace to N. for ever:
Lord, have mercy.

R. Lord, have mercy.

Lord Jesus, you bless those who mourn and are in pain. Bless
N.'s family and friends who gather around him/her today:
Lord, have mercy.

R. Lord, have mercy.

3   A deceased child

The minister begins:

Let us pray for N., his/her family and friends, and for all God's
people.

An assisting minister or reader then continues:

For N., child of God, that he/she be held securely in God's loving embrace now and for all eternity.
We pray to the Lord.

R. Lord, hear our prayer.

For N.'s family, especially his/her mother and father, [his/her
brother(s) and sister(s),] that they feel the healing power of
Christ in the midst of their pain and grief.
We pray to the Lord.

R. Lord, hear our prayer.

For N.'s friends, those who played with him/her and those who cared for him/her, that they be consoled in their loss and strengthened in their love for one another.
We pray to the Lord.

R. Lord, hear our prayer.

For all parents who grieve over the death of their children, that they be comforted in the knowledge that their children dwell with God.
We pray to the Lord.

R. Lord, hear our prayer.

For children who have died of hunger and disease, that these little ones be seated close to the Lord at his heavenly table.
We pray to the Lord.

R. Lord, hear our prayer.

For the whole Church, that we prepare worthily for the hour of our death, when God will call us by name to pass from this world to the next.
We pray to the Lord.

R. Lord, hear our prayer.

The minister concludes:

Lord God,
you entrusted N. to our care
and now you embrace him/her in your love.

Take N. into your keeping
together with all children who have died.

Comfort us, your sorrowing servants,
who seek to do your will
and to know your saving peace.

We ask this through Christ our Lord.

R. Amen.

FINAL COMMENDATION AND FAREWELL

Prayer of Commendation

527 The following prayer is used as an alternative to the prayer of commendation.

To you, O Lord, we commend the soul of N. your servant;   192
in the sight of this world he/she is now dead;
in your sight may he/she live for ever.
Forgive whatever sins he/she committed through human
    weakness
and in your goodness grant him/her everlasting peace.

We ask this through Christ our Lord.

R. Amen.

RITE OF COMMITTAL

Concluding Prayer

528 The following prayer is used as an alternative to the concluding prayer.

Loving God, from whom all life proceeds   197
and by whose hand the dead are raised again,
though we are sinners, you wish always to hear us.
Accept the prayers we offer in sadness for your servant N.:
deliver his/her soul from death,
number him/her among your saints,
and clothe him/her with the robe of salvation
to enjoy for ever the delights of your kingdom.

We ask this through Christ our Lord.

R. Amen.

PART IV
OFFICE
FOR THE DEAD

*With the Lord there is mercy
and fullness of redemption*

PART IV
OFFICE
FOR THE DEAD

529 The vigil for the deceased may be celebrated in the form of some part of the office for the dead. To encourage this form of the vigil, the chief hours, 'Morning Prayer' and 'Evening Prayer', are provided here. When the funeral liturgy is celebrated the evening before the committal, it may be appropriate to celebrate morning prayer before the procession to the place of committal.

530 In the celebration of the office for the dead members of the Christian community gather to offer praise and thanks to God especially for the gifts of redemption and resurrection, to intercede for the dead, and to find strength in Christ's victory over death. When the community celebrates the hours, Christ the Mediator and High Priest is truly present through his Spirit in the gathered assembly, in the proclamation of God's word, and in the prayer and song of the Church.[1] The community's celebration of the hours acknowledges that spiritual bond that links the Church on earth with the Church in heaven, for it is in union with the whole Church that this prayer is offered on behalf of the deceased.

531 At morning prayer the Christian community recalls 'the resurrection of the Lord Jesus, the true light enlightening all people (see John 1:9) and "the sun of justice" (Malachi 4:2) "rising from on high" (Luke 1:78).'[2] The celebration of morning prayer from the office for the dead relates the death of the Christian to Christ's victory over death and affirms the hope that those who have received the light of Christ at baptism will share in that victory.

532 At evening prayer the Christian community gathers to give thanks for the gifts it has received, to recall the sacrifice of Jesus Christ and the saving works of redemption, and to call upon Christ, the evening star and unconquerable light.[3] Through evening prayer from the office for the dead the community gives thanks to God for the gift of life received by the deceased and praises the Father for the redemption brought about by the sacrifice of his Son, who is the joy-giving light and the true source of hope.

---

[1] See General Instruction of the Liturgy of the Hours, no. 13.

[2] General Instruction of the Liturgy of the Hours, no. 38.

[3] See General Instruction of the Liturgy of the Hours, no. 39.

STRUCTURE AND CONTENT OF
MORNING PRAYER AND EVENING PRAYER

533 Morning prayer and evening prayer from the office for the dead include the introduction (or the reception of the body), hymn, psalmody, reading, response to the word of God, gospel canticle, intercessions, concluding prayer, and dismissal.

In parishes and religious communities where it is appropriate, a simple form of morning and evening prayer may be celebrated. This may include an adapted introductory verse, a thanksgiving prayer, if the hymn cannot be sung, and one psalm. Other parts of the celebration may be adapted in accordance with the General Instruction on the Liturgy of the Hours.

INTRODUCTORY VERSE OR RECEPTION OF THE BODY

534 Morning prayer and evening prayer begin with the introductory verse, *O God, come to our aid*, except when the invitatory replaces it, or when the rite of reception of the body is celebrated, since this replaces both the introductory verse and the hymn.

HYMN

535 To set the tone for the hour, a hymn is sung.

PSALMODY

536 In praying the psalms of the office for the dead, the assembly offers God praise and intercedes for the deceased person and the mourners in the words of prayer that Jesus himself used during his life on earth. Through the psalms the assembly prays in the voice of Christ, who intercedes on its behalf before the Father. In the psalms of petition and lament it expresses its sorrow and its firm hope in the redemption won by Christ. In the psalms of praise the assembly has a foretaste of the destiny of its deceased member and its own destiny, participation in the liturgy of heaven, where every tear will be wiped away and the Lord's victory over death will be complete.

537 Since the psalms are songs, whenever possible, they should be sung. The manner of singing them may be:

    1. antiphonal, that is, two groups alternate singing the stanzas; the last stanza, the doxology, is sung by both groups;
    2. responsorial, that is, the antiphon is sung by all before and after each stanza and the stanzas are sung by a cantor;
    3. direct, that is, the stanzas are sung without interruption by all, by a choir, or by a cantor.

The rubrics for each psalm in morning prayer and evening prayer indicate a way for singing it; other ways may be used.

538 The psalmody of morning prayer from the office for the dead consists of Psalm 50(51), a psalm of lament and petition, Psalm 145(146) or Psalm 150, a psalm of praise, and an Old Testament canticle from Isaiah.

539 The psalmody of evening prayer consists of Psalm 120(121) and Psalm 129(130), two psalms of lament and petition, and a New Testament canticle from the letter of Paul to the Philippians.

540 For pastoral reasons, psalms other than those given in the office for the dead may be chosen, provided they are appropriate for the time of day and suitable for use in the office for the dead.[4]

READING

541 The reading of the word of God in the office for the dead proclaims the paschal mystery and conveys the hope of being gathered together again in God's kingdom. The short reading in place in the hour or a longer Scripture reading from the Lectionary, Volume III, may be used.[5] For pastoral reasons and if circumstances allow, a non-biblical reading may be included at morning or evening prayer in addition to the reading from Scripture, as is the practice in the office of readings.

RESPONSE TO THE WORD OF GOD

542 A period of silence may follow the reading, then a brief homily based on the reading. After the homily the short responsory or another responsorial song may be sung or recited.

GOSPEL CANTICLE

543 After the response to the word of God, the Canticle of Zechariah is sung at morning prayer and the Canticle of Mary at evening prayer as an expression of praise and thanksgiving for redemption.[6]

544 During the singing of the gospel canticle, the altar, then the presiding minister and the congregation may be incensed.

---

[4] See General Instruction of the Liturgy of the Hours, no. 252.

[5] See General Instruction of the Liturgy of the Hours, no. 46.

[6] See General Instruction of the Liturgy of the Hours, no. 50.

545 In the intercessions of the office for the dead, the assembly prays that the deceased and all who die marked with the sign of faith may rise again together in glory with Christ. The intercessions provided in the hour may be used or adapted to the circumstances, or new intercessions may be composed.

The minister introduces the intercessions. An assisting minister sings or says the intentions. In keeping with the form of the intentions in the liturgy of the hours, the assembly responds with either the second part of the intention or the response. After a brief introduction by the minister the assembly sings or says the Lord's Prayer.

CONCLUDING PRAYER AND DISMISSAL

546 The concluding prayer, proclaimed by the minister, completes the hour.

547 After the concluding prayer and before the dismissal a member of the family or a friend of the deceased may be invited to speak in remembrance of the deceased.

548 When the funeral liturgy is celebrated the evening before the committal, it may be appropriate to celebrate morning prayer before the procession to the place of committal. In such an instance the dismissal is omitted and the rite continues with the procession to the place of committal.

MINISTRY AND PARTICIPATION

549 The celebration of the office for the dead requires careful preparation, especially in the case of communities that may not be familiar with the liturgy of the hours. Priests and other ministers should provide catechesis on the place and significance of the liturgy of the hours in the life of the Church and the purpose of the celebration of the office for the dead. They should also encourage members of the parish community to participate in the celebration as an effective means of prayer for the deceased, as a sign of their concern and support for the family and close friends, and as a sign of faith and hope in the paschal mystery. This catechesis will help to ensure the full and active participation of the assembly in the celebration of the office for the dead.

550 The office for the dead may be celebrated in the home, the chapel of rest, or in the church. In special circumstances, when the office is com-

bined with the funeral liturgy, care should be taken that the celebration not be too lengthy.[7]

551 The place in which the celebration occurs will often suggest adaptations. A celebration in the home of the deceased, for example, may be simplified or shortened.

552 A priest or deacon should normally preside whenever the office for the dead is celebrated with a congregation; other ministers (a reader, a cantor, an acolyte) should exercise their proper ministries. In the absence of a priest or deacon, a layperson presides.

Whenever possible, ministers should involve the family of the deceased in the planning of the hour and in the designation of ministers.

The minister vests according to local custom. If morning prayer or evening prayer is celebrated in the church, a priest or a deacon who presides wears an alb or surplice with stole (a cope may also be worn).

553 The sung celebration of the liturgy of the hours 'is more in keeping with the nature of this prayer, and a mark of both higher solemnity and closer union of hearts in offering praise to God.'[8] Whenever possible, therefore, singing at morning or evening prayer should be encouraged.

In the choice of music preference should be given to the singing of the hymn, the psalmody, and the gospel canticle. The introductory verse, the responsory, the intercessions, the Lord's Prayer, and the dismissal may also be sung.

An organist or other instrumentalist and a cantor should assist the assembly in singing the hymn, psalms, and responses. The parish community should also prepare booklets or participation aids that contain an outline of the hour, the texts and music belonging to the people, and directions for posture, gesture, and movement.

---

[7] See General Instruction of the Liturgy of the Hours, nos. 93-97.

[8] Congregation of Rites, Instruction *Musicam Sacram*, 5 March 1967, no. 37: AAS 59 (1967), 310; DOL 508, no. 4158.

OUTLINE OF THE RITE

Introductory Verse
Hymn
Psalmody
Reading
[Homily]
Responsory
Canticle of Zechariah
Intercessions
The Lord's Prayer
Concluding Prayer
Dismissal
[Procession to the Place of Committal]

24 MORNING PRAYER

554 When morning prayer begins with the invitatory, the introductory verse is omitted.

INTRODUCTORY VERSE

555 All stand and make the sign of the cross as the minister sings or says:

O God, come to our aid.

R. O Lord, make haste to help us.

Glory be to the Father and to the Son and to the Holy Spirit:

R. As it was in the beginning, is now, and ever shall be, world without end. Amen [alleluia].

HYMN

556 The following or another suitable hymn is sung.

Remember those, O Lord,
Who in your peace have died,
Yet may not gain love's high reward
Till love is purified!

With you they faced death's night,
Sealed with your victory sign.
Soon may the splendour of your light
On them for ever shine!

Sweet is their pain, yet deep,
Till perfect love is born;
Their lone night-watch they gladly keep
Before your radiant morn!

Your love is their great joy;
Your will their one desire;
As finest gold without alloy
Refine them in love's fire!

For them we humbly pray:
Perfect them in your love!
O may we share eternal day
With them in heaven above.

Text: James Quinn, S.J.

PSALMODY

557 The psalms may be sung or recited in various ways (see
no. 537). For pastoral reasons other psalms may be chosen, or
the number of psalms may be reduced.

Ant. 1 The bones you have crushed will rejoice in you, Lord.

Psalm 50 (51)

Have mércy on me, Gód, in your kíndness.*
In your compássion blot óut my offénce.
O wásh me more and móre from my guílt*
and cléanse me fróm my sín.

My offénces trúly I knów them;*
my sín is álways befóre me.
Against yóu, you alóne, have I sínned;*
what is évil in your síght I have dóne.

That you may be jústified whén you give séntence*
and be withóut repróach when you júdge,
O sée, in guílt I was bórn,*
a sínner was Í concéived.

Indéed you love trúth in the héart;*
then in the sécret of my héart teach me wísdom.
O púrify me, thén I shall be cléan;*
O wásh me, I shall be whíter than snów.

Make me héar rejóicing and gládness,*
that the bónes you have crúshed may revíve.
From my síns turn awáy your fáce*
and blót out áll my guílt.

A púre heart créate for me, O Gód,*
put a stéadfast spírit withín me.
Do not cást me awáy from your présence,*
nor depríve me of your hóly spírit.

Give me agáin the jóy of your hélp;*
with a spírit of férvour sustáin me,
that I may téach transgréssors your wáys*
and sínners may retúrn to yóu.

O réscue me, Gód, my hélper,*
and my tóngue shall ríng out your góodness.
O Lórd, ópen my líps*
and my móuth shall decláre your práise.

For in sácrifice you táke no delíght,*
burnt óffering from mé you would refúse,
my sácrifice, a cóntrite spírit.*
A húmbled, contrite héart you will not spúrn.

In your góodness, show fávour to Síon:*
rebuíld the wálls of Jerúsalem.
Thén you will be pléased with lawful sácrifice,*
hólocausts óffered on your áltar.

Ant. The bones you have crushed will rejoice in you, Lord.

Ant. 2 Rescue my soul, Lord, from the gate of death.

Canticle: Isaiah 38:10-14, 17-20

I said, In the noontide of my days I must depart;†
I am consigned to the gates of Sheol*
for the rest of my years.

I said, I shall not see the Lord*
in the land of the living;
I shall look upon man no more*
among the inhabitants of the world.

My dwelling is plucked up and removed from me*
like a shepherd's tent;
like a weaver I have rolled up my life;*
he cuts me off from the loom;

From day to night you bring me to an end;*
I cry for help until morning;
like a lion he breaks all my bones;*
from day to night you bring me to an end.

Like a swallow or a crane I clamour,*
I moan like a dove.
My eyes are weary with looking upward.*
O Lord, I am oppressed; be my security.

Lo, it was for my welfare*
that I had great bitterness;
but you have held back my life*
from the pit of destruction,
for you have cast all my sins*
behind your back.

For Sheol cannot thank you,*
death cannot praise you;
those who go down to the pit*
cannot hope for your faithfulness.

The living, the living, he thanks you†
as I do this day;*
the fathers make known to the children your
    faithfulness.

The Lord will save me,*
and we will sing to stringed instruments
all the days of our life,*
at the house of the Lord.

Ant. Rescue my soul, Lord, from the gate of death.

Ant. 3 I will praise God all my days.

Psalm 145 (146)

My sóul, give práise to the Lórd;†
I will práise the Lórd all my dáys,*
make músic to my Gód while I líve.

Pút no trúst in prínces,*
in mortal mén in whóm there is no hélp.
Take their bréath, they retúrn to cláy*
and their pláns that dáy come to nóthing.

He is háppy who is hélped by Jacob's Gód,*
whose hópe is in the Lórd his Gód,
who alóne made héaven and éarth,*
the séas and áll they contáin.

It is hé who keeps fáith for éver,*
who is júst to thóse who are oppréssed.
It is hé who gives bréad to the húngry,*
the Lórd, who sets prísoners frée,

the Lórd who gives síght to the blínd,*
who ráises up thóse who are bowed dówn,
the Lórd, who protécts the stránger*
and uphólds the wídow and órphan.

It is the Lórd who lóves the júst*
but thwárts the páth of the wícked.
The Lórd will réign for éver,*
Sion's Gód, from áge to áge.

Ant. I will praise God all my days.

Alternative Psalm

Ant. 3 Let everything that lives praise the Lord.

Psalm 150

Praise Gód in his hóly pláce,*
práise him in his míghty héavens.
Práise him for his pówerful déeds,*
práise his surpássing gréatness.

O práise him with sóund of trúmpet,*
práise him with lúte and hárp.
Práise him with tímbrel and dánce,*
práise him with stríngs and pípes.

O práise him with resóunding cýmbals,*
práise him with cláshing of cýmbals.
Let éverything that líves and that bréathes*
give práise to the Lórd.

Ant. Let everything that lives praise the Lord.

READING

558 All are seated during the reading. The following reading
or one of those provided in the Lectionary, Volume III, may be
proclaimed by the reader.

1 Thessalonians 4:14

We believe that Jesus died and rose again; so we believe that
God will bring with Jesus those who have died believing in him.

After the reading a period of silence is recommended.

HOMILY

559 A brief homily may follow the reading.

560 After the homily the short responsory or another responsorial song may be sung or recited.

R. I will praise you, Lord. You have rescued me.

Repeat R.

V. You have changed my mourning into gladness.

R. Glory be. R.

CANTICLE OF ZECHARIAH

561 If morning prayer is celebrated in the church, the altar, the
minister, and the congregation may be incensed in turn during
the canticle. All stand as one of the following antiphons is sung
by the cantor and then repeated by all.

Ant. I am the resurrection and the life; he who believes in me,
though he die, yet shall he live, and whoever lives and believes
in me shall never die.

During the Easter season

Ant. Christ has risen; he is the light of his people, whom he has
redeemed with his blood, alleluia.

Blessed be the Lord, the God of Israel!*
He has visited his people and redeemed them.

He has raised up for us a mighty saviour*
in the house of David his servant,
as he promised by the lips of holy men,*
those who were his prophets from of old.

A saviour who would free us from our foes,*
from the hands of all who hate us.
So his love for our fathers is fulfilled*
and his holy covenant remembered.

He swore to Abraham our father to grant us,*
that free from fear, and saved from the hands of our foes,
we might serve him in holiness and justice*
all the days of our life in his presence.

As for you, little child,*
you shall be called a prophet of God, the Most High.
You shall go ahead of the Lord*
to prepare his ways before him,

To make known to his people their salvation*
through forgiveness of all their sins,
the loving-kindness of the heart of our God*
who visits us like the dawn from on high.

He will give light to those in darkness,†
those who dwell in the shadow of death,*
and guide us into the way of peace.

Ant. I am the resurrection and the life; he who believes in me,
though he die, yet shall he live, and whoever lives and believes
in me shall never die.

During the Easter season

Ant. Christ has risen; he is the light of his people, whom he has
redeemed with his blood, alleluia.

INTERCESSIONS

562 The following intercessions may be used or adapted to the
circumstances, or new intercessions may be composed.

God the Father almighty, raised Jesus from the dead and he
will give life to our own mortal bodies. We pray to him in faith:

R. Lord, bring us to life in Christ.

Holy Father, we have been buried with your Son in baptism
to rise with him in glory; — may we always live in Christ and
not see death for ever. R.

Father, you have given us the living bread from heaven to be
eaten with faith and love; — grant that we may have eternal life
and be raised up on the last day. R.

Lord, when your Son was in agony you sent an angel to console him; — at the hour of our death take away all fear and fill
our hearts with hope. R.

You delivered the three young men from the blazing furnace; — free the souls of the dead from the punishments their sins have deserved. R.

God of the living and the dead, you brought Jesus back to life; — raise up the faithful departed, and let us come with them into your heavenly glory. R.

THE LORD'S PRAYER

563 In the following or similar words, the minister introduces the Lord's Prayer.

With God there is mercy and fullness of redemption; let us pray as Jesus taught us:

Our Father . . .

CONCLUDING PRAYER

364 The minister says one of the following prayers or one of those provided in nos. 580-581, p. 407.

A   God of loving kindness,   173
listen favourably to our prayers:
strengthen our belief that your Son has risen from the dead
and our hope that your servant N. will also rise again.

We ask this through our Lord Jesus Christ, your Son,
who lives and reigns with you and the Holy Spirit,
one God, for ever and ever.

R. Amen.

B   O God,   171
glory of believers and life of the just,
by the death and resurrection of your Son, we are redeemed:
have mercy on your servant N.,
and make him/her worthy to share the joys of paradise,
for he/she believed in the resurrection of the dead.

We ask this through our Lord Jesus Christ, your Son,
who lives and reigns with you and the Holy Spirit,
one God, for ever and ever.

R. Amen.

C
Lord, in our grief we turn to you.
Are you not the God of love
always ready to hear our cries?

Listen to our prayers for your servant N.,
whom you have numbered among your own people:
lead him/her to your kingdom of light and peace
and count him/her among the saints in glory.

We ask this through our Lord Jesus Christ, your Son,
who lives and reigns with you and the Holy Spirit,
one God, for ever and ever.

R. Amen.

> A member of the family or a friend of the deceased may speak
> in remembrance of the deceased.

> If the procession to the place of committal is to follow morning
> prayer, the dismissal is omitted.

DISMISSAL

565 The minister then blesses the people.

A   A minister who is a priest or deacon says the following or an-
           other form of blessing, as at Mass.

The Lord be with you.

R. And also with you.

May almighty God bless you,
the Father, ✠ and the Son, and the Holy Spirit.

R. Amen.

B   A lay minister invokes God's blessing and signs himself or her-
           self with the sign of the cross, saying:

The Lord bless us, and keep us from all evil, and bring us to
everlasting life.

R. Amen.

> The minister then dismisses the people:

Go in the peace of Christ.

R. Thanks be to God.

Procession to the Place of Committal

566 The deacon or, in the absence of a deacon, the minister says:

In peace let us take N. to his/her place of rest.

If a symbol of the Christian life has been placed on the coffin, it should be removed at this time.

The procession then begins: the minister and assisting ministers precede the coffin; the family and mourners follow.

One or more of the following texts or other suitable songs may be sung during the procession to the entrance of the church. The singing may continue during the journey to the place of committal.

A   The following antiphon may be sung with verses from Psalm 24 (25), p. 429.

May the angels lead you into paradise;   50
may the martyrs come to welcome you
and take you to the holy city,
the new and eternal Jerusalem.

B   The following antiphon may be sung with verses from Psalm 114 (116), p. 430, or separately.

May choirs of angels welcome you   50
and lead you to the bosom of Abraham;
and where Lazarus is poor no longer
may you find eternal rest.

C   May saints and angels lead you on,
Escorting you where Christ has gone.
Now he has called you, come to him
Who sits above the seraphim.

Come to the peace of Abraham
And to the supper of the Lamb:
Come to the glory of the blessed,
And to perpetual light and rest.

D   Another suitable psalm may also be used.

OUTLINE OF THE RITE

Introductory Verse
Hymn
Psalmody
Reading
[Homily]
Responsory
Canticle of Mary
Intercessions
The Lord's Prayer
Concluding Prayer
Dismissal

25 EVENING PRAYER

> 567 When the celebration begins with the rite of reception of the body at the church the introductory verse and the hymn are omitted and the celebration continues with the psalmody.

INTRODUCTORY VERSE

> 568 All stand and make the sign of the cross as the minister sings or says:

O God, come to our aid.

R. O Lord, make haste to help us.

Glory be to the Father and to the Son and to the Holy Spirit:

R. As it was in the beginning, is now, and ever shall be, world without end. Amen [alleluia].

HYMN

> 569 The following or another suitable hymn is sung.

For all the saints who from their labours rest,
Who thee by faith before the world confessed,
Thy name, O Jesus, be for ever blest:
Alleluia, alleluia!

Thou wast their rock, their fortress and their might;
Thou, Lord, their captain in the well-fought fight;
Thou in the darkness drear their one true light:
Alleluia, alleluia!

O blest communion, fellowship divine!
We feebly struggle, they in glory shine;
Yet all are one in thee, for all are thine:
Alleluia, alleluia!

But, lo, there breaks a yet more glorious day;
The saints triumphant rise in bright array:
The King of glory passes on his way:
Alleluia, alleluia!

Text: William W. How, 1823-1897
Tune: Sine Nomine 10.10.10 with Alleluias
Music: R. Vaughan Williams, 1872-1958

570 The psalms may be sung or recited in various ways (see no. **537**). For pastoral reasons other psalms may be chosen, or the number of psalms may be reduced.

Ant. 1 The Lord will guard you from every evil, he will guard your soul.

Psalm 120 (121)

I líft up my éyes to the móuntains:*
from whére shall come my hélp?
My hélp shall cóme from the Lórd*
who made héaven and éarth.

May he néver állow you to stúmble!*
Let him sléep not, your guárd.
Nó, he sléeps not nor slúmbers,*
Ísrael's guárd.

The Lórd is your guárd and your sháde;*
at your ríght side he stánds.
By dáy the sún shall not smíte you*
nor the móon in the níght.

The Lórd will guárd you from évil,*
he will guárd your sóul.
The Lord will guárd your góing and cóming*
both nów and for éver.

Ant. The Lord will guard you from every evil, he will guard your soul.

Ant. 2 If you, O Lord, should mark our guilt, Lord, who would survive?

Psalm 129 (130)

Out of the dépths I crý to you, O Lórd,*
Lórd, hear my vóice!
O lét your éars be atténtive*
to the vóice of my pléading.

If you, O Lórd, should márk our guílt,*
Lórd, who would survíve?
But with yóu is fóund forgíveness:*
for thís we revére you.

My sóul is wáiting for the Lórd,*
I cóunt on his wórd.
My sóul is lónging for the Lórd*
more than wátchman for dáybreak.
Let the wátchman cóunt on dáybreak*
and Ísrael on the Lórd.

Becáuse with the Lórd there is mércy
and fúlness of redémption,
Ísrael indéed he will redéem*
from áll its iníquity.

Ant. If you, O Lord, should mark our guilt, Lord, who would
survive?

Ant. 3 As the Father raises the dead and gives them life, so the
Son gives life to anyone he chooses.

    Canticle: Philippians 2:6-11

Though he was in the form of God,*
Jesus did not count equality with God
    a thing to be grasped.

He emptied himself,†
taking the form of a servant,*
being born in the likeness of men.

And being found in human form,*
he humbled himself and became obedient unto death,*
even death on a cross.

Therefore God has highly exalted him*
and bestowed on him the name which is above every name,

That at the name of Jesus every knee should bow,*
in heaven and on earth and under the earth,

And every tongue confess that Jesus Christ is Lord,*
to the glory of God the Father.

Ant. As the Father raises the dead and gives them life, so the
Son gives life to anyone he chooses.

READING

571 All are seated during the reading. The following reading
or one of those provided in the Lectionary, Volume III, may be
proclaimed by the reader.

1 Corinthians 15:55-57

Death, where is your victory? Death, where is your sting? Now
the sting of death is sin, and sin gets its power from the Law.
So let us thank God for giving us the victory through our Lord
Jesus Christ.

After the reading a period of silence is recommended.

HOMILY

572 A brief homily may follow the reading.

RESPONSORY

573 After the homily the short responsory or another responsorial song may be sung or recited.

R. In you, O Lord, I take refuge. Let me not be lost for ever.
   Repeat R.

V. I will rejoice and be glad because of your merciful love.

R. Glory be. R.

CANTICLE OF MARY

574 If evening prayer is celebrated in the church, the altar, the minister, and the congregation may be incensed in turn during the canticle. All stand as one of the following antiphons is sung by the cantor and then repeated by all.

Ant. All that the Father gives me will come to me; and I will never turn away the one who comes to me.

During the Easter season

Ant. Christ was crucified and rose from the dead; he has redeemed us, alleluia.

My soul glorifies the Lord,*
my spirit rejoices in God, my Saviour.
He looks on his servant in her lowliness;*
henceforth all ages will call me blessed.

The Almighty works marvels for me.*
Holy his name!
His mercy is from age to age,*
on those who fear him.

He puts forth his arm in strength*
and scatters the proud-hearted.
He casts the mighty from their thrones*
and raises the lowly.

He fills the starving with good things,*
sends the rich away empty.

He protects Israel, his servant,*
remembering his mercy,
the mercy promised to our fathers,*
to Abraham and his sons for ever.

Ant. All that the Father gives me will come to me; and I will never turn away the one who comes to me.

During the Easter season

Ant. Christ was crucified and rose from the dead; he has redeemed us, alleluia.

INTERCESSIONS

575 The following intercessions may be used or adapted to the circumstances, or new intercessions may be composed.

Let us pray to Christ who gives us the hope that our mortal bodies will become like his in glory.

R. Lord, you are our life and our resurrection.

Christ, Son of the living God, you raised your friend Lazarus from the dead; — grant life and glory to the faithful departed, redeemed by your precious blood. R.

Compassionate Saviour, you wiped away all tears when you gave back to the widow of Naim her only son; — comfort those who mourn because the one they love has died. R.

Christ, our Redeemer, destroy the reign of sin in our mortal bodies; — let us not receive the wages of death but the reward of eternal life. R.

Christ, our Saviour, look on those who live without hope and do not know you; — let them believe in the resurrection and the life of the world to come. R.

You restored sight to the man born blind and opened the eyes of his faith; — reveal your face to the dead who have not seen your glory. R.

Lord, be merciful to us when we leave this earthly dwelling; — make for us a home in heaven that will last for ever. R.

THE LORD'S PRAYER

576 In the following or similar words, the minister introduces the Lord's Prayer.

With God there is mercy and fullness of redemption; let us pray as Jesus taught us:

All:

Our Father . . .

577 The minister says one of the following prayers or one of those
provided in nos. 580-581, p. 407.

A   God of loving kindness,   173
listen favourably to our prayers:
strengthen our belief that your Son has risen from the dead
and our hope that your servant N. will also rise again.

We ask this through our Lord Jesus Christ, your Son,
who lives and reigns with you and the Holy Spirit,
one God, for ever and ever.

R. Amen.

B   O God,   171
glory of believers and life of the just,
by the death and resurrection of your Son, we are redeemed:
have mercy on your servant N.,
and make him/her worthy to share the joys of paradise,
for he/she believed in the resurrection of the dead.

We ask this through our Lord Jesus Christ, your Son,
who lives and reigns with you and the Holy Spirit,
one God, for ever and ever.

R. Amen.

C   During the Easter season
Lord, in our grief we turn to you.   33
Are you not the God of love
always ready to hear our cries?

Listen to our prayers for your servant N.,
whom you have numbered among your own people:
lead him/her to your kingdom of light and peace
and count him/her among the saints in glory.

We ask this through our Lord Jesus Christ, your Son,
who lives and reigns with you and the Holy Spirit,
one God, for ever and ever.

R. Amen.

A member of the family or a friend of the deceased may speak in remembrance of the deceased.

Dismissal

578 The minister then blesses the people.

A A minister who is a priest or deacon says the following or another form of blessing, as at Mass.

The Lord be with you.

R. And also with you.

May almighty God bless you,
the Father, ✠ and the Son, and the Holy Spirit.

R. Amen.

B A lay minister invokes God's blessing and signs himself or herself with the sign of the cross, saying:

The Lord bless us, and keep us from all evil, and bring us to everlasting life.

R. Amen.

The minister then dismisses the people:

Go in the peace of Christ.

R. Thanks be to God.

PART V
ADDITIONAL TEXTS

The one who raised Christ Jesus from the dead
will give your mortal bodies
life through his Spirit living in you

579 The following prayers for the dead and prayers for the mourners are for use in the various rites of Parts I, II, and IV.

The prayers and psalms are grouped as follows:

580 The following prayers for the dead may be used in the various rites of Parts I and II and in Part IV. The prayers should be chosen taking the character of the text into account as well as the place in the rite where it will occur. All of the prayers in this section end with the shorter conclusion. When a prayer is used as the opening prayer at the funeral liturgy, the longer conclusion is used.

1   General

God of faithfulness,
in your wisdom you have called your servant N.
  out of this world;
release him/her from the bonds of sin,
and welcome him/her into your presence,
so that he/she may enjoy eternal light and peace
and be raised up in glory with all your saints.

We ask this through Christ our Lord.

R. Amen.

2   General

Lord, in our grief we turn to you.
Are you not the God of love
always ready to hear our cries?

Listen to our prayers for your servant N.,
whom you have called out of this world:
lead him/her to your kingdom of light and peace
and count him/her among the saints in glory.

We ask this through Christ our Lord.

R. Amen.

3   General

Holy Lord, almighty and eternal God,
hear our prayers for your servant N.,
whom you have summoned out of this world.
Forgive his/her sins and failings
and grant him/her a place of refreshment, light,
  and peace.

Let him/her pass unharmed through the gates of death
to dwell with the blessed in light,
as you promised to Abraham and his children for ever.
Accept N. into your safe-keeping
and on the great day of judgment
raise him/her up with all the saints
to inherit your eternal kingdom.

We ask this through Christ our Lord.

R. Amen.

General

Into your hands, O Lord,   168
we humbly entrust our brother/sister N.
In this life you embraced him/her with your tender love;
deliver him/her now from every evil
and bid him/her enter eternal rest.

The old order has passed away:
welcome him/her then into paradise,
where there will be no sorrow, no weeping nor pain,
but the fullness of peace and joy
with your Son and the Holy Spirit
for ever and ever.

R. Amen.

General

Almighty God and Father,   170
it is our certain faith
that your Son, who died on the cross, was raised from the dead,
the firstfruits of all who have fallen asleep.
Grant that through this mystery
your servant N., who has gone to his/her rest in Christ,
may share in the joy of his resurrection.

We ask this through Christ our Lord.

R. Amen.

O God,
glory of believers and life of the just,
by the death and resurrection of your Son, we are redeemed:
have mercy on your servant N.,
and make him/her worthy to share the joys of paradise,
for he/she believed in the resurrection of the dead.

We ask this through Christ our Lord.

R. Amen.

Almighty God and Father,
by the mystery of the cross, you have made us strong;
by the sacrament of the resurrection
you have sealed us as your own.
Look kindly upon your servant N.,
now freed from the bonds of mortality,
and count him/her among your saints in heaven.

We ask this through Christ our Lord.

R. Amen.

God of loving kindness,
listen favourably to our prayers:
strengthen our belief that your Son has risen from the dead
and our hope that your servant N. will also rise again.

We ask this through Christ our Lord.

R. Amen.

To you, O God, the dead do not die,
and in death our life is changed, not ended.
Hear our prayers
and command the soul of your servant N.
to dwell with Abraham, your friend,
and be raised at last on the great day of judgment.

In your mercy cleanse him/her of any sin
which he/she may have committed through human frailty.

We ask this through Christ our Lord.

R. Amen.

10   General

Lord God, in whom all find refuge,   175
we appeal to your boundless mercy:
grant to the soul of your servant N.
a kindly welcome,
cleansing of sin,
release from the chains of death,
and entry into everlasting life.

We ask this through Christ our Lord.

R. Amen.

11   General

God of all consolation,   176
open our hearts to your word,
so that, listening to it, we may comfort one another,
finding light in time of darkness
and faith in time of doubt.

We ask this through Christ our Lord.

R. Amen.

12   General

O God,
to whom mercy and forgiveness belong,
hear our prayers on behalf of your servant N.,
whom you have called out of this world;
and because he/she put his/her hope and trust in you,
command that he/she be carried safely home to heaven
and come to enjoy your eternal reward.

We ask this through Christ our Lord.

R. Amen.

13   General

O God,
in whom sinners find mercy and the saints find joy,
we pray to you for our brother/sister N.,
whose body we honour with Christian burial,
that he/she may be delivered from the bonds of death.
Admit him/her to the joyful company of your saints
and raise him/her on the last day
to rejoice in your presence for ever.

We ask this through Christ our Lord.

R. Amen.

14   A pope

O God,
from whom the just receive an unfailing reward,
grant that your servant N., our Pope,
whom you made vicar of Peter and shepherd of your Church,
may rejoice for ever in the vision of your glory,
for he was a faithful steward here on earth
of the mysteries of your forgiveness and grace.

We ask this through Christ our Lord.

R. Amen.

15   A diocesan bishop

Almighty and merciful God,
eternal Shepherd of your people,
listen to our prayers
and grant that your servant, N., our bishop,
to whom you entrusted the care of this Church,
may enter the joy of his eternal Master,
there to receive the rich reward of his labours.

We ask this through Christ our Lord.

R. Amen.

16   Another bishop

O God,
from the ranks of your priests
you chose your servant N.
to fulfil the office of bishop.

Grant that he may share
in the eternal fellowship of those priests
who, faithful to the teachings of the apostles,
dwell in your heavenly kingdom.

We ask this through Christ our Lord.

R. Amen.

17   A priest

God of mercy and love,
grant to N., your servant and priest,
a glorious place at your heavenly table,
for you made him here on earth
a faithful minister of your word and sacrament.

We ask this through Christ our Lord.

R. Amen.

18   A priest

O God,
listen favourably to our prayers
offered on behalf of your servant and priest,
and grant that N.,
who committed himself zealously to the service of your name,
may rejoice for ever in the company of your saints.

We ask this through Christ our Lord.

R. Amen.

19   A priest

Lord God,
you chose our brother N. to serve your people as a priest
and to share the joys and burdens of their lives.

Look with mercy on him
and give him the reward of his labours,
the fulness of life promised to those who preach your
    holy Gospel.

We ask this through Christ our Lord.

R. Amen.

20   A deacon

God of mercy,
as once you chose seven men of honest repute
to serve your Church,
so also you chose N. as your servant and deacon.
Grant that he may rejoice in your eternal fellowship
with all the heralds of your Gospel,
for he was untiring in his ministry here on earth.

We ask this through Christ our Lord.

R. Amen.

21   A deacon

Lord God,
you sent your Son into the world
to preach the Good News of salvation
and to pour out his Spirit of grace upon your Church.

Look with kindness on your servant N.
As a deacon in the Church
he was strengthened by the gift of the Spirit
to preach the Good News,
to minister in your assembly,
and to do the works of charity.

Give him the reward promised
to those who show their love of you
by service to their neigbour.

We ask this through Christ our Lord.

R. Amen.

22   A religious

All-powerful God,
we pray for our brother/sister N.,
who responded to the call of Christ
and pursued wholeheartedly the ways of perfect love.
Grant that he/she may rejoice
on that day when your glory will be revealed
and in company with all his/her brothers and sisters
share for ever the happiness of your kingdom.

We ask this through Christ our Lord.

R. Amen.

23   A religious

God of blessings,
source of all holiness,
the voice of your Spirit has drawn countless men and women
to follow Jesus Christ
and to bind themselves to you
with ready will and loving heart.

Look with mercy on N.
who sought to fulfill his/her vows to you,
and grant him/her the reward promised to all good and
    faithful servants.

May he/she rejoice in the company of the saints
and with them praise you for ever.

We ask this through Christ our Lord.

R. Amen.

24   One who worked in the service of the Gospel

Faithful God,   178
we humbly ask your mercy for your servant N.,
who worked so generously to spread the Good News:
grant him/her the reward of his/her labours
and bring him/her safely to your promised land.

We ask this through Christ our Lord.

R. Amen.

25   A baptized child

Lord, in our grief we call upon your mercy: 223
open your ears to our prayers,
and one day unite us again with N.,
who, we firmly trust,
already enjoys eternal life in your kingdom.

We ask this through Christ our Lord.

R. Amen.

26   A baptized child

To you, O Lord,   224
we humbly entrust this child,
so precious in your sight.
Take him/her into your arms
and welcome him/her into paradise,
where there will be no sorrow, no weeping nor pain,
but the fullness of peace and joy
with your Son and the Holy Spirit
for ever and ever.

R. Amen.

27   A young person

Lord,   177
your wisdom governs the length of our days.
We mourn the loss of N.,
whose life has passed so quickly,
and we entrust him/her to your mercy.
Welcome him/her into your heavenly dwelling
and grant him/her the happiness of everlasting youth.

We ask this through Christ our Lord.

R. Amen.

28   A young person

Lord God,
source and destiny of our lives,
in your loving providence
you gave us N.
to grow in wisdom, age, and grace.
Now you have called him/her to yourself.

As we grieve the loss of one so young,
we seek to understand your purpose.

Draw him/her to yourself
and give him/her full stature in Christ.
May he/she stand with all the angels and saints,
who know your love and praise your saving will.

We ask this through Christ our Lord.

R. Amen.

29   Parents

Lord God, who commanded us to honour father and mother,   181
look kindly upon your servants N. and N.,
have mercy upon them
and let us see them again in eternal light.

We ask this through Christ our Lord.

R. Amen.

30   A parent

God of our ancestors in faith,
by the covenant made on Mount Sinai
you taught your people to strengthen the bonds of family
through faith, honour, and love.
Look kindly upon N.,
a father/mother who sought to bind his/her children to you.
Bring him/her one day to our heavenly home
where the saints dwell in blessedness and peace.

We ask this through Christ our Lord.

R. Amen.

31   A married couple

Lord God, whose covenant is everlasting,   182
have mercy upon the sins of your servants N. and N.;
as their love for each other united them on earth,
so let your love join them together in heaven.

We ask this through Christ our Lord.

R. Amen.

32   A married couple

Eternal Father,
in the beginning you established the love of man and woman
as a sign of creation.
Your own Son loves the Church as a spouse.
Grant mercy and peace to N. and N. who,
by their love for each other,
were signs of the creative love
which binds the Church to Christ.

We ask this in the name of Jesus the Lord.

R. Amen.

33   A married couple

Lord God,
giver of all that is true and lovely and gracious,
you created in marriage a sign of your covenant.
Look with mercy upon N. and N.
You blessed them in their companionship,
and in their joys and sorrows you bound them together.
Lead them into eternal peace,
and bring them to the table
where the saints feast together in your heavenly home.

We ask this through Christ our Lord.

R. Amen.

34   A wife

Eternal God,
you made the love of man and woman
a sign of the bond between Christ and the Church.

Grant mercy and peace to N.,
who was united in love with her husband.
May the care and devotion of her life on earth
find a lasting reward in heaven.
Look kindly on her husband and family/children
as now they turn to your compassion and love.
Strengthen their faith and lighten their loss.

We ask this through Christ our Lord.

R. Amen.

35   A husband

Eternal God,
you made the love of man and woman
a sign of the bond between Christ and the Church.

Grant mercy and peace to N.,
who was united in love with his wife.
May the care and devotion of his life on earth
find a lasting reward in heaven.
Look kindly on his wife and family/children
as now they turn to your compassion and love.
Strengthen their faith and lighten their loss.

We ask this through Christ our Lord.

R. Amen.

Almighty and faithful Creator,
all things are of your making,
all people are shaped in your image.
We now entrust the soul of N. to your goodness.
In your infinite wisdom and power,
work in him/her your merciful purpose,
known to you alone from the beginning of time.
Console the hearts of those who love him/her
in the hope that all who trust in you
will find peace and rest in your kingdom.

We ask this in the name of Jesus the Lord.

R. Amen.

37   An elderly person

God of endless ages,
from one generation to the next
you have been our refuge and strength.
Before the mountains were born
or the earth came to be,
you are God.
Have mercy now on your servant N.
whose long life was spent in your service.
Give him/her a place in your kingdom,
where hope is firm for all who love
and rest is sure for all who serve.

We ask this through Christ our Lord.

R. Amen.

38   An elderly person

God of mercy,
look kindly on your servant N.
who has set down the burden of his/her years.
As he/she served you faithfully throughout his/her life,
may you give him/her the fullness of your peace and joy.
We give thanks for the long life of N.,
now caught up in your eternal love.
We make our prayer in the name of Jesus who is our risen Lord
now and for ever.

R. Amen.

39   One who died after a long illness

God of deliverance,
you called our brother/sister N.
to serve you in weakness and pain,
and gave him/her the grace of sharing the cross of your Son.
Reward his/her patience and forbearance,
and grant him/her the fullness of Christ's victory.

We ask this through Christ our Lord.

R. Amen.

40   One who died after a long illness

Most faithful God,
lively is the courage of those who hope in you.
Your servant N. suffered greatly
but placed his/her trust in your mercy.
Confident that the petition of those who mourn
pierces the clouds and finds an answer,
we beg you, give rest to N.
Do not remember his/her sins
but look upon his/her sufferings
and grant him/her refreshment, light, and peace.

We ask this through Christ our Lord.

R. Amen.

41   One who died after a long illness

O God,
you are water for our thirst
and manna in our desert.
We praise you for the life of N.
and bless your mercy
that has brought his/her suffering to an end.
Now we beg that same endless mercy
to raise him/her to new life.
Nourished by the food and drink of heaven,
may he/she rest for ever
in the joy of Christ our Lord.

R. Amen.

179

42   One who died suddenly

Lord,
as we mourn the sudden death of our brother/sister,
show us the immense power of your goodness
and strengthen our belief
that N. has entered into your presence.

We ask this through Christ our Lord.

R. Amen.

43   One who died accidentally or violently

Lord our God,
you are always faithful and quick to show mercy.
Our brother/sister N.
was suddenly [and violently] taken from us.
Come swiftly to his/her aid,
have mercy on him/her,
and comfort his/her family and friends
by the power and protection of the cross.

We ask this through Christ our Lord.

R. Amen.

44   One who died by suicide

God, lover of souls,
you hold dear what you have made
and spare all things, for they are yours.
Look gently on your servant N.,
and by the blood of the cross
forgive his/her sins and failings.

Remember the faith of those who mourn
and satisfy their longing for that day
when all will be made new again
in Christ, our risen Lord,
who lives and reigns with you for ever and ever.

R. Amen.

45   One who died by suicide

Almighty God and Father of all,
you strengthen us by the mystery of the cross
and with the sacrament of your Son's resurrection.
Have mercy on our brother/sister N.
Forgive all his/her sins and grant him/her peace.
May we who mourn this sudden death be comforted
    and consoled by your power and protection.

We ask this through Christ our Lord.

R. Amen.

46   Several persons

O Lord,
you gave new life to N. and N.
in the waters of baptism;
show mercy to them now,
and bring them to the happiness of life in your kingdom.

We ask this through Christ our Lord.

R. Amen.

47   Several persons

All-powerful God,
whose mercy is never withheld
from those who call upon you in hope,
look kindly on your servants N. and N.,
who departed this life confessing your name,
and number them among your saints for evermore.

We ask this through Christ our Lord.

R. Amen.

PRAYERS FOR THE MOURNERS

581 The following prayers for the mourners may be used in the various rites of Parts I and II. The prayers should be chosen taking the character of the text into account as well as the place in the rite where it will occur.

1   General

Father of mercies and God of all consolation,   34
you pursue us with untiring love
and dispel the shadow of death
with the bright dawn of life.

[Comfort your family in their loss and sorrow.
Be our refuge and our strength, O Lord,
and lift us from the depths of grief
into the peace and light of your presence.]

Your Son, our Lord Jesus Christ,
by dying has destroyed our death,
and by rising, restored our life.
Enable us therefore to press on toward him,
so that, after our earthly course is run,
he may reunite us with those we love,
when every tear will be wiped away.

We ask this through Christ our Lord.

R. Amen.

2   General

Lord Jesus, our Redeemer,   169
you willingly gave yourself up to death,
so that all might be saved and pass from death to life.
We humbly ask you to comfort your servants in their grief
and to receive N. into the arms of your mercy.
You alone are the Holy One,
you are mercy itself;
by dying you unlocked the gates of life
   for those who believe in you.
Forgive N. his/her sins,
and grant him/her a place of happiness, light, and peace
in the kingdom of your glory for ever.

R. Amen.

3   General

God, all-compassionate,   202
ruler of the living and the dead,
you know beforehand
those whose faithful lives reveal them as your own.
We pray for those who belong to this present world
and for those who have passed to the world to come:
grant them pardon for all their sins.
We ask you graciously to hear our prayer
through the intercession of all the saints
and for your mercy's sake.

For you are God, for ever and ever.

R. Amen.

4   General

Lord our God,
the death of our brother/sister N.
recalls our human condition
and the brevity of our lives on earth.
But for those who believe in your love
death is not the end,
nor does it destroy the bonds
that you forge in our lives.
We share the faith of your Son's disciples
and the hope of the children of God.
Bring the light of Christ's resurrection
to this time of testing and pain
as we pray for N. and for those who love him/her,
through Christ our Lord.

R. Amen.

5   General

Lord God,
you are attentive to the voice of our pleading.
Let us find in your Son
comfort in our sadness,
certainty in our doubt,
and courage to live through this hour.
Make our faith strong
through Christ our Lord.

R. Amen.

Lord,
N. is gone now from this earthly dwelling
and has left behind those who mourn his/her absence.
Grant that as we grieve for our brother/sister
we may hold his/her memory dear
and live in hope of the eternal kingdom
where you will bring us together again.

We ask this through Christ our Lord.

R. Amen.

General

Most merciful God,
whose wisdom is beyond our understanding,
surround the family of N. with your love,
that they may not be overwhelmed by their loss,
but have confidence in your goodness,
and strength to meet the days to come.

We ask this through Christ our Lord.

R. Amen.

A baptized child

Lord of all gentleness,
surround us with your care
and comfort us in our sorrow,
for we grieve at the loss of this [little] child.

As you washed N. in the waters of baptism
and welcomed him/her into the life of heaven,
so call us one day
to be united with him/her
and share for ever the.joy of your kingdom.

We ask this through Christ our Lord.

R. Amen.

225

9   A baptized child

Eternal Father,
through the intercession of Mary,
who bore your Son and stood by the cross as he died,
grant to these parents in their grief
the assistance of her presence,
the comfort of her faith,
and the reward of her prayers.

We ask this through Christ our Lord.

R. Amen.

10   A baptized child

Lord God,
source and destiny of our lives,
in your loving providence
you gave us N.
to grow in wisdom, age, and grace.
Now you have called him/her to yourself.

We grieve over the loss of one so young
and struggle to understand your purpose.

Draw him/her to yourself
and give him/her full stature in Christ.
May he/she stand with all the angels and saints,
who know your love and praise your saving will.

We ask this through Jesus Christ, our Lord.

R. Amen.

11   A baptized child

Merciful Lord,
whose wisdom is beyond human understanding,
you adopted N. as your own in baptism
and have taken him/her to yourself
even as he/she stood on the threshold of life.
Listen to our prayers and extend to us your grace,
that one day we may share eternal life with N.,
for we firmly believe that he/she now rests with you.

We ask this through Christ our Lord.

R. Amen.

12   A baptized child

Lord God,
from whom human sadness is never hidden,
you know the burden of grief
that we feel at the loss of this child.

As we mourn his/her passing from this life,
comfort us with the knowledge
that N. lives now in your loving embrace.

We ask this through Christ our Lord.

R. Amen.

13   A child who died before baptism

O Lord, whose ways are beyond understanding,   235
listen to the prayers of your faithful people:
that those weighed down by grief
at the loss of this [little] child
may find reassurance in your infinite goodness.

We ask this through Christ our Lord.

R. Amen.

14   A child who died before baptism

God of all consolation,   236
searcher of mind and heart,
the faith of these parents [N. and N.] is known to you.

Comfort them with the knowledge
that the child for whom they grieve
is entrusted now to your loving care.

We ask this through Christ our Lord.

R. Amen.

15　　　A stillborn child

Lord God,
ever caring and gentle,
we commit to your love this little one,
quickened to life for so short a time.
Enfold him/her in eternal life.

We pray for his/her parents
who are saddened by the loss of their child.
Give them courage
and help them in their pain and grief.
May they all meet one day
in the joy and peace of your kingdom.

We ask this through Christ our Lord.

R. Amen.

582 The following psalms may be used during a procession to the church or to the place of committal.

Psalm 24 (25)

To you, O Lord, I lift my soul.
I trust you, let me not be disappointed;
do not let my enemies triumph.
Those who hope in you shall not be disappointed,
but only those who wantonly break faith.

Lord, make me know your ways.
Lord, teach me your paths.
Make me walk in your truth, and teach me:
for you are God my saviour.

In you I hope all day long
because of your goodness, O Lord.
Remember your mercy, Lord,
and the love you have shown from of old.
Do not remember the sins of my youth.
In your love remember me.

The Lord is good and upright.
He shows the path to those who stray,
he guides the humble in the right path;
he teaches his way to the poor.

His ways are faithfulness and love
for those who keep his covenant and will.
Lord, for the sake of your name
forgive my guilt; for it is great.

If anyone fears the Lord
he will show him the path he should choose.
His soul shall live in happiness
and his children shall possess the land.
The Lord's friendship is for those who revere him;
to them he reveals his covenant.

My eyes are always on the Lord;
for he rescues my feet from the snare.
Turn to me and have mercy
for I am lonely and poor.

Relieve the anguish of my heart
and set me free from my distress.
See my affliction and my toil
and take all my sins away.

See how many are my foes;
how violent their hatred for me.
Preserve my life and rescue me.
Do not disappoint me, you are my refuge.
May innocence and uprightness protect me:
for my hope is in you, O Lord.

Redeem Israel, O God, from all its distress.

2   Psalm 114 (116)

Alleluia!

I love the Lord for he has heard
the cry of my appeal;
for he turned his ear to me
in the day when I called him.

They surrounded me, the snares of death,
with the anguish of the tomb;
they caught me, sorrow and distress.
I called on the Lord's name.

O Lord my God, deliver me!

How gracious is the Lord, and just;
our God has compassion.
The Lord protects the simple hearts;
I was helpless so he saved me.

Turn back, my soul, to your rest
for the Lord has been good;
he has kept my soul from death,
my eyes from tears
and my feet from stumbling.

I will walk in the presence of the Lord
in the land of the living.

I trusted, even when I said:
'I am sorely afflicted,'
and when I said in my alarm:
'No man can be trusted.'

How can I repay the Lord
for his goodness to me?
The cup of salvation I will raise;
I will call on the Lord's name.

My vows to the Lord I will fulfil
before all his people.
O precious in the eyes of the Lord
is the death of his faithful.

Your servant, Lord, your servant am I;
you have loosened my bonds.
A thanksgiving sacrifice I make:
I will call on the Lord's name.

My vows to the Lord I will fulfil
before all his people,
in the courts of the house of the Lord,
in your midst, O Jerusalem.

APPENDIX

ORDO EXSEQUIARUM, 1969, INTRODUCTION*

1   At the funerals of its children the Church confidently celebrates Christ's paschal mystery. Its intention is that those who by baptism were made one body with the dead and risen Christ may with him pass from death to life. In soul they are to be cleansed and taken up into heaven with the saints and elect; in body they await the blessed hope of Christ's coming and the resurrection of the dead.

The Church, therefore, offers the eucharistic sacrifice of Christ's Passover for the dead and pours forth prayers and petitions for them. Because of the communion of all Christ's members with each other, all of this brings spiritual aid to the dead and the consolation of hope to the living.

2   As they celebrate the funerals of their brothers and sisters, Christians should be intent on affirming their hope for eternal life. They should not, however, give the impression of either disregard or contempt for the attitudes or practices of their own time and place. In such matters as family traditions, local customs, burial societies, Christians should willingly acknowledge whatever they perceive to be good and try to transform whatever seems alien to the Gospel. Then the funeral ceremonies for Christians will both manifest paschal faith and be true examples of the spirit of the Gospel.

3   Although any form of empty display must be excluded, it is right to show respect for the bodies of the faithful departed, which in life were the temple of the Holy Spirit. This is why it is worthwhile that there be an expression of faith in eternal life and the offering of prayers for the deceased, at least at the more significant times between death and burial.

Depending on local custom, such special moments include the vigil at the home of the deceased, the laying out of the body, and the carrying of the body to the place of burial. They should be marked by the gathering of family and friends and, if possible, of the whole community to receive in the liturgy of the word the consolation of hope, to offer together the eucharistic sacrifice, and to pay last respects to the deceased by a final farewell.

4   To take into account in some degree conditions in all parts of the world, the present rite of funerals is arranged on the basis of three models:

1. The first envisions three stations, namely, at the home of the deceased, at the church, and at the cemetery.

2. The second covers only two stations, at the church and at the cemetery.

3. The third involves only one station, which is at the home of the deceased.

5   The first model for a funeral is practically the same as the former rite in the Roman Ritual. It includes as a rule, at least in country places, three stations, namely, at the home of the deceased, at the church, and at the cemetery, with two processions in between. Especially in large cities, however, processions are seldom held or are inconvenient for various reasons. As for the stations at home and at the cemetery, priests sometimes are unable to lead them because of a shortage of clergy or the distance of the cemetery from the church. In view of these considerations, the faithful must be urged to recite the usual psalms and prayers themselves when there is no deacon or priest present. If that is impossible, the home and cemetery stations are to be omitted.

6   In this first model the station at the church consists as a rule in the celebration of the funeral Mass; this is forbidden only during the Easter triduum, on solemnities, and on the Sundays of Advent, Lent, and the Easter season. Pastoral reasons may on occasion require that a funeral be celebrated in the church without a Mass (which in all cases must, if possible, be celebrated on another day within a reasonable time); in that case a liturgy of the word is prescribed absolutely. Therefore, the station at the church always includes a liturgy of the word, with or without a Mass, and the rite hitherto called 'absolution' of the

---

* As emended by the Congregation for the Sacraments and Divine Worship, 12 September 1983.

dead and henceforth to be called 'the final commendation and farewell.'

7   The second funeral plan consists of only two stations, namely, at the cemetery, that is, at the cemetery chapel, and at the grave. This plan does not envision a eucharistic celebration, but one is to take place, without the body present, before the actual funeral or after the funeral.

8   A funeral rite, following the third model, to be celebrated in the deceased's home may perhaps in some places be regarded as pointless. Yet in certain parts of the world it seems needed. In view of the many diversities, the model purposefully does not go into details. At the same time it seemed advisable at least to set out guidelines so that this plan might share certain elements with the other two, for example, the liturgy of the word and the rite of final commendation or farewell. The detailed directives will be left to the conferences of bishops to settle.

9   In the future preparation of particular rituals conformed to the Roman Ritual, it will be up to the conference of bishops either to keep the three models or to change their arrangement or to omit one or other of them. For it is quite possible that in any particular country one model, for example, the first with its three stations, is the only one in use and as such the one to be kept. Elsewhere all three may be needed. The conference of bishops will make the arrangements appropriate to what particular needs require.

10 After the funeral Mass the rite of final commendation and farewell is celebrated.

The meaning of the rite does not signify a kind of purification of the deceased; that is what the eucharistic sacrifice accomplishes. Rather it stands as a farewell by which the Christian community together pays respect to one of its members before the body is removed or buried. Death, of course, always has involved an element of separation, but Christians as Christ's members are one in him and not even death can part them from each other.[1]

The priest's opening words are to introduce and explain this rite, a few moments of silence are to follow, then the sprinkling with holy water and the incensation, then a song of farewell. Not only is it useful for all to sing this song, composed of a pertinent text set to a suitable melody, but all should have the sense of its being the high point of the entire rite.

Also to be seen as signs of farewell are the sprinkling with holy water, a reminder that through baptism the person was marked for eternal life, and the incensation, signifying respect for the body as the temple of the Holy Spirit.

The rite of final commendation and farewell may only be held during an actual funeral service, that is, when the body is present.

11 In any celebration for the deceased, whether a funeral or not, the rite attaches great importance to the readings from the word of God. These proclaim the paschal mystery, they convey the hope of being gathered together again in God's kingdom, they teach remembrance of the dead, and throughout they encourage the witness of a Christian life.

12 In its good offices on behalf of the dead, the Church turns again and again especially to the prayer of the psalms as an expression of grief and a sure source of trust. Pastors are, therefore, to make an earnest effort through an effective catechesis to lead their communities to a clearer and deeper grasp of at least some of the psalms provided for the funeral liturgy. With regard to other chants that the rite frequently assigns on pastoral grounds, they are also to seek to instil a 'warm and living love of Scripture'[2] and a sense of its meaning in the liturgy.

13 In its prayers the Christian community confesses its faith and makes compassionate intercession for deceased adults that they may reach their final happiness with God. The community's belief is that deceased children whom through baptism God has adopted as his own have already attained that blessedness. But the commu-

---

[1] See Simeon of Thessalonica, *De ordine sepulturae*: PG 155, 685 B.

[2] Vatican Council II, Constitution on the Liturgy *Sacrosanctum Concilium*, art. 24.

nity pours forth its prayers on behalf of their parents, as well as for all the loved ones of the dead, so that in their grief they will experience the comfort of faith.

14 The practice of reciting the office of the dead on the occasion of funerals or at other times is based in some places on particular law, on an endowment for this purpose, or on custom. The practice may be continued, provided the office is celebrated becomingly and devoutly. But in view of the circumstances of contemporary life and for pastoral considerations, a Bible vigil or celebration of God's word may be substituted.

14bis Funeral rites are to be celebrated for catechumens. In keeping with the provisions of CIC, can. 1183, celebration of funeral rites may also be granted to:

1. children whose baptism was intended by their parents but who died before being baptized;
2. baptized members of another Church or non-Catholic Ecclesial Community at the discretion of the local Ordinary, but not if it is known that they did not wish this nor if a minister of their own is available.

15 Funeral rites are to be granted to those who have chosen cremation, unless there is evidence that their choice was dictated by anti-Christian motives.

The funeral is to be celebrated according to the model in use in the region. It should be carried out in a way, however, that clearly expresses the Church's preference for the custom of burying the dead, after the example of Christ's own will to be buried, and that forestalls any danger of scandalizing or shocking the faithful.

The rites usually held in the cemetery chapel or at the grave may in this case take place within the confines of the crematorium and, for want of any other suitable place, even in the crematorium room. Every precaution is to be taken against the danger of scandal or religious indifferentism.

Offices and Ministries toward the Dead

16 In the celebration of a funeral all the members of the people of God must remember that to each one a role and an office is entrusted: to relatives and friends, funeral directors, the Christian community as such, finally, the priest, who as the teacher of faith and the minister of comfort presides at the liturgical rites and celebrates the eucharist.

17 All should also be mindful, and priests especially, that as they commend the deceased to God at a funeral, they have a responsibility as well to raise the hopes of those present and to build up their faith in the paschal mystery and the resurrection of the dead. They should do so in such a way, however, that as bearers of the tenderness of the Church and the comfort of faith, they console those who believe without offending those who grieve.

18 In preparing and planning a funeral, priests are to keep in mind with delicate sensitivity not only the identity of the deceased and the circumstances of the death, but also the grief of the bereaved and their needs for a Christian life. Priests are to be particularly mindful of those who attend the liturgical celebration or hear the Gospel because of the funeral, but are either non-Catholics or Catholics who never or seldom take part in the eucharist or have apparently lost the faith. Priests are, after all, the servants of Christ's Gospel on behalf of all.

19 Except for the Mass, a deacon may conduct all the funeral rites. As pastoral needs require, the conference of bishops, with the Apostolic See's permission, may even depute a layperson for this.

When there is no priest or deacon, it is recommended that in funerals according to the first model laypersons carry out the stations at the home and cemetery; the same applies generally to all vigils for the dead.

20 Apart from the marks of distinction arising from a person's liturgical function or holy orders and those honours due to civil authorities according to liturgical law,[3] no special honours are to be paid in the

---

[3] See Vatican Council II, Constitution on the Liturgy *Sacrosanctum Concilium*, art. 32.

celebration of a funeral to any private persons or classes of persons.

Adaptations Belonging to the
Conferences of Bishops

21 In virtue of the Constitution on the Liturgy (art. 63 b), the conferences of bishops have the right to prepare a section in particular rituals corresponding to the present section of the Roman Ritual and adapted to the needs of the different parts of the world. This section is for use in the regions concerned, once the *acta* of the conferences have been reviewed by the Apostolic See.

In making such adaptations it shall be up to the conferences of bishops:

1. to decide on the adaptations, within the limits laid down in the present section of the Roman Ritual;

2. to weigh carefully and prudently which elements from the traditions and culture of individual peoples may be appropriately admitted and accordingly to propose to the Apostolic See further adaptations considered to be useful or necessary that will be introduced into the liturgy with its consent;

3. to retain elements of particular rituals that may now exist, provided they are compatible with the Constitution on the Liturgy and contemporary needs, or to adapt such elements;

4. to prepare translations of the texts that are truly suited to the genius of the different languages and cultures and, whenever appropriate, to add suitable melodies for singing;

5. to adapt and enlarge this Introduction in the Roman Ritual in such a way that the ministers will fully grasp and carry out the meaning of the rites;

6. in editions of the liturgical books to be prepared under the direction of the conferences of bishops, to arrange the material in a format deemed to be best suited to pastoral practice; this is to be done in such a way, however, that none of the contents of this *editio typica* are omitted.

When added rubrics or texts are judged useful, these are to be set off by some typographical symbol or mark from the rubrics and texts of the Roman Ritual.

22 In drawing up particular rituals for funerals, it shall be up to the conferences of bishops:

1. to give the rite an arrangement patterned on one or more of the models, in the way indicated in no. 9;

2. to replace the formularies given in the basic rite with others taken from those in Chapter VI, should this seem advantageous;

3. to add different formularies of the same type whenever the Roman Ritual provides optional formularies (following the rule given in no. 21, 6);

4. to decide whether laypersons should be deputed to celebrate funerals (see no. 19);

5. to decree, whenever pastoral considerations dictate, omission of the sprinkling with holy water and the incensation or to substitute another rite for them;

6. to decree for funerals the liturgical colour that fits in with the culture of peoples, that is not offensive to human grief, and that is an expression of Christian hope in the light of the paschal mystery.

Function of the Priest in Preparing
and Planning the Celebration

23 The priest is to make willing use of the options allowed in the rite, taking into consideration the many different situations and the wishes of the family and the community.

24 The rite provided for each model is drawn up in such a way that it can be carried out with simplicity; nevertheless the rite supplies a wide selection of texts to fit various contingencies. Thus, for example:

1. As a general rule all texts are interchangeable, in order to achieve, with the help of the community or the family, a closer reflection of the actual circumstances of each celebration.

2. Some elements are not assigned as obligatory, but are left as optional additions, as, for example, the prayer for

the mourners at the home of the deceased.

3. In keeping with liturgical tradition, a wide freedom of choice is given regarding the texts provided for processions.

4. When a psalm listed or suggested for a liturgical reason may present a pastoral problem, another psalm may be substituted. Even within the psalms a verse or verses that seem to be unsuitable from a pastoral standpoint may be omitted.

5. The texts of prayers are always written in the singular, that is, for one deceased male. Accordingly, in any particular case the text is to be modified as to gender and number.

6. In prayers the lines within parentheses may be omitted.

25 Like the entire ministry of the priest to the dead, celebration of the funeral liturgy with meaning and dignity presupposes a view of the priestly office in its inner relationship with the Christian mystery.

Among the priest's responsibilities are:

1. to be at the side of the sick and dying, as is indicated in the proper section of the Roman Ritual;

2. to impart catechesis on the meaning of Christian death;

3. to comfort the family of the deceased, to sustain them amid the anguish of their grief, to be as kind and helpful as possible, and, through the use of the resources provided and allowed in the ritual, to prepare with them a funeral celebration that has meaning for them;

4. finally, to fit the liturgy for the dead into the total setting of the liturgical life of the parish and his own pastoral ministry.

BIBLICAL INDEX